Vagabon

Frances Hodgson Burnett

Alpha Editions

This edition published in 2024

ISBN : 9789362091642

Design and Setting By
Alpha Editions
www.alphaedis.com
Email - info@alphaedis.com

Contents

CHAPTER I.
IN WHICH WE HOLD COUNSEL.

It was a nondescript sort of a room, taking it altogether. A big, sunny room, whose once handsome papering and corniceing had grown dingy, and whose rich carpeting had lost its color and pile in places, and yet asserted its superiority to its surroundings with an air of lost grandeur in every shabby medallion. There were pictures in abundance on the walls, and more than one of them were gems in their way, despite the evidence all bore to being the work of amateurs. The tables were carved elaborately, and the faded, brocaded chairs were of the order *pouf*, and as inviting as they were disreputable in appearance; there was manuscript music among the general litter, a guitar hung from the wall by a tarnished blue and silver ribbon, and a violin lay on the piano; and yet, notwithstanding the air of free-and-easy disorder, one could hardly help recognizing a sort of vagabond comfort and luxury in the Bohemian surroundings. It was so very evident that the owners must enjoy life in an easy, light-hearted, though perhaps light-headed fashion; and it was also so very evident that their light hearts and light heads rose above their knowledge of their light purses.

They were congregated together now, holding a grand family council around the centre-table, and Dolly was the principal feature, as usual; and, embarrassing as the subject of said council was, not one of them looked as if it was other than a most excellent joke that Dolly, having been invited into the camps of the Philistines, should find she had nothing to put on to grace the occasion. And as to Dolly,—well, that young person stood in the midst of them in her shabby, Frenchy little hat, slapping one pink palm with a shabby, shapely kid glove, her eyes alight, her comical dismay and amusement displaying itself even in the arch of her brows.

"And so the Philistine leader pounced upon me herself," she was saying. "You know the 'Ark,' Phil? Well, they were all in the Ark,—the Rev. Bilberry in front, and the boys and girls filling up the corners; so you may imagine the effect produced when they stopped, and Lady Augusta bent over the side to solemnly proclaim her intention of inviting me to partake of coffee and conversation on Friday night, with an air of severely wondering whether I would dare to say 'No!'"

"Why did n't you say it?" said Aimée. "You know it will be an awful bore, Dolly. Those Bilberry clan gatherings always are. You have said so yourself often enough."

"Of course I have," returned Dolly. "And of course it will be, but it would be dreadfully indiscreet to let the Bilberry element know I thought so. The

Bilberry doors once closed against us, where is our respectability, and Phil's chance of success among the Philistines? It is bad enough, of course, but there is reason to be thankful that I am the only victim. The rest of you would be sure to blunder into the B. B. B.'s [meaning the Bilberry black books], and that *would* be an agreeable state of affairs. 'Toinette, look at Tod, he is sitting in the coal-box eating Phil's fusees."

In 'Toinette we find Mrs. Phil, a handsome creature, young enough to have been in the school-room, but with the face and figure of a Greek goddess, and a pair of eyes lovely enough to haunt one's dreams as a memory for a lifetime, and as to the rest, an inconsistent young madcap, whose beauty and spirit seemed only a necessary part of the household arrangements, and whose son and heir, in the person of the enterprising Tod (an abbreviate of Theodore), was the source of unlimited domestic enjoyment and the object of much indiscreet adoration. It was just like Philip Crewe, this marrying on probabilities; and it was equally like the rest of them to accept the state of affairs as an excellent joke, and regard the result as an exquisite piece of pleasantry. 'Toinette herself was only another careless, unworldly addition to the family circle, and enjoyed her position as thoroughly as the rest did; and as to Tod, what a delicate satire upon responsibilities Tod was, and how tranquilly he comported himself under a *régime* which admitted of free access into dangerous places, and a lack of personal restraint which allowed him all the joys the infantile mind can revel in!

At Dolly's exclamation Toinette rushed at him in his stronghold, and extricated him from the coal-box with demonstrations of dismay.

"Look at his white dress!" she wailed pathetically. "I only put it on a few minutes ago; and he has eaten two dozen fusees, if this was n't an empty box when he found it. I hope they won't disagree with him, Phil."

"They won't," said Phil, composedly. "Nothing does. Dust him, and proceed to business. I want to hear the rest of Dolly's story."

"I *think*," said Mollie, "that he ate Shem and Ham this morning, for I could only find Japheth after he had been playing with his Noah's Ark. Go on, Dolly."

"Wait until I have taken off my things," said Dolly, "and then we 'll talk it over. We must talk it over, you know, if I am to go."

She took off her hat, and then laid her shawl aside,—a little scarlet shawl, draped about her figure and tossed over one shoulder smartly, and by no means ungracefully,—and so stood revealed; and it must be admitted she was well worth looking at. Not a beauty, but a fresh, wholesome little body, with a real complexion, an abundance of hair, and large-irised, wide-awake eyes, changeable as to color, because capricious in expression; the sort of girl, in fact, who would be likely to persuade people ultimately that, considering circumstances, absolute beauty could be easily dispensed with, and, upon the whole, would rather detract from the general charm of novelty, which, in her case, reigned supreme.

"It is n't the mere fact of being a beauty that makes women popular," she would say; "it's the being able to persuade people that you are one,—or better than one. Don't some historians tell us that Cleopatra had red hair and questionable eyes, and yet she managed to blind the world so completely, that no one is sure whether it is true or not, and to this day the generality of people are inclined to believe that it was her supernatural beauty that dragged Marc Antony to the dust at her feet."

Aimée's face was more nearly perfect than Dolly's; Mollie's was more imposing, child as she was; 'Toinette threw her far into the shade in the matter of statuesque splendor; but still it was Dolly who did all the difficult things, and had divers tragic adventures with questionable adorers, whose name was legion, and who were a continual source of rejoicing and entertainment to the family.

Having tossed hat and shawl on to the table, among the manuscript music, paint-brushes, and palettes, this young person slipped into the most comfortable chair near the fire, and, having waited for the rest to seat themselves, proceeded to open the council. Mollie, who was sixteen, large, fair, beautiful, and not as tidy as she might have been, dropped into a not ungraceful position at her feet. Aimée, who was a little maiden with a tender, *spirituelle* face, and all the forethought of the family, sat near, with some grave perplexity in her expression. 'Toinette and Tod, *posed* in the low nursery-chair,—the girl's firm, white arm flung around the child,—swung lightly to and fro, fit models for an artist.

"You would make a first-class picture,—the lot of you," commented Phil, amicably.

"Never mind the picture," said Mollie, drawing her disreputable slippers up under her wrapper. "We want to hear how Dolly thinks of going to the Bilberrys'. Oh, Dolly, how heavenly it would be if you had a turquoise-blue sat—"

"Heavenly!" interrupted Dolly. "I should think so. Particularly celestial for Lady Augusta, who looks mahogany-colored in it, and peculiarly celestial for a poor relation from Vagabondia. It would be as much as my reputation was worth. She would never forgive me. You must learn discretion, Mollie."

"There is some consolation in knowing you can't get it," said 'Toinette. "You won't be obliged to deny yourself or be indiscreet. But what *are* you going to wear, Dolly?"

"That is for the council to decide," Dolly returned. "First, we must settle on what we want, and then we must settle on the way to get it."

"Other people go the other way about it," said Aimée.

"If we were only rich!" said Mollie.

"But it is a most glaringly patent fact that we are not," said Dolly. "There is one thing certain, however,—it must be white."

"A simple white muslin," suggested 'Toinette, struggling in the grasp of the immortal Tod,—"a simple white muslin, with an equally simple wild flower in your hair, *à la* Amanda Fitzallan. How the Dowager Bilberry *would* like that."

"And a wide blue sash," suggested Mollie. "And the sleeves tied up with bows. *And* tucks, Dolly. Girls, just think of Dolly making great eyes at an eligible Philistine, in white muslin and a sash and tucks!"

She was a hardened little sinner, this Dolly, her only redeeming point being that she was honest enough about her iniquities,—so honest that they were really not such terrible iniquities after all, and were regarded as rather good fun by the *habitués* of Vagabondia proper. She laughed just as heartily as the rest of them at Mollie's speech. She could no more resist the temptation of making great eyes at eligible Philistines than she could help making them at the entertaining but highly ineligible Bohemians, who continually frequented Phil's studio. The fear of man was not before her eyes; and the life she had led had invested her with a whimsical yet shrewd knowledge of human nature, and a business-like habit of looking matters in the face, which made her something of a novelty; and when is not novelty irresistible? And as to the masculine Philistines,—well, the audacity of Dolly's successes in the very midst of the enemy's camp had been the cause of much stately demoralization of Philistine battalions.

At her quietest she created small sensations and attracted attention; but in her wicked moods, when she was in a state of mind to prompt her to revenge the numerous small slights and overt acts of lofty patronage she met with, the dowagers stood in some secret awe of her propensities, and not without reason. Woe betide the daring matron who measured swords with her at such times. Great would be her confusion and dire her fall before the skirmish was over, and nothing was more certain than that she would retire from the field a wiser if not a better woman. After being triumphantly routed with great slaughter on two or three occasions, the enemy had discovered this, and decided mentally that it was more discreet to let "little Miss Crewe" alone, considering that, though it was humiliating to be routed, even by one of their own forces, it was infinitely more so to be routed by an innocent-looking young person, whose position was questionable, and who actually owed her vague shadow of respectability to her distant but august relative, the Lady Augusta Decima Crewe Bilberry, wife of the Rev. Marmaduke Sholto Bilberry, and mother of the plenteous crop of young Bilberrys, to whom little Miss Crewe was music teacher and morning governess.

So it was that Mollie's joke about the tucks and white muslin gained additional point from the family recollection of past experiences.

"But," said Dolly, when the laugh had subsided, "it won't do to talk nonsense all day. Here 's where we stand, you know. Coffee and conversation on Friday night on one side, and nothing but my draggled old green tarlatan on the other, and it's Tuesday now."

"And the family impecuniosity being a fact well established in the family mind," began Phil, with composure.

"But that 's nonsense," interrupted Aimée. "And, as Dolly says, nonsense won't do now. But," with a quaint sigh, "we always *do* talk nonsense."

But here a slight diversion was created. Mrs. Phil jumped up, with an exclamation of delight, and, dropping Tod on to Mollie's lap, disappeared through the open door.

"I will be back in a minute," she called back to them, as she ran up-stairs. "I have just thought of something."

"Girls," said Mollie, "it's her white merino."

And so it was. In a few minutes she reappeared with it,—a heap of soft white folds in her arms, and a yard or so of the train dragging after her upon the carpet,—the one presentable relic of a once inconsistently elaborate bridal trousseau, at present in a rather tumbled and rolled-up condition, but still white and soft and thick, and open to unlimited improvement.

"I had forgotten all about it," she said, triumphantly. "I have never needed it at all, and I knew I never should when I bought it, but it looked so nice when I saw it that I could n't help buying it. I once thought of cutting it up into things for Tod; but it seems to me, Dolly, it 's what you want exactly, and Tod can trust to Providence,—things always come somehow."

It was quite characteristic of Vagabondia that there should be more rejoicing over this one stray sheep of good luck than there would have been over any ninety and nine in the ordinary folds of more prosperous people. And Mrs. Phil rejoiced as heartily as the rest. It was her turn now, and she was as ready to sacrifice her white merino on the shrine of the household impecuniosity as she would be to borrow Dolly's best bonnet, or Mollie's shoes, or Aimée's gloves, when occasion demanded such a course. So the merino was laid upon the table, and the council rose to examine, comment, and suggest.

"A train," said Dolly, concisely; "no trimming, and swan's-down. Even the Bilberry could n't complain of that, I 'm sure."

Mollie, resting her smooth white elbows on the table in a comfortably lounging posture, regarded the garment with great longing in her drowsy brown eyes.

"I wish it was white satin," she observed, somewhat irrelevantly, "and I was going to wear it at a real ball, with real lace, you know, and a court train, and flowers, and a fan."

Dolly looked down at her handsome childish face good-naturedly. She was such an incongruous mixture of beauty and utter simplicity, this easy-going baby of sixteen, that Dolly could not have helped liking her heartily under any circumstances, even supposing there had been no tie of relationship between them.

"I wish it was white satin and you were going to wear it," she said. "White satin is just the sort of thing for you, Mollie. Never mind, wait until the figurative ship comes in."

"And in the interval," suggested Aimée, "put a stitch or so in that wrapper of yours. It has been torn for a week now, and Tod tumbles over it half a dozen times every morning before breakfast."

Mollie cast her eyes over her shoulder to give it an indifferent glance as it rested on the faded carpet behind her.

"I wish Lady Augusta would mend things before she sends them to us," she said, with sublime _naïveté_, and then, at the burst of laughter which greeted her words, she stopped short, staring at the highly entertained circle with widely opened, innocent eyes. "What are you laughing at?" she said. "I 'm sure she might. She is always preaching about liking to have something to occupy her time, and it would be far more charitable of her to spend her time in that way than in persistently going into poor houses where the people don't want her, and reading tracts to them that they don't want to hear."

Dolly's appreciation of the audacity of the idea reached a climax in an actual shriek of delight.

"If I had five pounds, which I have not, and never shall have," she said, "I would freely give it just to see Lady Augusta hear you say that, my dear. Five pounds! I would give ten—twenty—fifty, if need be. It would be such an exquisite joke."

But Mollie did not regard the matter in this light. To her unsophisticated mind Lady Augusta represented nothing more than periodical boredom in the shape of occasional calls, usually made unexpectedly, when the house was at its worst, and nobody was especially tidy,—calls invariably enlivened by severe comments upon the evil propensities of poor relations in general, and the shocking lack of respectability in this branch of the order in particular. Worldly wisdom was not a family trait, Dolly's half-whimsical assumption of it being the only symptom of the existence of such a gift, and Mollie was the most sublimely thoughtless of the lot. Mrs. Phil had never been guilty of a discreet act in her life. Phil himself regarded consequences less than he regarded anything else, and Aimée's childish staidness and forethought had certainly not an atom of worldliness in it. Accordingly, Dolly was left to battle with society, and now and then, it must be admitted, the result of her brisk affrays did her no small credit.

For a very short space of time the merino was being disposed of to an advantage; Dolly seating herself in her chair again to renovate the skirt; Aimée unpicking the bodice, and Mollie looking on with occasional comments.

"Here is Griffith," she said, at last, glancing over her shoulder at a figure passing the window; and the next minute the door was opened without ceremony, and "Grif" made his appearance upon the scene.

Being called upon to describe Griffith Donne, one would hardly feel inclined to describe him as being imposing in personal appearance. He was a thin, undersized young man, rather out at elbows and shabby of attire, and with a decided air of Bohemia about him; but his youthful face was singularly pleasing and innocent, and his long-lashed, brown-black eyes were more than good-looking,—they were absolutely beautiful in a soft, pathetic way,— beautiful as the eyes of the loveliest of women.

He came into the room as if he was used to coming into it in an every-day fashion; and Dolly, looking up, gave him a smile and a nod.

"Ah, you are all here, are you?" he said. "What is on hand now? What is all this white stuff for?" And he drew a chair up close by Dolly's side, and lifted the merino in his hand.

"For Friday night," answered Aimée. "Bilberry's again, Griffith. Coffee and conversation this time."

Griffith looked at Dolly inquiringly, but Dolly only laughed and shrugged her plump shoulders wickedly.

"Look here," he said, with a disapproving air, "it ain't true, is it, Dolly? You are not going to make a burnt-offering of yourself on the Bilberry shrine again, are you?"

But Dolly only laughed the more as she took the merino from him.

"If you want a breadth of merino to hold, take another one," she said. "I want that. And as to being a burnt-offering on the shrine of Bilberry, my dear Griffith, you must know it is policy," and immediately went on with her unpicking again, while Griffith, bending over in an attitude more remarkable for ease than grace, looked on at her sharp little glancing scissors with an appearance of great interest.

It would perhaps be as well to pause here to account for this young man's evident freedom in the family circle. It was very plain that he was accustomed to coming and going when he pleased, and it was easy to be adduced from his manner that, to him, Dolly was the chief attraction in the establishment. The fact was, he was engaged to Dolly, and had been engaged to her for years, and in all probability, unless his prospects altered their aspect, would be engaged to her for years to come. In past time, when both were absurdly young, and ought to have been at school, the two had met,—an impressionable, good-natured, well-disposed couple of children, who fell in love with each other unreasoningly and honestly, giving no thought to the future. They were too young to be married, of course, and indeed had not troubled themselves about anything so matter of fact; they had fallen in love, and enjoyed it, and, strange to say, had been enjoying it ever since, and falling in love more deeply every day of their affectionate, inconsequent, free-and-easy lives. What did it matter to them that neither owned a solitary sixpence, for which they had not a thousand uses? What did it matter to Dolly that Griffith's literary career had so far been so unremunerative that a new suit is as an event, and an extra shilling an era? What did it matter to Griffith that Dolly's dresses were re-trimmed and re-turned and re-furbished, until their reappearance with the various seasons was the opening of a High Carnival of jokes? Love is not a matter of bread and butter in Vagabondia, thank Heaven! Love is left to Bohemia as well as to barren Respectability, and, as Griffith frequently observed with no slight enthusiasm, "When it comes to figure, where's the feminine Philistine whose silks and satins and purple and fine raiment fit like Dolly's do?" So it went on, and the two adored each other with mutual simplicity, and, having their little quarrels, always made them up again with much affectionate remorse, and, scorning the prudential advice of outsiders, believed in each other and the better day which was to come, when one or the other gained worldly goods enough to admit of a marriage in which they were to be happy in their own way,—which, I may add, was a way simple and tender, unselfish and faithful, enough.

It was quite evident, however, that Griffith was not in the best of spirits this morning. He was not as sanguine as Dolly by nature, and outward influences tended rather to depress him occasionally. But he never was so low-spirited that Dolly could not cheer him, consequently he always came to her with his troubles; and to her credit, be it said, she never failed to understand and deal with them tenderly, commonplace though they were. So she understood his mood very well to-day. Something had gone wrong at "the office." ("The office" was the editorial den which swallowed him up, and held him in bondage from morning until night; appropriating his labor for a very small pecuniary compensation, too, it may be added.) "Old Flynn," as the principal was respectfully designated, had been creating one of his periodical disturbances, or he had been snubbed, which, by the way, was not a rare event, and to poor Griffith slights were stings and patronage poison. He could not laugh at the enemy and scorn discomfiture as Dolly could, and the consequence of an encounter with the Philistines on his part was usually a desperate fit of low spirits, which made him wretched, bitter, and gloomy by turns.

This morning it appeared that his spirits had reached their lowest ebb, and before many minutes had passed he was pouring forth his tribulations with much frankness and simplicity. Mr. Griffith Donne's principal trial was the existence of an elderly maiden aunt, who did not approve of him, and was in the habit of expressing her disapproval in lengthy epistolary correspondence, invariably tending to severe denunciation of his mode of life, and also invariably terminating with the announcement that unless he "desisted" (from what, or in what manner, not specified) she should consider it her bounden duty to disinherit him forthwith. One of these periodical epistles, having arrived before he had breakfasted, had rather destroyed Griffith's customary equanimity, and various events of the morning had not improved his frame of mind; consequently he came to Dolly for comfort.

"And she's coming to London, too," he ended, after favoring the assemblage with extracts from the letter. "And, of course, she will expect me to do the dutiful. Confound her money! I wish she would build an asylum for irate, elderly spinsters with it, and retire into it for the remainder of her natural life. I don't want it, and"—with praiseworthy ingenuousness—"I shouldn't get it if I did!"

"But," said Dolly, when they found themselves alone for a few minutes, "it would be an agreeable sort of thing to have, Griffith, upon the whole, wouldn't it?"

They were standing close together by the fire, Griffith with his arm thrown round the girl's waist, and she with both her plump, flexible hands clasped on his shoulder and her chin resting on them, and her big, round eyes gazing up into his. She was prone to affectionate, nestling attitudes and coaxing ways—with Griffith it may be understood—her other adorers were treated cavalierly enough.

"A nice sort of thing," echoed Griffith. "I should think it would. I should like to have it for your sake. I don't care for it so much for myself, you know,

Dolly, but I want the time to come when I can buy you such things as Old Flynn's nieces wear. It would n't be a waste of good material on such a figure as yours. I have an idea of my own about a winter dress I intend you to have when we are rich,—a dark blue velvet, and a hat with a white plume in, and one of those muff affairs made of long white silky fur—"

"Angora," said Dolly, her artless enjoyment of the idea shining in her eyes. "Angora, Griffith."

"I don't know what it's called," answered Griffith, "but it is exactly your style, and I have thought about it a dozen times. Ah, if we were only rich!"

Dolly laughed joyously, clasping her hands a little closer over his shoulder. Their conversations upon prospects generally ended in some such pleasantly erratic remarks. They never were tired of supposing that they were rich; and really, in default of being rich, it must be admitted that there is some consolation in being in a frame of mind which can derive happiness from such innocent day-dreams.

"Just think of the house we would have," she said, "and the fun we could all have together, if you and I were rich and—and married, Griffith. We should be happy if we were married, and not rich, but if we were rich *and* married— goodness, Griffith!" and she opened her eyes wide and looked so enjoyable altogether, that Griffith, being entirely overcome by reason of the strength of his feelings upon the subject, caught her in both arms and embraced her heartily, and only released her in an extremely but charmingly crushed and dishevelled condition, after he had kissed her about half a dozen times.

It did not appear, upon the whole, that she objected to the proceeding. She took it quite naturally and unaffectedly, as if she was used to it, and regarded it as a part of the programme. Indeed, it was quite a refreshing sight to see her put both her little hands up to her disarranged hair and settle the crimps serenely.

"We should have the chances to find true people if we were rich," she said. "And then we could take care, of Aimée and Mollie, and help them to make grand marriages."

But that very instant Griffith's face fell somewhat.

"Dolly," he said, "have you never thought—not even *thought* that you would like to have made a grand marriage yourself?" And though there was not the least shade of a reason for the change in his mood, it was glaringly evident that he was at once rendered absolutely prostrate with misery at the thought.

These sudden pangs of remorse at his own selfishness in holding the girl bound to him, were his weakness, and Dolly's great difficulty was to pilot him safely through his shoals of doubt and self-reproach, and she had her own way of managing it. Just now her way of managing it was to confront him bravely, coming quite close to him again, and taking hold of one of his coat buttons.

"I have thought of it a hundred times," she said, "but not since I have belonged to you; and as I have belonged to you ever since I was fifteen years old, I should think what I thought before then can hardly have the right to trouble us now. *You* never think of marrying any one but me, do you, Griffith?"

"Think of marrying any one else!" exclaimed Griffith, indignantly. "I would n't marry a female Rajah with a diamond—"

"I know you wouldn't," Dolly interrupted. "I believe in you, Griffith. Why won't you believe in me?" And the eyes lifted to his were so perfectly honest and straightforward that the sourest of cynics must have believed them, and Griffith was neither sour nor a cynic, but simply an unsuccessful, affectionate, contradictory young man, too susceptible to outward influences for his own peace of mind.

He was a *very* unfortunate young man, it may as well be observed at once, and his misfortunes were all the harder to bear because he was not to blame for them. He had talent, and was industrious and indefatigable, and yet, somehow or other, the Fates seemed to be against him. If he had been less honest or less willing, he might perhaps have been more successful; but in his intercourse with the world's slippery ones he customarily found himself imposed upon. He had done hard work for which he had never been paid, and work for which he had been paid badly; he had fought honestly to gain footing, and, somehow or other, luck had seemed to be against him, for certainly he had not gained it yet. Honest men admired and respected him, and men of intellectual worth prophesied better days; but so far it had really seemed that the people who were willing to befriend him were powerless, and those who were powerful cared little about the matter. So he alternately struggled and despaired, and yet retained his good nature, and occasionally enjoyed life heartily in defiance of circumstances. With every member of the Crewe household he was popular, from Tod to Mrs. Phil. His engagement to Dolly they regarded as a satisfactory arrangement. That he was barely able to support himself, and scarcely possessed a presentable suit of clothes, was to their minds the most inconsequent of trifles. It was unfortunate, perhaps, but unavoidable; and their sublime trust in the luck which was to ripen in all of them at some indefinite future time, was their hope in this case. Some time or other he would "get into something," they had decided, and then he would marry Dolly, and they would all enjoy the attendant festivities. And in the mean time they allowed the two to be happy, and made Griffith welcome, inviting him to their little impromptu suppers, and taking care never to be *de trop* on the occasion of *tête-à-tête* conversations.

The *tête-à-tête* of the morning ended happily as usual. Dolly went back to her unpicking, and Griffith, finding his ghost of self-reproach laid for the time being, watched her in a supremely blissful state of mind. He never tired of watching her, he frequently told her in enthusiastic confidence. The charm in Dolly Crewe was her adaptability; she was never out of place, and it had been said that she suited herself to her accompaniments far oftener than her accompaniments suited themselves to her. Seeing her in a shabby dress, seated in the shabby parlor, one instinctively felt that shabbiness was not so utterly unbearable after all, and acknowledged that it had a brightness of its own. Meeting her at a clan gathering in the camps of the Philistines, one always found her in excellent spirits, and quite undamped in her enjoyment of the frequently ponderous rejoicings. In the Bilberry school-room, among dog-eared French grammars and lead-pencilled music, education did not appear actually dispiriting; and now, as she sat by the fire, with the bright, sharp little scissors in lier hand, and the pile of white merino on her knees and trailing on the hearth-rug at her feet, Griffith found her simply irresistible. Ah! the bliss that revealed itself in the prospect of making her Mrs. Donne, and taking possession of her entirely! The joy of seeing her seated in an arm-chair of his own, by a fire which was solely his property, in a room which was nobody else's paradise! He could imagine so well how she would regard such a state of affairs as a nice little joke, and would pretend to adapt herself to her position with divers daring witcheries practised upon himself to the dethroning of his reason; how she would make innocent, wicked speeches, and be coaxing and dazzling and mock-matronly by turns; and above all, how she would enjoy it, and make him enjoy it, too; and yet sometimes, when they were quiet and alone, would drop all her whimsical little airs and graces, and make such tender, unselfish, poetic little speeches, that he would find himself startled in life wonder at the depth and warmth and generosity of her girlish heart. He often found her surprising him after this manner, and the surprise usually came when he had just been most nearly betrayed into thinking of her as an adorable little collection of witcheries and whimsicalities, and forgetting that she had other moods. More than once she had absolutely brought tears into his eyes, and a thrill to his heart, by some sudden, pathetic, trustful speech, made after she had been dazzling and bewildering for hours with her pretty coquetries and daring flashes of wit. No one but Griffith ever saw her in these intense moods. The rest of them saw her intense enough sometimes but the sudden, uncontrollable flashes of light Griffith saw now and then, fairly staggered him. And the poor fellow's love for her was something akin to adoration. There was only this one woman upon earth to him, and his whole soul was bound up in her. It was for her he struggled against disappointment, it was for her he hoped, it was only the desperate strength of his love for her that made disappointment so terribly bitter to him. Certainly his love made him better and sweeter-tempered and more energetic than he would have been if his life had not been so full of it. His one ambition was to gain success to lay at her feet. To him success meant Dolly, and Dolly meant Paradise, an honest Paradise, in which primeval bliss reigned supreme and trial was unknown. Consequently the bright little scissors glanced before his eyes a sort of loadstar.

"I did n't tell you that nephew of Old Flynn's had come back, did I?" he said, at length.

"No," answered Dolly, snipping diligently. "You never mentioned him. What nephew, and where did he come from?"

"A fellow of the name of Gowan, who has been travelling in the East for no particular reason for the last ten years. He called on Flynn, at the office, today, for the first time; and if I had been called upon to kick him out, I should have regarded it as a cheerful and improving recreation."

"Why?" laughed Dolly. "Is he one of the Philistines?"

"Philistine!" echoed Griffith, with disgust. "I should think so. A complacent idiot in a chronic state of fatigue. Drove up to the door in a cab,—his own, by the way, and a confoundedly handsome affair it is,—gave the reins to his tiger, and stared at the building tranquilly for at least two minutes before he came in, stared at Old Flynn when he *did* come in, stared at me, shook hands with Old Flynn exhaustedly, and then subsided into listening and paring his nails during the remainder of the interview."

"Which might or might not be discreet under the circumstances," said Dolly. "Perhaps he had nothing to say. Never mind, Grif. Let us console ourselves with the thought that we are not as these utterly worthless explorers of the East are," with a flourish of the scissors.

"Better is a dinner of herbs in Vagabondia, with a garnish of conversation and *bon-mots*, than a stalled ox among the Philistines with dulness."

But about an hour after Griffith had taken his departure, as she was bending over the table, industriously clipping at the merino, a thought suddenly crossed her mind, which made her drop her scissors and look up meditatively.

"By the way," she began, all at once. "Yes, it must be! How was it I did not think of it when Grif was talking? I am sure, it was Gowan, Lady Augusta said. To be sure it was. Mollie, this exploring nephew of the Flynns is to partake of coffee and conversation with us at the Bilberrys' on Friday, if I am not mistaken, and I never remembered it until now."

CHAPTER II
IN THE CAMPS OF THE PHILISTINES.

A TOILET in Vagabondia was an event. Not an ordinary toilet, of course, but a toilet extraordinary,—such as is necessarily called forth by some festive gathering or unusual occasion. It was also an excitement after a manner, and not a disagreeable one. It made demands upon the inventive and creative powers of the whole family, and brought to light hidden resources. It also aroused energy, and, being a success, was rejoiced over as a brilliant success. Respectability might complacently retire to its well-furnished chamber, and choose serenely from its unlimited supply of figurative purple and legendary fine linen, without finding a situation either dramatic or amusing; but in Vagabondia this was not the case. Having contrived to conjure up, as it were, from the secret places of the earth an evening dress, are not gloves still necessary? and, being safe as regards gloves, do not the emergencies of the toilet call for minor details seemingly unimportant, but still not to be done without? Finding this to be the case, the household of Crewe rallied all its forces upon such occasions, and set aside all domestic arrangements for the time being. It was not impossible that Dolly should have prepared for a rejoicing without the assistance of Mollie and Aimée, Mrs. Phil and Tod, with occasional artistic suggestions from Phil and any particular friend of the family who chanced to be below-stairs, within hearing distance. It might not have appeared an impossibility, I should say, to ordinary people, but the household of Crewe regarded it as such, and accordingly, on the night of the Bilberry gathering, accompanied Dolly in a body to her tiring-room.

Upon the bed lay the merino dress, white, modest, and untrimmed, save for the swan's-down accompaniments, but fitting to a shade and exhibiting an artistic sweep of train.

"It is a discreet sort of garment," said Dolly, by way of comment; "and it is 'suitable to our social position.' Do you remember when Lady Augusta said that about my black alpaca, girls? Pleasant little observation, was n't it? 'Toinette, I trust hair-pins are not injurious to infantile digestive organs. If they are, perhaps it would be as well to convince Tod that such is the case. What is the matter, Mollie?"

Mollie, leaning upon the dressing-table in her favorite attitude, was looking rather discontented. She was looking very pretty, also, it might be said. Her sleepy, warm brown eyes, being upraised to Dolly, showed larger and warmer and browner than usual; the heavy brown locks, tumbling down over her shoulders, caught a sort of brownish, coppery shade in the flare of gas-light; there was a flush on her soft cheeks, and her ripe lips were curved in a lovely dissatisfaction. Hence Dolly's remark.

"I wish I was going," said the child.

Dolly's eyes flew open wide, in a very sublimity of astonishment.

"Wish you were going?" she echoed. "To the Bilberrys'?"

Mollie nodded.

"Yes, even there. I want to go somewhere. I think I should enjoy myself a little anywhere. I should like to see the people, and hear them talk, and find out what they do, and wear an evening dress."

Dolly gazed at her in mingled pity and bewilderment.

"Mollie," she said, "you are very innocent; and I always knew you were very innocent; but I did not know you were as innocent as this,—so utterly free from human guile that you could imagine pleasure in a Bilberry rejoicing. And I believe," still regarding her with that questioning pity, "—I believe you really *could*. I must keep an eye on you, Mollie. You are too unsophisticated to be out of danger."

It was characteristic of her good-natured sympathy for the girl that it should occur to her the next minute that perhaps it might please her to see herself donned even in such modest finery as the white merino. She understood her simple longings after unattainable glories so thoroughly, and she was so ready to amuse her to the best of her ability. So she suggested it.

"Put it on, Mollie," she said, "and let us see how you would look in it. I should like to see you in full dress."

The child rose with some faint stir of interest in her manner and went to the bed.

"It wouldn't be long enough for me if it wasn't for the train," she said; "but the train will make it long enough nearly, and I can pull it together at the waist."

She put it on at the bedside, and then came forward to the toilet-table; and Dolly, catching sight of her in the glass as she advanced, turned round with a start.

Standing in the light; the soft heavy white folds draping themselves about her statuesque curves of form as they might have draped themselves about the limbs of some young marble Grace or Goddess, with her white arms and shoulders uncovered, with her unchildish yet youthful face, with her large-irised eyes, her flush of momentary pleasure and half awkwardness, she was just a little dazzling, and Dolly did not hesitate to tell her so.

"You are a beauty, Mollie," she said. "And you are a woman in that dress. If you were only a Bilberry now, what a capital your face would be to you, and what a belle you would be!"

Which remarks, if indiscreet, were affectionate, and made in perfect good faith.

But when, having donned the merino herself, she made her way down the dark staircase to the parlor, there was a vague ghost of uneasiness in her mind, and it was the sight of Mollie in full dress which had aroused it.

"She is so very pretty," she said to herself. "I scarcely knew how very pretty she was until I turned round from the glass to look at her. What a pity it is that we are not rich enough to do her justice, and let her enjoy herself as other girls do. And—and," with a little sigh, "I am afraid we are a dreadfully careless lot. I wonder if Phil ever thinks about it? And she is so innocent and ignorant too. I hope she won't fall in love with anybody disreputable. I wish I knew how to take care of her."

And yet when she went into the parlor to run the gauntlet of family inspection, and walked across the floor to show the sweep of her train, and tried her little opera hood on Tod before putting it on herself, a casual observer would certainly have decided that she had never had a serious thought in her life. Griffith was there, of course. At such times his presence was considered absolutely necessary, and his admiration was always unbounded. His portion it was to tuck her under his arm and lead her out to the cab when the train and wraps were arranged and the hood put on. This evening, when he had made her comfortable and shut the door, she leaned out of the window at the last moment to speak to him.

"I forgot to tell you, Griffith," she said, "Lady Augusta said something about a Mr. Gowan to Mr. Bilberry the other day when she invited me. I wonder if it is the Gowan you were telling me about? He is to be there to-night."

"Of course it is," answered Griffith, with sudden discontent. "He is just the sort of fellow the Bilberrys would lionize."

It was rather incorrect of Dolly to feel, as she did, a sudden flash of anticipation. She could not help it. This intense appreciation of a novel or dramatic encounter with an eligible Philistine was her great weakness, and she made no secret of it even with her lover, which was unwise if frank.

She gave her fan a wicked flirt, and her eyes flashed as she did it.

"A mine of valuable information lies unexplored before me," she said. "I must make minute inquiries concerning the habits and peculiarities of the people of the East. I shall take the lion in tow, and Lady Augusta's happiness will be complete."

Griffith turned pale—his conquering demon was jealousy.

"Look here, Dolly," he began.

But Dolly settled herself in her seat again, and waved her hand with an air of extreme satisfaction. She did not mean to make him miserable, and would have been filled with remorse if she had quite understood the extent of the suffering she imposed upon him sometimes merely through her spirit, and the daring onslaughts she made upon people for whom she cared little or nothing. She understood his numerous other peculiarities pretty thoroughly, but she did not understand his jealousy, for the simple reason that she had never been jealous in her life.

"Tell the cabman to drive on," she said, with a flourish. "There is balm to be found even in Bilberry."

And when the man drove on she composed herself comfortably in a corner of the vehicle, in perfect unconsciousness of the fact that she had left a thorn behind, rankling in the bosom of the poor fellow who watched her from the pavement.

She was rather late, she found, on reaching her destination. The parlors were full, and the more enterprising of the guests were beginning to group themselves in twos and threes, and make spasmodic efforts at conversation. But conversation at a Bilberry assemblage was rarely a success,—it was so evident that to converse was a point of etiquette, and it was so patent that conversation was expected from everybody, whether they had anything to say or not.

Inoffensive individuals of retiring temperament, being introduced to each other solemnly and with ceremony, felt that to be silent was to be guilty of a glaring breach of Bilberry decorum, and, casting about in mental agony for available remarks, found none, and were overwhelmed with amiable confusion. Lady Augusta herself, in copper-colored silk of the most unbending quality and make, was not conducive to cheerfulness. Yet Dolly's first thought on catching sight of her this evening was a cheerful if audacious one.

"She looks as if she was dressed in a boiler," she commented, inwardly. "I wonder if I shall ever live so long—I wonder if I ever *could* live long enough to submit to a dress like that. And yet she seems to be almost happy in the possession of it. But, I dare say, that is the result of conscious virtue."

It was a very fortunate thing for Dolly that she was not easily discomposed. Most girls entering a room full of people, evidently unemployed, and in consequence naturally prone to not too charitable criticism of new-comers, might have lost self-possession. Not so Dolly Crewe. Being announced, she came in neither with unnecessary hurry nor timidly, and with not the least atom of shrinking from the eyes turned toward her; and, simple and unassuming a young person as she appeared on first sight, more than one pair of eyes in question found themselves attracted by the white merino, the white shoulders, the elaborate tresses, and the serene, innocent-looking orbs.

Lady Augusta advanced slightly to meet her, with a grewsome rustling of copper-colored stiffness. She did not approve of Dolly at any time, but she specially disapproved of her habit of setting time at defiance and ignoring the consequences.

"I am very glad to see you," she said, with the air of a potentate issuing a proclamation. "I *thought*"—somewhat severely—"that you were not coming at all."

"Did you?" remarked Dolly, with tranquillity.

"Yes," returned her ladyship. "And I could not understand it. It is nine o'clock now, and I *believe* I mentioned eight as the hour."

"I dare say you did," said Dolly, unfurling her small downy fan, and using it with much serene grace; "but I wasn't ready at eight. I hope you are very well."

"Thank you," replied her ladyship, icily. "I am very well. Will you go and take a seat by Euphemia? I allowed her to come into the room to-night, and I notice that her manner is not so self-possessed as I should wish."

Dolly gave a little nod of acquiescence, and looked across the room to where the luckless Euphemia sat edged in a corner behind a row of painfully conversational elderly gentlemen, who were struggling with the best intentions to keep up a theological discourse with the Rev. Marmaduke. Euphemia was the eldest Miss Bilberry. She was overgrown and angular, and suffered from chronic embarrassment, which was not alleviated by the eye of her maternal parent being upon her. She was one of Dolly's pupils, and cherished a secret but enthusiastic admiration for her. And, upon the whole, Dolly was fond of the girl. She was good-natured and unsophisticated, and bore the consciousness of her physical and mental imperfections with a humility which was almost touching to her friend sometimes. Catching Dolly's eye on this occasion, she glanced at her imploringly, and then, catching the eye of her mother, blushed to the tips of her ears, and relapsed into secret anguish of mind.

But Dolly, recognizing her misery, smiled reassuringly, and made her way across the room to her, insinuating herself through the theological phalanx.

"I am so glad you are here at last," said the girl. "I was so afraid you would n't come. And oh, how nice you look, and how beautifully you manage your train! I could never do it in the world. I should be sure to tumble over it. But nothing ever seems to trouble you at all. You haven't any idea how lovely you were when you went across the room to mamma. Everybody looked at you, and I don't wonder at it."

"They would have looked at anybody," answered Dolly, laughing. "They had nothing else to do."

"That is quite true, poor things," sighed Euphemia, sympathetically. "You don't know the worst yet, either. You don't know how stupid they are and can be, Dolly. That old gentleman near the screen has not spoken one word yet, and he keeps sighing and wiping the top of his bald head with his pocket-handkerchief until I can't keep my eyes off him, and I am afraid he has noticed me. I don't mean any harm, I'm sure, but I have got nothing to do myself, and I can't help it. But what I was going to say was, that people looked at you as they did not look at others who came in. You seem different some way. And I'm sure that Mr. Gowan of mamma's has been staring at you until it is positively rude of him."

Dolly's slowly moving fan became stationary for a moment.

"Mr. Gowan," she said. "Who is Mr. Gowan?"

"One of mamma's people," answered Euphemia, "though I'm sure I can't quite understand how he can be one of them. He looks so different from the rest. He is very rich, you know, and very aristocratic, and has travelled a great deal He has been all over the world, they say. There he is at that side-table."

Dolly's eyes, travelling round the assemblage with complacent indifference, rested at last on the side-table where the subject of Euphemia's remarks sat.

He really was an eligible Philistine, it seemed, despite Griffith's unflattering description of him.

He was a long-limbed, graceful man, with an aquiline face and superb eyes, which at this moment were resting complacently upon Dolly herself. It was not exactly admiration, either, which they expressed, it was something of a more entertaining nature, at least so Dolly found it,—it was nothing more nor less than a slowly awakening interest in her which paid her the compliment of rising above the surface of evident boredom and overcoming lassitude. It looked as if he was just beginning to study her, and found the game worth the candle. Dolly met his glance with steadiness, and as she met it she measured him. Then she turned to Euphemia again and fluttered the fan slowly and serenely.

"He's nice, is n't he?" commented the guileless Phemie. "If the rest of them were like him, I don't think we should be so stupid, but as it is, you know, he can't talk when there is nobody to talk to."

"No," said Dolly. "One could hardly expect it of him. But I wonder why he does not say something to that thin lady in the dress-cap."

"Oh, dear!" exclaimed Phemie, "I don't wonder in the least. That is Miss Berenice MacDowlas, Dolly."

"Miss Berenice MacDowlas!" echoed Dolly, with a start. "You don't say so?"

"Yes," answered Euphemia. "Do you know her? You spoke as if you did."

"Well—yes—no," answered Dolly, with a half laugh. "I should say I know somebody who does."

And she looked as if she was rather enjoying some small joke of her own. The fact was that Miss MacDowlas was no other than Griffith's amiable aunt. But, of course, it would not have done to tell this to Euphemia Bilberry. Euphemia's ideas on the subject of the tender passion were as yet crude and unformed, and Dolly Crewe was not prone to sentimental confidences, so, as yet, Euphemia and indeed the whole Bilberry family, remained in blissful ignorance of the very existence of such a person as Mr. Griffith Donne.

If personal appearance was to be relied upon, Miss MacDowlas was not a promising subject for diplomatic beguiling.

"We have no need to depend upon her," was Dolly's mental decision. "One glimpse of life in Vagabondia would end poor Griffith's chances with her. I wonder what she would think if she could see Tod in all his glory when 'Toinette and Phil are busy painting."

And her vivid recollection of the personal adornments of Tod at such times brought a smile to her lips.

She made herself very comfortable in her corner, and, exerting herself to her utmost to alleviate Euphemia's sufferings, succeeded so far that the girl forgot everything else but her enjoyment of her friend's caustic speeches and satirical little jokes. Dolly was not afraid of results, and, standing in due awe of public opinion, gave herself up to the encouraging of any shadow of amusement quite heartily. She was so entertaining in a small way upon this occasion, that Euphemia's frame of mind became in some degree ecstatic. From her place of state across the room, Lady Augusta regarded them with disapproval. It was so very evident that they were enjoying themselves, and that this shocking Dorothea Crewe was not to be suppressed. (Dorothea, be it known, was Dolly's baptismal name, and Lady Augusta held to its full pronunciation as a matter of duty.) It was useless, however, to disapprove. Behind the theological phalanx Dolly sat enthroned plainly in the best of spirits, and in rather a dangerous mood, to judge from outward appearances. There was nothing of the poor relation about her at least. The little snowy fan was being manipulated gracefully and with occasional artistic nourishes, her enjoyable roulades of laughter tinkled audaciously, her white shoulders were expressive, her gestures charming, and, above all, people were beginning to look at her admiringly, if not with absolute envy. Something must be done.

Lady Augusta moved across the room, piloting her way between people on ottomans and people on chairs, rustling with awe-inspiring majesty; and, reaching the corner at last, she spoke to the daring Dolly over the heads of the phalanx.

"Dorothea," she said, "we should like a little music."

This she had expected would be a move which could not fail to set the young person in her right place. It would show her that her time was not her own, and that she was expected to make herself useful; and it would also set to rights any little mistake lookers-on might have previously labored under as to her position. But even this did not destroy Dolly's equanimity. She finished the small joke she had been making to Phemie, and then turned to her august relative with a sweet but trying smile.

"Music?" she said. "Certainly." And arose at once.

Then Lady Augusta saw her mistake. It was only another chance for Miss Dolly to display herself to advantage, after all. When she arose from her seat in the corner, and gave a glance of inspection to her train over her bare white shoulder, people began to look at her again; and when she crossed the room, she was an actual Sensation,—and to create a sensation in the Bilberry parlors was to attain a triumph. Worse than this, also, as her ladyship passed the bald-headed individual by the screen, that gentleman—who was a lion as regarded worldly possessions—condescended to make his first remark for the evening.

"Pretty girl, that," he said. "Nice girl,—fine figure. Relative?"

"My daughter's governess, sir," replied her ladyship, rigidly.

And in Dolly's passage across the room another incident occurred which was not lost upon the head of the house of Bilberry. Near the seat of Mr. Ralph Gowan stood a vacated chair, which obstructed the passage to the piano, and, observing it, the gentleman in question rose and removed it, bowing obsequiously in reply to Dolly's slight gesture of thanks, and when she took her place at the instrument he moved to a seat near by, and settled himself to listen with the air of a man who expected to enjoy the performance.

And he evidently did enjoy it, for a very pleasant little performance it was. The songs had a thrill of either pathos or piquancy in every word and note, and the audience found they were listening in spite of themselves.

When they were ended, Ralph Gowan sought out Lady Augusta in her stronghold, and placidly proposed being introduced to her young guest; and since it was evident that he intended to leave her no alternative, her ladyship was fain to comply; and so, before half the evening was over, Dolly found herself being entertained as she had never been entertained before in the camps of the Philistines at least. And as to the Eastern explorer, boredom was forgotten for the time, and he gave himself up entirely to the amusing and enjoying of this piquant young person with the white shoulders.

"Crewe," he said to her during the course of their first conversation. "I am sure Lady Augusta said 'Crewe.' Then you are relatives, I suppose?"

"Poor relations," answered Dolly, coolly, and without a shadow of discomfiture. "I am the children's governess. Trying, is n't it?"

Ralph Gowan met the gaze of the bright eyes admiringly. Even at this early period of their acquaintance he was falling into the snare every other man fell into,—the snare of finding that Dolly Crewe was startlingly unlike anybody else.

"Not for the children," he said. "Under such circumstances education must necessarily acquire a new charm."

"Thank you," said Dolly.

When supper was announced, Lady Augusta made another attack and was foiled again. She came to their corner, and, bending over Dolly, spoke to her in stage-whisper.

"I will bring young Mr. Jessup to take you into the supper-room, Dorothea," she said.

But Dolly's plans were already arranged, and even if such had not been the case she would scarcely have rejoiced at the prospect of the escort of young Mr. Jessup, who was a mild young idiot engaged in the study of theology.

"Thank you, Lady Augusta," she said, cheerfully, "but I have promised Mr. Gowan."

And Lady Augusta had the pleasure of seeing her leave the room a minute later, with her small glove slipped through Ralph Gowan's arm, and the plainly delighted face of that gentleman inclined attentively toward the elaborate Frenchy coiffure.

At the supper-table little Miss Crewe was a prominent feature. At her end of the table conversation flourished and cheerfulness reigned. Even Euphemia and young Mr. Jessup, who had come down together in a mutual agony of embarrassment, began to pluck up spirit and hazard occasional remarks, and finally even joined in the laughter at Dolly's witticism.

People lower down the table glanced up across the various dishes, and envied the group who seemed to set the general heaviness and discontent at defiance.

Dolly, accompanied by coffee and cakes, was more at home and more delightful than ever, so delightful, indeed, that Ralph Gowan began to regard even Lady Augusta with gratitude, since it was to her he was, to some extent, indebted for his new acquaintance.

"She is a delightful—yes, a delightful girl!" exclaimed young Mr. Jessup, confidentially addressing-Euphemia, and blushing vividly at his own boldness. "I never heard such a laugh as she has in my life. It is actually exhilarating. It quite raises one's spirits," with mild *naïveté*.

Euphemia began to brighten at once. She could talk about Dolly Crewe if she could talk about nothing else.

"Oh, but you have n't seen *anything* of her yet," she said, in a burst of enthusiasm. "If you could only see her every day, as I do, and hear the witty things she says, and see how self-possessed she is, when other people would be perfectly miserable with confusion, there would be no wonder at your saying you never saw anybody like her. *I* never did, I am sure. And then, you know, somehow or other, she always looks so well in everything she wears,— even in the shabbiest things, and her things are nearly always shabby enough, for they are dreadfully poor. She is always finding new ways of wearing things or new ways of doing her hair or—or something. It is the way her dresses fit, I think. Oh, dear, how I do wish the dressmaker could make mine fit as hers do! Just look at that white merino, now, for instance. It is the plainest dress in the room, and there is not a bit of fuss or trimming about it, and yet see how soft the folds look and how it hangs,—the train, you know. It reminds me of a picture,—one of those pictures in fashionable monthlies,— illustrations of love stories, you know."

"It is a very pretty dress," said young Mr. Jessup, eying it with great interest. "What did you say the stuff was called?"

"Merino," answered Phemie.

"Merino," repeated Mr. Jessup. "I will try and remember. I should like my sister Lucinda Maria to have a dress like it."

And he regarded it with growing admiration just tempered by the effect of a mental picture of Lucinda Maria, who was bony and of remarkable proportions, attired in its soft and flowing counterpart, with white swan's-down adorning her bare shoulders.

"May I ask," said Miss MacDowlas, at the bottom of the table, to Lady Augusta,—"may I ask who that young lady with the fresh completion is,—the young lady in white at the other end?"

"That is my governess," replied her ladyship, freezingly. "Miss Dorothea Crewe."

And Miss MacDowlas settled her eye-glass and gave Miss Dorothea Crewe the benefit of a prolonged examination.

"Crewe," she said, at length. "Poor relation, I suppose?" with some sharpness of manner. Dignity was lost upon Miss MacDowlas.

"A branch of my family who are no great credit to it," was the majestic rejoinder.

"Oh, indeed," was the lady's sole remark, and then Miss MacDowlas returned to her coffee, still, however, keeping her double eye-glass across her nose and casting an occasional glance at Dolly.

And just at this particular moment Dolly was unconsciously sealing Ralph Gowan's fate for him. Quite unconsciously, I repeat, for the most serious of Dolly's iniquities were generally unconscious. When she flirted, her flirtations were of so frank and open a nature, that, bewildered and fascinated though her victims might be, they must have been blind indeed to have been deceived, and so there were those who survived them and left the field safe, though somewhat sore at heart. But when she was in her honest, earnest, life-enjoying moods, and meant no harm,—when she was simply enjoying herself and trying to amuse her masculine companion, when her gestures were unconscious and her speeches unstudied, when she laughed through sheer merriment and was charmingly theatrical because she could not help it and because little bits of pathos and comedy were natural to her at times, then it was that the danger became deadly; then it was that her admirers were regardless of consequences, and defied results. And she was in just such a mood to-night.

"Come and see us?" she was saying. "Of course you may; and if you come, you shall have an insight into the domestic workings of modern Vagabondia. You shall be introduced to half a dozen people who toil not, neither do they spin successfully, for their toiling and spinning seems to have little result, after all. You shall see shabbiness and the spice of life hand-in-hand; and, I dare say, you will find that the figurative dinner of herbs is not utterly destitute of a flavor of *piquancy*. You shall see people who enjoy themselves in sheer defiance of circumstances, and who find a pathos in every-day events, which, in the camps of the Philistines, mean nothing. Yes, you may come if you care to." And Ralph Gowan, looking down at the changeful eyes, saw an almost tender light shining in their depths,—summoned up all at once perhaps by one of those inexplicable touches of pathos of which she had spoken.

But even coffee and conversation must come to an end at last, and so the end of this evening came. People began to drop away one by one, bidding their hostess good-night with the air of individuals who had performed a duty, and were relieved to find it performed and disposed of for the time being. So Dolly, leaving her companion with a bright farewell, and amiably disposing of Lady Augusta, slipped up-stairs to the retiring-room for her wraps. In the course of three minutes she came down again, the scarlet shawl draped around her, and the highly ornamental hood donned. She was of so little consequence in the Bilberry household that no one met her when she reappeared. Even the servants knew that her convenience or inconvenience was of small moment, so the task of summoning her cab would have devolved upon herself, had it not been for a little incident, which might have been either an accident or otherwise. As she came down the staircase a gentleman crossed the threshold of the parlor and came to meet her,—and this gentleman was no other than Ralph Gowan.

"Let me have the pleasure of putting you into your—"

"Cab," ended Dolly, with a trill of a laugh,—it was so evident that he had been going to say "carriage." "Thank you, with the greatest of pleasure. Indeed, it is rather a relief to me, for they generally keep me waiting. And I detest waiting."

He handed her into her seat, and lingered to see that she was comfortable, perhaps with unnecessary caution; and then, when she gave him her hand through the window, he held it for a moment longer than was exactly called for by the exigencies of the occasion.

"You will not forget that you have given me permission to call," he said, hesitating slightly.

"Oh, dear no!" she answered. "I shall not forget. We are always glad to see people—in Vagabondia."

And as the cab drove off, she waved the hand he had held in an airy gesture of adieu, gave him a bewildering farewell nod, and, withdrawing her face from the window, disappeared in the shadow within.

"Great Jove!" meditated Ralph Gowan, when he had seen the last of her. "And this is a nursery governess,—a sort of escape-valve for the spleen and ill moods of that woman in copper-color. She teaches them French and music, I dare say, and makes those spicy little jokes of hers over the dog-eared arithmetic. Ah, well! such is impartial Fortune," And he strolled back into the house again, to make his adieus to Lady Augusta, with the bewitching Greuze face fresh in his memory.

But, for her part, Dolly, having left him behind in the Philistine camp, was nestling comfortably in the dark corner of her cab, thinking of Griffith, as she always did think of him when she found herself alone for a moment.

"I wonder if he will be at home when I get there," she said. "Poor fellow! he would find it dull enough without me, unless they were all in unusually good spirits. I wonder if the time ever will come when we shall have a little house of our own, and can go out together or stay at home, just as we like."

CHAPTER III.
IN WHICH THE TRAIN IS LAID.

"After a holiday comes a rest day." The astuteness of this proverb continually proved itself in Vagabondia, and this was more particularly the case when the holiday had been Dolly's, inasmuch as Dolly was invariably called upon to "fight her battles o'er again," and recount her experiences the day following a visit, for the delectation of the household. Had there appeared in the camps a Philistine of notoriety, then that Philistine must play his or her part again through the medium of Dolly's own inimitable powers of description or representation; had any little scene occurred possessing a spice of flavoring, or illustrating any Philistine peculiarity, then Dolly was quite equal to the task of putting it upon the family stage, and re-enacting it with iniquitous seasonings and additions of her own. And yet the fun was never of an ill-natured sort. When Dolly gave them a correct embodiment of Lady Augusta in reception of her guests, with an accurate description of the "great Copper-Boiler costume," the bursts of applause meant nothing more than that Dolly's imitative gifts were in good condition, and that the "great Copper-Boiler costume" was a success. Then, the feminine mind being keenly alive to an interest in earthly vanities, an enlargement on Philistine adornments was considered necessary, and Dolly always rendered herself popular by a minute description of the reigning fashions, as displayed by the Bilberry element. She found herself quite repaid for the trouble of going into detail, by the unsophisticated pleasure in Mollie's eyes alone, for to Mollie outward furnishings seemed more than worthy of description and discussion.

Accordingly, the morning after Lady Augusta's *conversazione*, Dolly gave herself up to the task of enlivening the household. It was Saturday morning, fortunately, and on Saturday her visits to the Bilberry mansion were dispensed with, so she was quite at liberty to seat herself by the fire, with Tod in her arms, and recount the events of the evening. Somehow or other, she had almost regarded him as a special charge from the first. She had always been a favorite with him, as she was a favorite with most children. She was just as natural and thoroughly at home with Tod in her arms, or clambering over her feet, or clutching at the trimmings of her dress, as she was under any other circumstances; and when on this occasion Griffith came in at noon to hear the news, and found her kneeling upon the carpet with outstretched hands teaching the pretty little tottering fellow to walk, he felt her simply irresistible.

"Come to Aunt Dolly," she was saying. "Tod, come to Aunt Dolly." And then she looked up laughing. "Look at him, Griffith," she said. "He has walked all the way from that arm-chair." And then she made a rush at the child, and caught him in her arms with a little whirl, and jumped up with such a light-hearted enjoyment of the whole affair that it was positively exciting to look at her.

It was quite natural—indeed, it would have been quite unnatural if she had not found her usual abiding-place in her lover's encircling arm at once, even with Tod conveniently established on one of her own, and evidently regarding his own proximity upon such an occasion as remarkable if nothing else. That arm of Griffith's usually *did* slip around her waist even at the most ordinary times, and long use had so accustomed Dolly to the habit that she would have experienced some slight feeling of astonishment if the familiarity had been omitted.

It was rather a surprise to the young man to find that Miss MacDowlas had appeared upon the scene, and that she had partaken of coffee and conversation in the flesh the evening before.

"But it's just like her," he said. "She is the sort of relative who always *does* turn up unexpectedly, Dolly. How does she look?"

"Juvenescent," said Dolly; "depressingly so to persons who rely upon her for the realizing of expectations. A very few minutes satisfied me that I should never become Mrs. Griffith Donne upon *her* money. It is a very fortunate thing for us that we are of Vagabondian antecedents, Griffith,—just see how we might trouble ourselves, and wear our patience out over Miss MacDowlas, if we troubled ourselves about anything. This being utterly free from the care of worldly possessions makes one touchingly disinterested. Since we have nothing to expect, we are perfectly willing to wait until we get it."

She had thought so little about Ralph Gowan,—once losing sight of him, as he stood watching her on the pavement, that in discussing other subjects she had forgotten to mention him, and it was only Mollie's entrance into the room that brought him upon the carpet.

Coming in, with her hair bunched up in a lovely, disorderly knot, and the dimple on her left cheek artistically accentuated by a small patch of black, the youngest Miss Crewe yet appeared to advantage, when, after appropriating Tod, she slipped down into a sitting posture with him on the carpet, in the midst of the amplitude of folds of Lady Augusta's once gorgeous wrapper.

"Have you told him about the great Copper-Boiler costume, Dolly?" she said, bending down so that one brown tress hung swaying before Tod's eyes. "Has she, Griffith?"

"Yes," answered Griffith, looking at her with a vague sense of admiration. He shared all Dolly's enthusiasm on the subject of Mollie's prettiness.

"Was n't it good? I wish I was as cool as Dolly is. And poor Phemie—and the gentleman who made love to you all the evening, Dolly. What was his name? Was n't it Gowan?"

Griffith's eyes turned toward Dolly that instant.

"Gowan!" he exclaimed. "You didn't say anything about him. You didn't even say he was there."

"Did n't she?" said Mollie, looking up with innocently wide-open eyes. "Why, he made love to her all—"

"I wish you would n't talk such rubbish, Mollie," Dolly interrupted her—a trifle sharply because she understood the cloud on her lover's face so well. "Who said Mr. Gowan made love to me? Not I, you may be sure. I told you he talked to me, and that was all."

"You did not tell *me* that much," said Griffith, dryly.

It would scarcely have been human nature for Dolly not to have fired a little then, in spite of herself. She was constitutionally good-natured, but she was not seraphic, and her lover's rather excusable jealousy was specially hard to bear, when, as upon this occasion, it had no real foundation.

"I did not think it necessary," she said; "and, besides, I forgot; but if you wish to know the particulars," with a stiff little air of dignity, "I can give them you. Mr. Gowan was there, and found the evening stupid, as every one else did. There was no one else to talk to, so he talked to me, and when I came home he put me into the cab. And, the fact is, he is a good-natured Philistine enough. That is all, I believe, unless you would like me to try to record all he said."

"No, thank you," answered Griffith, and instantly began to torture himself with imagining what he really had said, making the very natural mistake of imagining what he would have said himself, and then giving Ralph Gowan credit for having perpetrated like tender gallantries. He never could divest himself of the idea that every living man found Dolly as entrancing as he found her himself. It could only be one man's bitter-sweet portion to be as desperately and inconsolably in love with her as he was himself, and no other than himself, or a man who might be his exact prototype, could have cherished a love at once so strong and so weak. There had been other men who had loved Dolly Crewe,—-adored her for a while, in fact, and imagined themselves wretches because they had been unsuccessful; but they had generally outlived their despair, and their adoration, cooling for want of sustenance, had usually settled down into a comfortable admiring liking for the cause of their misery, but it would never have been so with Griffith. This ordinary, hard-working, ill-paid young man had passionate impulse and hidden power of suffering enough in his restive nature to make a broken hope a broken life to him. His long-cherished love for the shabbily attired, often-snubbed, dauntless young person yclept Dorothea Crewe was the mainspring of his existence. He would have done daring deeds of valor for her sake, if circumstances had called upon him to comport himself in such tragic manner; had he been a knight of olden time, he would just have been the chivalrous, hotheaded, but affectionate young man to have entered the lists in his love's behalf, and tilted against tremendous odds, and died unvanquished; but living in the nineteenth century, his impetuosity, being necessarily restrained, became concentrated upon one point, and chafed him terribly at times. Without Dolly, he would have been without an object in life; with Dolly, he was willing to face any amount of discouragement and misfortune; and at this stage of his affection—after years of belief in that far-off blissful future—to lose her would have brought him wreck and ruin.

So when Dolly, in the full consciousness of present freedom from iniquity, withdrew herself from his encircling arm and turned her attention to Tod and Mollie, he was far more wretched than he had any right to be, and stood watching them, and gnawing his slender mustache, gloomy and distrustful.

But this could not last long, of course. They might quarrel, but they always made friends; and when in a short time Mollie, doubtless feeling herself a trifle in the way, left the room with the child, Dolly's impulsive warm-heartedness got the better of her upon this occasion as upon all others.

She came back to her lover's side and laid her hand on his arm.

"Don't let us quarrel about Ralph Gowan, Griffith," she said. "It was my fault; I ought to have told you."

He fairly crushed her in his remorseful embrace almost before she had finished her appeal. His distrust of her was as easily overcome as it was roused; one touch of her hand, one suspicion of a tremor in her voice, always conquered him and reduced him to penitent submission.

"You are an angel," he said, "and I am an unfeeling clod. No other woman would bear with me as you do. God bless you, Dolly."

She nestled within his arms and took his caresses almost gratefully. Perhaps it would have been wiser to have shown him how deep a sting his want of faith gave her sometimes, but she was always so glad when their misunderstandings were at an end, that she would not have so revenged herself upon him for the world. The cool, audacious self she exhibited in the camps of the Philistines was never shown to Griffith; in her intercourse with him she was only a slightly intensified edition of the child he had fallen in love with years before,—a bright, quick-witted child, with a deep nature and an immense faculty for loving and clinging to people. Dolly at twenty-two was pretty much what she had been at fifteen, when they had quarrelled and made up again, loved each other and romanced over the future brilliancy of prospect which now seemed just as far off as ever.

In five minutes after the clearing away of the temporary cloud, they were in a seventh heaven of bliss, as usual. In some of his wanderings about town, Griffith had met with a modest house, which would have been the very thing for them if they had possessed about double the income of which they were at present in receipt. He often met with houses of this kind; they seemed, in fact, to present themselves to his longing vision every week of his life; and I think it rather to his credit to mention that he never failed to describe them to Dolly, and enlarge upon their merits with much eloquence. Furniture warehouses also were a source of some simple pleasure to them. *If* they possessed the income (not that they had the remotest prospect of possessing it), and rented the house, naturally they would require furniture, and it was encouraging to know that the necessary articles might be bought *if* the money was forthcoming. Consequently a low-priced table or a cheap sofa was a consolation, if not a source of rejoicing, and their happiest hours were spent in counting the cost of parlor carpets never to be purchased, and window curtains of thin air. They even economized sternly in minor matters, and debated the expenditure of an extra shilling as closely as if it had been a matter entailing the deepest anxiety; and on the whole, perhaps, practical persons might have condemned their affectionate, hopeful weakness as childish and nonsensical, but they were happy in the indulgence of it, at all events, and surely they might have been engaged in a less tender and more worldly pastime. There were other people, perhaps, weak and imprudent themselves it may be, who would have seen a touch of simple pathos in this unconsciously shown faith in Fortune and her not too kindly moods.

"Old Flynn ought to raise my salary, you know, Dolly," said Griffith. "I work hard enough for him, confound him!" somewhat irrelevantly, but with laudable and not unamiable vigor. He meant no harm to "Old Flynn;" he would have done a good-natured thing for him at any moment, the mild expletive was simply the result of adopted custom. "There is n't a fellow in the place who does as much as I do. I worked from seven in the morning till midnight every day last week, and I wrote half his editorials for him, and nobody knows he does n't get them up himself. If he would only give me two hundred instead of one, just see how we could live."

"We could live on a hundred and fifty," put in Dolly, with an air of practical speculation which did her credit, "if we were economical."

"Well, say a hundred and fifty, then," returned Griffith, quite as seriously, "for we should be economical. Say a hundred and fifty. It would be nothing to him,—confound him!—but it would be everything in the world to us. That house in the suburbs was only thirty pounds, taxes and all, and it was just the very thing we should want if we were married."

"How many rooms?" asked Dolly.

"Six, and kitchen and cupboards and all that sort of contrivances. I asked particularly—went to see the landlord to inquire and see what repairing he would do if we wanted the place. There is a garden of a few yards in the front, too, and one or two rose-bushes. I don't know whether they ever bloom, but if they do, you could wear them in your hair. I thought of that the minute I saw them. The first time I saw you, Dolly, you had a rose in your hair, and I remember thinking I had never seen a flower worn in the same way. Other girls do n't wear things as you wear them somehow or other."

Dolly acknowledged the compliment with a laugh and a coaxing, patronizing little squeeze of his arm.

"You think they don't," she said, "you affectionate old fellow, that is it. Well, and what did the landlord say? Would he beautify?"

"Well, yes, I think he would if the matter was pressed," said Griffith, returning to the subject with a vigor of enjoyment inspiriting to behold. "And, by the way, Dolly, I saw a small sofa at a place in town which was just the right size to fit into a sort of alcove there is in the front parlor."

"Did you inquire the price?" said Dolly.

"Well—no," cheerfully; "but I can, if you would like to know it. You see, I had n't any money, and did n't know when I should have any, and I felt rather discouraged at the time, and I had an idea the price would make me feel worse, so I did not go in. But it was a comfortable, plump little affair, covered with green,—the sort of thing I should like to have in our house, when we have one. It would be so comfortable to throw one's self down on to after a hard day's work, particularly if one had a headache."

"Yes," said Dolly; and then, half unconsciously and quite in spite of herself, the ghost of a sigh escaped her. She could not help wishing things were a trifle more real sometimes, bright and whimsically unworldly as she was.

"What did that mean?" Griffith asked her.

She wakened up, as it were, and looked as happy as ever in an instant, creeping a trifle closer to him in her loving anxiety to blind him to the presence of the little pain in her heart.

"Nothing," she said, briskly. And then—"We don't want much, do we, Griffith?"

"No," said Griffith, a certain grim sense of humor getting the better of him. "And we have n't got it."

She laughed outright at the joke quite enjoyably. Even the grimmest of jocosities wins its measure of respect in Vagabondia, and besides, her laugh removed the impression her sigh might have created. She was herself again at once.

"Never mind," she said. (It was always "never mind.") "Never mind, it will all come right in the end. Humble merit *must* be rewarded, and if humble merit isn't, we can only console ourselves with the reasonable reflection that there must be something radically wrong with the state of society. Who knows whether you may not 'get into something,' as Phil says, which may be twenty times better than anything Old Flynn can give you!" with characteristic Vagabondian hopefulness.

Just at this juncture Phil himself entered, or, rather, half entered, for he only put his head—a comely, curled head surmounted by a disreputable velvet cap—half into the room.

"Oh, you are here, are you?" he said. "You are the fellow I want. I am just touching up something I want to show you. Come into the studio for a minute or so, Grif."

"It is that picture Mollie sat for," he explained, as they followed him into the big, barren room, dignified by the name of studio. "I have just finished it."

Mollie was standing before the picture herself when they went in to look at it, but she did not turn round on hearing them. She had Tod in her arms yet, but she seemed to have forgotten his very existence in her preoccupation. And it was scarcely to be wondered at. The picture was only a head,— Mollie's own fresh, drowsy-eyed face standing out in contrast under some folds of dark drapery thrown over the brown hair like a monk's cowl, two or three autumn-tinted oak leaves clinging to a straying tress,—but it was effective and novel enough to be a trifle startling. And Mollie was looking at it with a growing shadow of pleasure in her expression. She was slowly awakening to a sense of its beauty, and she was by no means dissatisfied.

"It is lovely!" Dolly cried out, enthusiastically.

"So it is," said Griffith. "And as like her as art can make it. It's a success, Phil."

Phil stepped back with a critical air to give it a new inspection.

"Yes, it is a success," he said. "Just give me a chance to get it hung well, and it will draw a crowd next season. You shall have a new dress if it does, Mollie, and you shall choose it yourself."

Mollie roused herself for a moment, and lighted up.

"Shall I?" she said; and then all at once she blushed in a way that made Dolly stare at her in some wonder. It seemed queer to think that Mollie—careless child Mollie—was woman enough to blush over anything.

And then Aimée and 'Toinette came in, and looked on and admired just as openly and heartily as the rest, only Aimée was rather the more reticent of the two, and cast furtive glances at Mollie now and then. But Mollie was in a new mood, and had very little to say; and half an hour after, when her elder sister went into the family sitting-room, she found her curled up in an easy-chair by the fire, looking reflective. Dolly went to the hearth and stood near her.

"What are you thinking about?" she asked.

Mollie stirred uneasily, and half blushed again.

"I don't know," she answered.

"Yes, you do," contradicted Dolly, good-naturedly. "Are you thinking that it is a pleasant sort of a thing to be handsome enough to be made a picture of, Mollie?"

The brown eyes met hers with an innocent sort of deprecating consciousness. "I—I never thought about myself in that way before," admitted Mollie, naively.

"Why," returned Dolly, quite sincerely, "you must have looked in the glass."

"Ye-es," with a slow shake of the head; "but it did n't look the same way in the glass,—it did n't look as nice."

Dolly regarded her with a surprise which was not unmingled with affectionate pity. She was not as unsophisticated as Mollie, and never had been. As the feminine head of the family, she had acquired a certain shrewdness early in life, and had taken a place in the household the rest were hardly equal to. There had been no such awakening as this for her. At fourteen, she had been fully and complacently conscious of the exact status of her charms and abilities, physical and mental. She had neither under-nor over-rated them. She had smiled back at her reflection in her mirror, showing two rows of little milk-white teeth, and being well enough satisfied with being a charming young person with a secure complexion and enviable self-poise. She understood herself, and attained perfection in the art of understanding others. Her rather sharp experience had not allowed *her* to look in the glass in guileless ignorance of what she saw there, and perhaps this made her all the fonder of Mollie.

"What kind of a dress are you going to choose if Phil buys you one?" she asked.

"Maroon," answered Mollie. "Oh!" with a little shuddering breath of desperate delight, "how I wish I could have a maroon silk!"

Dolly shook her head doubtfully.

"It wouldn't be serviceable, because you could only have the one, and you could n't wear it on wet days," she said.

"I should n't care about its being serviceable," burst forth innocent Vagabondia, rebelling against the trammels of prudence. "I want something pretty. I do so detest serviceable things. I would stay in the house all the wet days if I might have a maroon silk to wear when it was fine."

"She is beginning to long for purple and fine linen," sighed Dolly, as she ran up to her bedroom afterward. "The saints forefend! It is a bad sign. She will fall in love the next thing. Poor, indiscreet little damsel!"

But, despite her sage lamentations, there was even at that moment a plan maturing in her mind which was an inconsistent mixture of Vagabondia's goodnature and whim. Mollie's fancy for the maroon silk had struck her as being artistic, and there was not a Crewe among them who had not a weakness for the artistic in effect. Tod himself was imaginatively supposed to share it and exhibit preternatural intelligence upon the subject. In Dolly it amounted to a passion which she found it impossible to resist. By it she was prompted to divers small extravagances at times, and by it she was assisted in the arranging of all her personal adornments. It was impossible to slight the mental picture of Mollie with maroon drapery falling about her feet, with her cheeks tinted with excited color, and with that marvel of delight in her eyes. She could not help thinking about it.

"She would be simply incomparable," she found herself soliloquizing. "Just give her that dress, put a white flower in her hair and set her down in a ballroom, or in the dress circle of a theatre, and she would set the whole place astir. Oh, she must have it."

It was very foolish and extravagant of course; even the people who are weakly tolerant enough to rather lean toward Dorothea Crewe, will admit this. The money that would purchase the maroon garment would have purchased a dozen minor articles far more necessary to the dilapidated household; but while straining at such domestic gnats as these articles were, she was quite willing and even a trifle anxious to swallow Mollie's gorgeous camel. Such impulsive inconsistency was characteristic, however, and she betook herself to her bedroom with the intention of working out the problem of accommodating supply to demand.

She took out her purse and emptied its contents on to her dressing-table. Two or three crushed bills, a scrap or so of poetry presented by Griffith upon various tender occasions, and a discouragingly small banknote, the sole remains of her last quarter's salary The supply was not equal to the demand, it was evident. But she was by no means overpowered. She was dashed, but not despairing. Of course, she had not expected to launch into such a reckless piece of expenditure all at once, she had only thought she might attain her modest ambition in the due course of time, and she thought so yet. She crammed bills and bank-note back into the purse with serene cheerfulness and shut it with a little snap of the clasp.

"I will begin to save up," she said, "and I will persuade Phil to help me. We can surely do it between us, and then we will take her somewhere and let her have her first experience of modern society. What a sensation she would create in the camps of the Philistines!"

She descended into the kitchen after this, appearing in those lower regions in the full glory of apron and rolled-up sleeves, greatly to the delight of the youthful maid-of-all-work, who, being feeble of intellect and fond of society, regarded the prospect of spending the afternoon with her as a source of absolute rejoicing. The "Sepoy," as she was familiarly designated by the family, was strongly attached to Dolly, as, indeed, she was to every other member of the household. The truth was, that the usefulness of the Sepoy (whose baptismal name was Belinda) was rather an agreeable fiction than a well-established fact. She had been adopted as a matter of charity, and it was charity rather than any recognized brilliance of parts which caused her to be retained. Phil had picked her up on the streets one night in time gone by, and had brought her home principally because her rags were soaked and she had asserted that she had nowhere to go for shelter, and partly, it must be confessed, because she was a curiosity. Having taken her in, nobody was stern enough to turn her out to face her fate again, and so she stayed. Nobody taught her anything in particular about household economy, because nobody knew anything particular to teach her. It was understood that she was to do what she could, and that what she could not do should be shared among them. She could fetch and carry, execute small commissions, manage the drudgery and answer the door-bell, when she was presentable, which was not often; indeed, this last duty had ceased to devolve upon her, after she had once confronted Lady Augusta with personal adornments so remarkable as to strike that august lady dumb and rigid with indignation upon the threshold, and cause her, when she recovered herself, to stonily, but irately demand an explanation of the gratuitous insult she considered had been offered her. Belinda's place was in the kitchen, after this, and to these regions she usually confined herself, happily vigorous in the discharge of her daily duties. She was very fond of Dolly, and hailed the approach of her days of freedom with secret demonstrations of joy. She hoarded the simple presents of finery given her by that young person with care, and regarded them in the light of sacred talismans. A subtle something in her dwarfed, feeble, starved-out nature was stirred, it may be, by the sight of the girl's life and brightness; and, apart from this, it would not have been like Dolly Crewe if she had not sympathized, half unconsciously, half because she was constitutionally sympathetic, with even this poor stray. If she had been of a more practical turn of mind, in all probability she would have taken Belinda in hand and attacked the work of training her with laudable persistence; but, as it was, private misgivings as to the strength of her own domestic accomplishments caused her to confine herself to more modest achievements. She could encourage her, at least, and encourage her she did with divers good-natured speeches and a leniency of demeanor which took the admiring Sepoy by storm.

Saturday became a white day in the eyes of Belinda, because, being a holiday, it left Dolly at liberty to descend into the kitchen and apply herself to the study of cookery as a science, with much agreeable bustle and a pleasant display of high spirit and enjoyment of the novelty of her position. She had her own innocent reasons for wishing to become a proficient in the art, and if her efforts were not always crowned with success, the appearance of her handiwork upon the table on the occasion of the Sunday's dinner never disturbed the family equilibrium, principally, perhaps, because the family digestion was unimpaired. They might be jocose, they had been ironical, but they were never severe, and they always addressed themselves to the occasionally arduous task of disposing of the viands with an indifference to consequences which nothing could disturb.

"One cannot possibly be married without knowing something of cookery," Dolly had announced oracularly; "and one cannot gain a knowledge of it without practising, so I am going to practise. None of you are dyspeptic, thank goodness, so you can stand it. The only risk we run is that Tod might get hold of a piece of the pastry and be cut off in the bloom of his youth; but we must keep a strict watch upon him."

And she purchased a cookery book and commenced operations, and held to her resolve with Spartan firmness, encouraged by private but enthusiastic bursts of commendation from Griffith, who, finding her out, read the tender meaning of the fanciful seeming whim, and was so touched thereby that the mere sight of her in her nonsensical little affectation of working paraphernalia raised him to a seventh heaven of bliss.

When she made her entrance into the kitchen on this occasion, and began to bustle about in search for her apron, Belinda, who was on her knees polishing the grate, amidst a formidable display of rags and brushes, paused to take breath and look at her admiringly.

"Are yer goin' to make yer pies 'n things, Miss Dolly?" she asked. "Which, if ye are, yer apern 's in the left 'and dror."

"So it is," said Dolly. "Thank you. Now where is the cookery book?"

"Left 'and dror agin," announced Belinda, with a faint grin. "I allus puts it there."

Whereupon Dolly, making industrious search for it, found it, and applied herself to a deep study of it, resting her white elbows on the dresser, and looking as if she had been suddenly called upon to master its contents or be led to the stake. She could not help being intense and in earnest even over this every-day problem of pies and puddings.

"Fricassee?" she murmured. "Fricassee was a failure, so was mock-turtle soup; it looked discouraging, and the fat *would* swim about in a way that attracted attention. Croquettes were not so bad, though they were a little stringy; but beef *à la mode* was positively unpleasant. Jugged hare did very well, but oyster *pâtés* were dubious. Veal pie Griffith liked."

"There's somebody a-ringin' at the door-bell," said Belinda, breaking in upon her. "He's rung twict, which I can go, mum, if I ain't got no smuts."

Dolly looked up from her book.

"Some one is going now, I think," she said. "I hope it is n't a visitor," listening attentively.

But it was a visitor, unfortunately. In a few minutes Mollie came in, studiously perusing a card she held in her hand.

"Ralph," she proclaimed, coming forward slowly. "Ralph Gowan. It's Lady Augusta's gentleman, Dolly, and he wants to see you."

Dolly took the card and looked at it, giving her shoulders a tiny shrug of surprise.

"He has not waited long," she said; "and it is rather inconvenient, but it can't be helped. I suppose I shall have to run up-stairs and present him to Phil."

She untied her apron, drew down her sleeves, settled the bit of ribbon at her throat, and in three minutes opened the parlor door and greeted her visitor, looking quite as much in the right place as she had done the night before in the white merino.

"I am very glad to see you," she said, shaking hands with him, "and I am sure Phil will be, too. He is always glad to see people, and just now you will be doubly welcome, because he has a new picture to talk about. Will you come into the studio, or shall I bring him here? I think it had better be the studio at once, because you will be sure to drift there in the end,—visitors always do."

"The studio let it be, if you please," answered Gowan, wondering, just as he had done the night before, at the indescribable something in her manner which was so novel because it was so utterly free from any suggestion of affectation. It would have been a difficult matter to tell her that he had not come for any other reason than to see herself again, and yet this really was the case.

But his rather fanciful taste found Phil a novelty also when she led him into the studio, and presented him to that young man, who was lying upon a couch with a cigar in his mouth.

Phil had something of the same cool friendliness of deportment, and, being used to the unexpected advent of guests at all hours, was quite ready to welcome him. He had the same faculty for making noticeable speeches, too, and was amiable, though languid and *débonnaire*, and by no means prone to ceremony. In ten minutes after he had entered the room Ralph Gowan understood, as by magic, that, little as the world was to these people, they had, in their Bohemian fashion, learned through sheer tact to comprehend and tolerate its weaknesses. He examined the pictures on the walls and in the folios, and now and then found himself roused into something more than ordinary admiration. But he was disappointed in one thing. He failed in accomplishing the object of his visit.

After she had seen that Phil and the paintings occupied his attention to some extent, Dolly left them.

"I was beginning to think about pies and puddings when you came," she said, "and I must go back to them. Saturday is the only day Lady Augusta leaves me, in which to improve in branches of domestic usefulness," with an iniquitous imitation of her ladyship's manner.

After which she went down to the kitchen again and plunged into culinary detail with renewed vigor, thinking of the six-roomed house in the suburbs, and the green sofa which was to fit into the alcove in the front parlor, growing quite happy over the mental picture, in blissful unconsciousness of the fact that a train had been that day laid, and that a spark would be applied that very night through the medium of a simple observation made by Phil to her lover.

"Gowan was here this morning, Grif, and Dolly brought him into the studio. He's not a bad sort of fellow for a Philistine, and he seems to know something about pictures. I should n't be surprised if he came again."

CHAPTER IV.
A LILY OF THE FIELD.

THIS was the significant and poetic appellation which at once attached itself to Ralph Gowan after his first visit to the studio in Bloomsbury Place, and, as might have been expected, it was a fancy of Dolly's, the affixing of significant titles being one of her *fortes*.

"The lilies of the field," she observed, astutely, "are a distinct class. They toil not, neither do they spin, and yet Solomon in all his glory was not arrayed like one of these. Yes, my young friends, Mr. Ralph Gowan is a lily of the field."

And she was not far wrong. Twenty-seven years before Mr. Ralph Gowan had been presented to an extended circle of admiring friends as the sole heir to a fortune large enough to have satisfied the ambitions of half a dozen heirs of moderate aspirations, and from that time forward his lines had continually fallen in pleasant places. As a boy he had been handsome, attractive, and thoroughbred, and consequently popular; his good looks made him a favorite with women, his good fortune with men; his friends were rather proud of him, and his enemies were powerless against him; he found it easy to be amiable because no obstacles to amiability lay in his path; and altogether he regarded existence as a comfortable enough affair.

At school his fellows had liked him just as boys as well as men are apt to like fortunate people; and as he had grown older he had always found himself a favorite, it may be for something of the same reason. But being, happily, a gentleman by nature, he had not been much spoiled by the general adulation. Having been born to it, he carried himself easily through it, scarcely recognizing the presence of what would have been patent to men less used to popularity. He was fond of travelling, and so had amused himself by comfortably arranging uncomfortable journeys and exploring pleasantly those parts of the earth which to ordinary tourists would appear unattainable.

He was not an ordinary young man, upon the whole, which was evinced by his making no attempt to write a book of travels, though he might safely have done so; and really, upon the whole, "lily of the field" though chance had made him, he was neither useless nor purposeless, and rather deserved his good luck than otherwise.

Perhaps it was because he was not an ordinary individual that his fancy was taken by the glimpse he had caught of life in Vagabondia. It was his first glimpse of the inner workings of such a life, and its novelty interested him. A girl of twenty-two who received attention and admiration in an enjoyable, matter-of-fact manner, as if she was used to and neither over- nor undervalued it, who could make coffee and conversation bearable and even exciting, who could hold her own against patronage and slights, and be as piquant and self-possessed at home as in society, who could be dazzling at night and charming in the morning, was novelty enough in herself to make Bloomsbury Place attractive, even at its dingiest, and there were other attractions aside from this one.

Phil in the studio, taking life philosophically, and regarding the world and society in general with sublime and amiable tolerance, was as unique in his way as Dolly was in hers; his handsome girl-wife, who had come in to them with her handsome child in her arms, was unique also; Mollie herself, who had opened the door and quite startled him with the mere sight of her face,— well, Mollie had impressed him as she impressed everybody. And he was quite observant enough to see the element of matter-of-fact, half-jocular affection that bound them one to another; he could not help seeing it, and it almost touched him. They were not a sentimental assembly, upon the whole, but they were fond of each other in a style peculiar to themselves, and ready to unite in any cause which was the cause of the common weal. The family habit of taking existence easily and regarding misfortunes from a serenely philosophical standpoint, amused Ralph Gowan intensely. It had spiced Dolly's conversation, and it spiced Phil's; indeed, it showed itself in more than words. They had banded themselves against unavoidable tribulation, and it could not fail to be beautifully patent to the far-seeing mind that, taking all things together, tribulation had the worst of it.

They were an artistic study, Ralph Gowan found, and so, in his character of a "lily of the field," he fell into the habit of studying them, as an amusement at first, afterwards because his liking for them became friendly and sincere.

It was an easy matter to call again after the first visit,—people always did call again at Bloomsbury Place, and Ralph Gowan was no exception to the rule. He met Phil in the city, and sauntered home with him to discuss art and look at his work; he invited him to first-class little dinners, and introduced him to one or two men worth knowing; in short, it was not long before the two were fond of each other in undemonstrative man fashion. The studio was the sort of place Gowan liked to drop into when time hung heavily on his hands, and consequently hardly a week passed without his having at least once or twice dropped into it to sit among the half dozen of Phil's fellow Bohemians, who were also fond of dropping in as the young man sat at his easel, sometimes furiously at work, sometimes tranquilly loitering over the finishing touches of a picture. They were good-natured, jovial fellows, too, these Bohemian visitors, though they were more frequently than not highly scented with the odor of inferior tobacco, and rarely made an ostentatious display in the matter of costume, or were conspicuously faultless in the matter of linen; they failed to patronize the hairdresser, and were prone to various convivialities, but they were neither vicious nor vulgar, and they were singularly faithful to their friendships for each other. They were all fond of Phil, and accordingly fraternized at once with his new friend, adopting him into their circle with the ease of manner and freedom of sentiment which seemed the characteristic of their class; and they took to him all the more kindly because, amateur though he was, he shared many of their enthusiasms.

Of course he did not always see Dolly when he went. During every other day of the week but Saturday she spent her time from nine in the morning until five in the afternoon in the rather depressing atmosphere of the Bilberry school-room. She vigorously assaulted the foundations of Lindley Murray, and attacked the rules of arithmetic; she taught Phemie French, and made despairing but continuous efforts at "finishing" her in music. But poor Phemie was not easily "finished," and hung somewhat heavily upon the hands of her youthful instructress; still, she was affectionate, if weak-minded, and so Dolly managed to retain her good spirits.

"I believe they are all fond of me in their way," she said to Griffith,—"all the children, I mean; and that is something to be thankful for."

"They couldn't help being fond of you," returned the young man. "Did any human being ever know you without being fond of you?"

"Yes," said Dolly; "Lady Augusta knows me; and I do not think—no," with a cheerfully resigned shake of the head, which did not exactly express deep regret or contrition, "I really do not think Lady Augusta is what you might call overwhelmed with the strength of her attachment for me."

"Oh, Lady Augusta!" said Griffith. "Confound Lady Augusta!"

Griffith was one of the very few people who did not like Ralph Gowan, and perhaps charitably inclined persons will be half inclined to excuse his weakness. It was rather trying, it must be admitted, for a desponding young man rather under stress of weather, so to speak, to find himself thrown into sharp contrast with an individual who had sailed in smooth waters all his life, and to whom a ripple would have been a by no means unpleasant excitement; it was rather chafing to constantly encounter this favorite of fortune in the best of humors, because he had nothing to irritate him; thoroughbred, unruffled, and *débonnaire* because he had nothing of pain or privation to face; handsome, well dressed, and at ease, because his income and his tastes balanced against each other accommodatingly. Human nature rose up and battled in the Vagabondian breast; there were times when, for the privilege of administering severe corporeal chastisement to Ralph Gowan, Griffith would have sacrificed his modest salary with a Christian fortitude and resignation beautiful to behold. To see him sitting in one of the faded padded chairs, roused all his ire, and his consciousness of his own weakness made the matter worse; to see him talking to Dolly, and see her making brisk little jokes for his amusement, was worse still, and drove him so frantic that more than once he had turned quite pale in his secret frenzy of despair and jealousy, and had quite frightened the girl, though he was wise enough to keep his secret to himself. It was plain enough that Gowan admired Dolly, but other men had admired her before; the sting of it was that this fellow, with his cool airs and graces and tantalizing repose of manner, had no need to hold back if he could win her. There would be no need for him to plan and pinch and despair; no need for faltering over odd shillings and calculating odd pence; *he* could marry her in an hour if she cared for him, and he could surround her with luxuries, and dress her like a queen, and make her happy, as she deserved to be. And then the poor fellow's heart would beat fiercely, and the very blood would tremble in his veins, at the mere thought of giving her up.

One night after they had been sitting together, and Gowan had just left the room with Phil, Dolly glanced up from her work and saw her lover looking at her with a face so pale and wretched that she was thrown into a passion of fear.

She tossed her work away in a second, and, making one of her little rushes at him, was caught in his arms and half suffocated. She knew the instant she caught sight of his face what he was suffering, though perhaps she did not know the worst.

"Oh, why will you?" she cried out, in tears, all at once. "It is cruel! You are as pale as death, and I know—I know so well what it means."

"Tell me you will never forget what we have been to each other," he said, when he could speak; "tell me you don't care for that fellow,—tell me you love me, Dolly, tell me you love me."

She did not hesitate a moment; she had never flirted with Griffith in her life, and she knew him too well to try him when he wore that desperate, feverish look of longing in his eyes. She burst into an impetuous sob, and clung to him with both hands.

"I love you with all my soul," she said. "I will never *let* you give me up; and as to forgetting, I might die, but I could never forget. Care for Ralph Gowan! I love *you*, Griffith, I love *you!*"

"And you don't regret?" he said, piteously. "Oh, Dolly, just think of what *he* could give you; and then think of our hopeless dreams about miserable six-roomed houses and cheap furniture."

"You will make me hate him," cried Dolly, her gust of love and pity making her fierce. "I don't want anything anybody could give me. I only want you, *dear* old fellow,—*darling* old fellow," holding him fast, as if she would never let him go, and shedding a shower of impassioned, tender tears. "Oh, my darling, only wait until I am your own wife, and see how happy I will be, and how happy I will make you,—for I *can* make you happy,—and see how I will work in our little home for your sake, and how content I will be with a little. Oh, what must I do to show you how I love you! Do you think I could have cared for Ralph Gowan all these years as I have cared for you? No indeed; but I shall care for you forever, and I would wait for you a *thousand* years if I might only be your wife, and die in your arms at the end of it."

And she believed every word she said, too, and would have been willing to lay down her young life to prove it, extravagant as it may all sound to the discreet. And she quite believed, too, that she could never have so loved any other man than this unlucky, jealous, tempestuous one; but I will take the liberty of saying that this was a mistake, for, being an impassioned, heart-ruled, unworldly young person, it is quite likely that if Ralph Gowan had stood in Mr. Griffith Donne's not exactly water-tight shoes, she would have clung to him quite as faithfully, and believed in his perfections quite as implicitly, and quite as scornfully would have depreciated the merits of his rival; but chance had arranged the matter for her years before, and so Mr. Griffith was the hero.

"Ralph Gowan!" she flung out. "What is Ralph Gowan, or any other man on earth, to me? Did I love *him* before I knew what love was, and scarcely understood my own heart? Did I grow into a woman loving *him* and clinging to *him* and dreaming about him? Have I ever had any troubles in common with *him*? Did we grow up together, and tell each other all our thoughts and help each other to bear things? Let him travel in the East, if he likes,"—with high and rather inconsistent disdain,—"and let him have ten thousand a year, if he will,—a hundred thousand millions a year wouldn't buy me from you— my own!" In another burst, "Let him ride in his carriage, if he chooses,"— rather, as if such a course would imply the most degraded weakness; but, as I have said before, she was illogical, if affectionate,—"let him ride in his carriage. I would rather walk barefoot through the world with you than ride in a hundred carriages, if every one of them was lined with diamonds and studded with pearls."

There was the true flavor of Vagabondia's indiscretion and want of forethought in this, I grant you; but such speeches as these were Dolly Crewe's mode of comforting her lover in his dark moods; at least, she was sincere,—and sincerity will excuse many touches of extravagance. And as to Griffith, every touch of loving, foolish rhapsody dropped upon his heart like dew from heaven, filling him with rapture and drawing him nearer to her than before.

"But," he objected,—a rather weak objection, offered rather weakly, because he was so full of renewed confidence and bliss,—"but he is a handsomer fellow than I am, Dolly, and it must be confessed he has good taste."

"Handsomer!" echoed Dolly. "What do I care about his beauty? He is n't *you*,—that is where he fails to come up to the mark. And as to his good taste, do you suppose for a second that I could ever admire the most imposing 'get-up' by Poole, as I love this threadbare coat of yours, that I have laid my cheek against for the last three years?" And she bent down all at once and kissed the shabby sleeve.

"No," she said, looking up the next minute with her eyes as bright as stars. "We have been *given* to each other, that is it. It was n't chance, it was something higher. We needed each other, and a higher power than Fate bound us together, and it was a power that is n't cruel enough to separate us now, after all these years have woven our lives in one chord, and drawn our hearts close, and taught us how to comfort and bear with each other. I was given to you because I could help to make your life brighter,—and you were given to me because you could help to brighten mine, and God will never part us so long as we are true."

The coat sleeve came into requisition again then, as it often did. Her enthusiastic burst ended in a gush of heart-full tears, and she hid her face on the coat sleeve until they were shed; Griffith in the mean time touching her partly bent head caressingly with his hand, but remaining silent because he could not trust himself to speak.

But she became quieter at last, and got over it so far as to look up and smile.

"I could n't give up the six-roomed house and the green sofa, Griffith," she said. "They are like a great many other things,—the more I don't get them the more I want them. And the long winter evenings we are to spend together, when you are to read and I am to sew, and we are both to be blissfully happy. I could n't give those up on any account. And how could I bear to see Ralph Gowan, or any one else, seated in the orthodox arm-chair?"

The very idea of this latter calamity occurring crushed Griffith completely. The long winter evenings they were to spend together were such a pleasant legend. Scarcely a day passed without his drawing a mental picture of the room which was to be their parlor, and of the fireside Dolly was to adorn. It required only a slight effort of imagination to picture her shining in the tiny room whose door closed upon an outside world of struggling and an inside world of love and hope and trust. He imagined Dolly under a variety of circumstances, but nothing pleased and touched him so tenderly as this fireside picture,—its ideal warmth and glow, and its poetic placing of Dolly as his wife sitting near to him with her smiles and winsome ways and looks—

his own, at last, unshared by any outsiders. Giving that long-cherished fancy up would have killed him, if he could have borne all the rest. And while these two experienced the recorded fluctuations of their romance in private, Ralph Gowan had followed Phil into the studio.

They found Mollie there on going into the room; and Mollie lying upon the sofa asleep, with her brown head upon a big soft purple cushion, was quite worthy a second glance. She had been rather overpowered in the parlor by the presence of Ralph Gowan, and, knowing there was a fire in the studio, and a couch drawn near it, she had retired there, and, appropriating a pile of cushions, had dropped asleep, and lay there curled up among them.

Seeing her, Gowan found himself smiling faintly. Mollie amused him just as she amused Dolly. It was so difficult a matter to assign her any settled position in the world; She was taller than the other girls, and far larger and more statuesque; indeed, there were moments when she seemed to be almost imposing in presence, but this only rendered her still more a charming incongruity. She might have carried herself like a royal princess, but she blushed up to the tips of her ears at a glance, and was otherwise as innocently awkward as a beauty may be. She was not fond of strangers either, and generally lapsed into silence when spoken to. Public admiration only disconcerted her, and made her pout, and the unceremonious but friendly compliments of Phil's brethren in art were her special grievance.

"They stare at me, and stare at me, and stare at me," she complained, pettishly, to Dolly, "and some of them say things to me. I wish they would attend to their pictures and leave me alone."

But she had never evinced any particular dislike to Ralph Gowan. She was overpowered by a secret sense of his vast superiority to the generality of mankind, but she rather admired him upon the whole. She liked to hear him talk to Dolly, and she approved of his style. It was such a novel sort of thing to meet with a man who was not shabby, and whose clothes seemed made for him and were worn with a grace. He was handsome, too, and witty and polite, and his cool, comfortable manner reminded her vaguely of Dolly's own. So she used to sit and listen to the two as they chatted, and in the end her guileless admiration of Dolly's eligible Philistine became pretty thoroughly established.

When the sound of advancing footsteps roused her from her nap she woke with great tranquillity, and sat up rubbing her drowsy eyes serenely for a minute or so before she discovered that Phil had a companion. But when she did discover that such was the fact she blushed all over, and looked up at Ralph Gowan in some naïve distress.

"I did n't know any one was coming," she said, "and I was so comfortable that I fell asleep. It was the cushions, I think."

"I dare say it was," answered Gowan, regarding her sleep-flushed cheeks and exquisite eyes with the pleasure he always felt in any beauty, animate or inanimate. "May I sit here, Mollie?" and then he looked at her again and decided that he was quite right in speaking to her as he would have spoken to a child, because she *was* such a very child.

"By me, on the sofa?" she answered. "Oh, yes."

"Are you going to talk business with Phil?" she asked him next, "or may I stay here? Griffith and Dolly won't want me in the parlor, and I don't want to go into the kitchen."

"I have no doubt you may stay here," he said, quite seriously; "but why won't they want you in the parlor?"

"They never want anybody," astutely. "I dare say they are making love,— they generally are."

"Making love," he repeated. "Ah, indeed!" and for the next few minutes was so absorbed in thought that Mollie was quite forgotten.

Making love were they,—this shabby, rather un-amiable young man and the elder Miss Crewe? It sounded rather like nonsense to Ralph Gowan, but it was not a pleasant sort of thing to think about. It is not to be supposed that he himself was very desperately in love with Dolly just yet, but it must be admitted he admired her decidedly. Beauty as Mollie was, he scarcely gave her a glance when Dolly was in the room,—he recognized the beauty, but it did not enslave him, it did not even attract him as Dolly's imperfect charms did. And perhaps he had his own ideas of what Dolly's love-making would be, of the spice and variety which would form its characteristics, and of the little bursts of warmth and affection that would render it delightful. It was not soothing to think of all this being lavished on a shabby young man who was not always urbane in demeanor and who stubbornly objected to being propitiated by politeness.

As was very natural, Mr. Ralph Gowan did not admire Mr. Griffith Donne enthusiastically. In his visits to Bloomsbury Place, finding an ill-dressed young man whose position in the household he could not understand, he began by treating him with good-natured suavity, being ready enough to make friends with him, as he had made friends with the rest of Phil's compatriots. But influenced by objections to certain things, Griffith was not to be treated suavely, but rather resented it. There was no good reason for his resenting it, but resent it he did, as openly as he could, without being an absolute savage and attracting attention. The weakness of such a line of conduct is glaringly patent, of course, to the well-regulated mind; but then Mr. Griffith Donne's mind was not well-regulated, and he was, on the contrary, a very hot-headed, undisciplined young man, and exceedingly sensitive to his own misfortunes and shabbiness, and infatuated in his passion for the object of his enemy's admiration. But Ralph Gowan could afford to be tolerant; in the matter of position he was secure, he had never been slighted or patronized in his life, and so had no shrinkings from such an ordeal; he was not disturbed by any bitter pang of jealousy as yet, and so, while he could not understand Griffith's restless anxiety to resent his presence, could still tolerate it and keep cool. Yet, as might be expected, he rather underrated his antagonist. Seeing him only in this one unfavorable light, he regarded him simply as a rather ill-bred, or, at least, aggressively inclined individual, whose temper and tone of mind might reasonably be objected to. Once or twice he had even felt his own blood rise at some implied ignoring of himself; but he was far the more urbane and well-disposed of the two, yet whether he was to be highly lauded for his forbearance, or whether, while lauding him, it would not be as well to think as well as possible of his enemy, is a matter for charity to decide.

It had not occurred to him before that Griffith's frequent and unceremonious visits implied anything very serious. There were so many free-and-easy visitors at the house, and they all so plainly cultivated Dolly, if they did not make actual love to her; and really outsiders would hardly have been impressed with her deportment toward her betrothed. She was not prone to exhibit her preference sentimentally in public. So Ralph Gowan had been deceived,—and so he was deceived still.

"This sort of fellow," as he mentally put it with unconscious high-handedness, was not the man to make such a woman happy, however ready she was to bear with him. It was just such men as he was, who, when the novelty of possession wore off, deteriorated into tyrannical, irritable husbands, and were not too well bred in their manners. So he became reflective and silent, when Mollie said that the two were "making love."

But at last it occurred to him that even to Mollie his preoccupation might appear singular, and he roused himself accordingly.

"Making love!" he said again. "Blissful occupation! I wonder how they do it. Do you know, Mollie?"

Mollie looked at him with a freedom from scruples or embarrassment at the conversation taking such a turn, which told its own story.

"Yes," she said. "They talk, you know, and say things to each other just as other people do, and he kisses her sometimes. I know that," with a decided air, "because I have seen him do it."

"Cool enough, that, upon my word," was her questioner's mental comment, "and not unpleasant for Donne; but hardly significant of a fastidious taste, if it is a public exhibition." "Ah, indeed!" he said, aloud.

"They have been engaged so long, you know," volunteered Mollie.

"Singularly enough, I did not know, Mollie," he replied. "Are you sure yourself?"

"Oh, yes!" exclaimed Mollie, opening her eyes. "I thought everybody knew that. They have been engaged ever since they were ever so much younger. Dolly was only fifteen, and Griffith was only eighteen, when they first fell in love."

"And they have been engaged ever since?" said Gowan, his curiosity getting decidedly the better of him.

"Yes, and would have been married long ago, if Griffith could have got into something; or if Old Flynn would have raised his salary. He has only a hundred a year," with unabashed frankness, "and, of course, they couldn't be married on that, so they are obliged to wait. A hundred and fifty would do, Dolly says,—but then, they have n't got a hundred and fifty."

Ralph Gowan was meanly conscious of not being overpowered with regret on hearing this latter statement of facts. And yet he was by no means devoid of generous impulse. He was quite honest, however deeply he might be mistaken, in deciding that it would be an unfortunate thing for Dolly if she married Griffith Donne. He thought he was right, and certainly if there had been no more good in his rival than he himself had seen on the surface, he would not have been far wrong; but as it was he was unconsciously very far wrong indeed. He ran into the almost excusable extreme of condemning Griffith upon circumstantial evidence. Unfair advantage had been taken of Dolly, he told himself. She had engaged herself before she knew her own heart, and was true to her lover because it was not in her nature to be false. Besides, what right has a man with a hundred a year to bind any woman to the prospect of the life of narrow economies and privations such an income would necessarily entail? And forthwith his admiration of Dolly became touched with pity, and increased fourfold. *She* was unselfish, at least, whatever her affianced might be. Poor little soul! (It is a circumstance worthy of note, because illustrative of the blindness of human nature, that at this very moment Miss Dorothea Crewe was enjoying her quiet *tête-à-tête* with her lover wondrously, and would not have changed places with any young lady in the kingdom upon any consideration whatever.)

It is not at all to be wondered at that, in the absence of other entertainment, Gowan drifted into a confidential chat with Mollie. She was the sort of girl few people could have remained entirely indifferent to. Her *naïveté* was as novel as her beauty, and her weakness, so to speak, was her strength. Gowan found it so at least, but still it must be confessed that Dolly was the chief subject of their conversation.

"You are very fond of your sister?" he said to the child.

Mollie nodded.

"Yes," she said, "I am very fond of her. We are all very fond of her. Dolly 's the clever one of the family, next to Phil. She is n't afraid of anybody, and things don't upset her. I wish I was like her. You ought to see her talk to Lady Augusta, I believe she is the only person in the world Lady Augusta can't patronize, and she is always trying to snub her just because she is so cool. But it never troubles Dolly. I have seen her sit and smile and talk in her quiet way until Lady Augusta could do nothing but sit still and stare at her as if she was choked, with her bonnet strings actually trembling."

Gowan laughed. He could imagine the effect produced so well, and it was so easy to picture Dolly smiling up in the face of her gaunt patroness, and all the time favoring her with a shower of beautiful little stabs, rendered pointed by the very essence of artfulness. He decided that upon the whole Lady Augusta was somewhat to be pitied.

"Dolly says," proceeded Mollie, "that she would like to be a beauty; but if I was like her I should n't care about being a beauty."

"Ah!" said Gowan, unable to resist the temptation to try with a fine speech,—"ah! it is all very well for *you* to talk about not caring to be a beauty."

It did not occur to him for an instant that it was indiscreet to say such a thing to her. He only meant it for a jest, and nine girls out of ten even at sixteen would have understood his languid air of grandiloquence in an instant. But Mollie at sixteen was extremely liberal-minded, and almost Arcadian in her simplicity of thought and demeanor.

Her brown eyes flew wide open, and for a minute she stared at him with mingled amazement and questioning.

"Me!" she said, ignoring all given rules of propriety of speech.

"Yes, you," answered Gowan, smiling, and looking down at her amusedly. "I have been paying you a compliment, Mollie."

"Oh!" said Mollie, bewilderment settling on her face. But the next instant the blood rushed to her cheeks, and her eyes fell, and she moved a little farther away from him.

It was the first compliment she had received in all her life, and it was the beginning of an era.

CHAPTER V.
IN WHICH THE PHILISTINES BE UPON US.

"We are going," Dolly to Ralph Gowan, "to have a family rejoicing, and we should like you to join us. We are going to celebrate Mollie's birthday."

"Thanks," he answered, "I shall be delighted." He had heard of these family rejoicings before, and was really pleased with the idea of attending one of them. They were strictly Vagabondian, which was one recommendation, and they were entirely free from the Bilberry element, which was another. They were not grand affairs, it is true, and set etiquette and the rules of society at open defiance, but they were cheerful, at least, and nobody attended them who had not previously resolved upon enjoying himself and taking kindly to even the most unexpected state of affairs. At Bloomsbury Place, Lady Augusta's "coffee and conversation" became "conversation and coffee," and the conversation came as naturally as the coffee. People who had jokes to make made them, and people who had not were exhilarated by the *bon-mots* of the rest.

"Mollie will be seventeen," said Dolly, "and it is rather a trial to me."

Gowan laughed.

"Why?" he asked.

She shook her head gravely.

"In the first place," she answered, "it makes me feel as if the dust of ages was accumulating in my pathway, and in the second, it is not safe for her."

"Why, again?" he demanded.

"She is far too pretty, and her knowledge of the world is far too limited. She secretly believes in Lord Burleigh, and clings to the poetic memory of King Cophetua and the Beggar-maid."

"And you do not?"

She held up her small forefinger and shook it at him.

"If ever there was an artful little minx," she said, "that Beggar-maid was one. I never believed in her. I doubted her before I was twelve. With her eyes cast down and her sly tricks! She did not cast them down for nothing. She did it because she had long eyelashes, and it was becoming. And it is my impression she knew more about the king than she professed to. She had studied his character and found it weak. Beggar-maid me no beggar-maids! She was as deep as she was handsome."

Of course he laughed again. Her air of severe worldly experience and that small warning forefinger were irresistible.

"But Mollie," he said, "with all her belief in Cophetua, you think there is not enough of the beggar-maid element in her character to sustain her under like circumstances?"

"If she met a Cophetua," she answered, "she would open her great eyes at his royal purple in positive delight, and if he caught her looking at him she would blush furiously and pout a little, and be so ashamed of her weakness that she would be ready to run away; but if he was artful enough to manage her aright, she would believe every word he said, and romance about him until her head was turned upside down. My fear is that some false Cophetua will masquerade for her benefit some day. She would never doubt his veracity, and if he asked her to run away with him I believe she would enjoy the idea. We shall have to keep sharp watch upon her."

"You never were so troubled about Aimée?" Gowan suggested.

"Aimée!" she exclaimed. "Aimée has kept us all in order, and managed our affairs for us ever since she wore Berlin wool boots and a coral necklace. She regulated the household in her earliest years, and will regulate it until she dies or somebody marries her, and what we are to do then our lares and pénates only know. Aimée! Nobody ever had any trouble with Aimée, and nobody ever will. Mollie is more like me, you see,—shares my weaknesses and minor sins, and always sees her indiscretions ten minutes too late for redemption. And then, since she is the youngest, and has been the baby so long, we have not been in the habit of regarding her as a responsible being exactly. It has struck me once or twice that Bloomsbury Place hardly afforded wise training to Mollie. Poor little soul!" And a faint shadow fell upon her face and rested there for a moment.

But it faded out again as her fits of gravity usually did, and in a few minutes she was giving him such a description of Lady Augusta's unexpected appearance upon a like occasion in time past, that he laughed until the room echoed, and forgot everything else but the audacious grotesqueness of her mimicry.

It being agreed upon that Mollie's birthday was to be celebrated, the whole household was plunged into preparations at once, though, of course, they were preparations upon a small scale and of a strictly private and domestic nature. Belinda, being promptly attacked with inflammation of the throat, which was a chronic weakness of hers, was rather inconveniently, but not at all to the surprise of her employers, incapacitated from service, and accordingly Dolly's duties became varied and multitudinous.

Sudden inflammation on the part of Belinda was so unavoidable a consequence of any approaching demand upon her services as to have become proverbial, and the swelling of that young person's "tornsuls," as she termed them, was anticipated as might be anticipated the rising of the sun. Not that it was Belinda's fault, however; Belinda's anxiety to be useful amounted at all times to something very nearly approaching a monomania; the fact simply was, that, her ailment being chronic, it usually evinced itself at inopportune periods. "It's the luck of the family," said Phil. "We never loved a tree or flower, etc."

And so Belinda was accepted as an unavoidable inconvenience, and was borne with cheerfully, accordingly.

It was not expected of her that she should appear otherwise on the eventful day than with the regulation roll of flannel about her neck. Dolly did not expect it of her at least, so she was not surprised, on entering the kitchen in the morning, to be accosted by her grimy young handmaiden in the usual form of announcement:—

"Which, if yer please, miss, my tornsuls is swole most awful."

"Are they?" said Dolly. "Well, I am very sorry, Belinda. It can't be helped, though; Mollie will have to run the errands and answer the door-bell, and you must stay with me and keep out of the draught. You can help a little, I dare say, if you are obliged to stay in the kitchen."

"Yes, 'm," said Belinda, and then sidling up to the dresser, and rubbing her nose in an abasement of spirit, which resulted in divers startling adornments of that already rather highly ornamented feature. "If yer please, 'm," she said, "I 'm very sorry, Miss Dolly. Seems like I ain't never o' no use to yer?"

"Yes, you are," said Dolly, cheerily, "and you can't help the sore throat, you know. You are a great deal of use to me sometimes. See how you save my hands from being spoiled; they would n't be as white as they are if I had to polish the grates and build the fires. Never mind, you will be better in a day or so. Now for the cookery-book."

"I never seen no one like her," muttered the delighted Sepoy, returning to her vigorous cleaning of kettles and pans. "I never seen no one like none on 'em, they 're that there good-natured an' easy on folk."

It was a busy day for Dolly, as well as for the rest of them, and there was a by no means unpleasant excitement in the atmosphere of business. The cookery, too, was a success, the game pâtés being a triumph, the tarts beautiful to behold, and the rest of the culinary experiments so marvellous, that Griffith, arriving early in the morning, and being led down into the pantry to look at them as a preliminary ceremony, professed to be struck dumb with admiration.

"There," said Dolly, backing up against the wall in her excitement, and thrusting her hands very far into her apron pockets indeed,—"there! what do you think of *that*, sir?" And she stood before him in a perfect glow of triumph, her cheeks like roses, her sleeves rolled above her dimpled elbows, her hair pushed on her forehead, and her general appearance so deliciously business-like and agreeably professional that the dusts of flour that were so prominent a feature in her costume seemed only an additional charm.

"Think of it?" said Griffith. "It is the most imposing display I ever saw in my life. The trimmings upon those tarts are positively artistic. You don't mean to say you did it all yourself?"

"Yes," regarding them critically,—"ev-er-y bit," with a little nod for every syllable.

"Won-der-ful!" with an air of complimentary incredulity. "May I ask if there is anything you can *not* do?"

"There is absolutely nothing," sententiously. And then somehow or other they were standing close together, as usual, his arm around her waist, her hands clasped upon his sleeve. "When we get the house in Putney, or Bayswater, or Peckham Eise, or whatever it is to be," she said, laughing in her most coaxing way, "this sort of thing will be convenient. And it *is* to come, you know,—the house, I mean."

"Yes," admitted Griffith, with dubious cheerfulness, "it *is* to come,—some time or other."

But her cheerfulness was not of a dubious kind at all. She only laughed again, and patted his arm with a charming air of proprietorship.

"I have got something else to show you," she said; "something up-stairs. Can you guess what it is? Something for Mollie,—something she wanted which is dreadfully extravagant."

"What!" exclaimed Griffith. "Not the maroon silk affair!"

"Yes," her doubt as to the wisdom of her course expressing itself in a whimsical little grimace. "I could n't help it. It will make her so happy; and I should so have liked it myself if I had been in her place."

She had been going to lead him up-stairs to show it to him as it lay in state, locked up in the parlor, but all at once she changed her mind.

"No," she said; "I think you had better not see it until Mollie comes down in state. It will look best then; so I won't spoil the effect by letting you see it now."

Griffith had brought his offering, too,—not much of an offering, perhaps, but worth a good deal when valued according to the affectionate good-will it represented. "The girls" had a very warm corner in the young man's tender heart, and the half-dozen pairs of gloves he produced from the shades of an inconvenient pocket of his great-coat, held their own modest significance.

"Gloves," he said, half apologetically, "always come in; and I believe I heard Mollie complaining of hers the other day."

Certainly they were appreciated by the young lady in question, their timely appearance disposing of a slight difficulty of addition to her toilet.

The maroon silk was to be a surprise; and surely, if ever surprise was a success, this was. Taking into consideration the fact that she had spent the earlier part of the day in plaintive efforts to remodel a dubious garment into a form fitting to grace the occasion, it is not to be wondered at that the sudden realization of one of her most hopelessly vivid imaginings rather destroyed the perfect balance of her equilibrium.

She had almost completed her toilet when Dolly produced her treasure; nothing, in fact, remained to be done but to don the dubious garment, when Dolly, slipping out of the room, returned almost immediately with something on her arm.

"Never mind your old alpaca, Mollie," she said. "I have something better for you here."

Mollie turned round in some wonder to see what she meant, and the next minute she turned red and pale with admiring amazement.

"Dolly," she said, rather unnecessarily, "it's a maroon silk." And she sat down with her hands clasped, and stared at it in the intensity of her wonder.

"Yes," said Dolly, "it is a maroon silk, and you are to wear it to-night. It is Phil's birthday present to you,—and mine."

The spell was broken at once. The girl got up and made an impulsive rush at her, and, flinging her bare white arms out, caught her in a tempestuous embrace, maroon silk and all, laughing and crying both together.

"Dolly," she said,—"Dolly, it is the grandest thing I ever had in my life, and you are the best two—you and Phil—that ever lived!" And not being as eloquent by nature as she was grateful and affectionate, she poured out the rest of her thanks in kisses and interjections.

Then Dolly, extricating herself, proceeded to add the final touches to the unfinished toilet, and in a very few minutes Miss Mollie stood before the glass regarding herself in such ecstatic content as she had perhaps never before experienced.

"Who is going to be here, Dolly?" she asked, after taking her first survey.

"Who?" said Dolly. "Well, I scarcely know. Only one or two of Phil's friends and Ralph Gowan."

Mollie gave a little start, and then blushed in the most pathetically helpless way.

"Ah!" she said, and looked at her reflection in the glass again, as if she did not exactly know what else to do.

A swift shadow of surprise showed itself in Dolly's eyes, and died out almost at the same moment.

"Are you ready?" she said, briefly. "If you are, we will go down-stairs."

There was a simultaneous cry of admiration from them all when the two entered the parlor below, and Miss Mollie appeared attired in all her glory.

"Here she is!" exclaimed 'Toinetté and Aimée, together.

"Just the right shade," was Phil's immediate comment. "Catches the lights and throws out her coloring so finely. Turn round, Mollie."

And Mollie turned round obediently, a trifle abashed by her own gorgeousness, and looking all the lovelier for her momentary abasement.

Griffith was delighted. He went to her and kissed her, and praised her with the enthusiastic frankness which characterized all his proceedings with regard to the different members of the family of his betrothed. He was as proud of the girl's beauty as if she were a sister of his own.

Then the object of their mutual admiration knelt down upon the hearth-rug, before Tod, who, attired in ephemeral splendor, had stopped in his tour across the room to stare up with bright baby wonder at the novelty of warm, rich color which had caught his fancy.

"I must kiss Tod," she said; no ceremony was ever considered complete, and no occasion perfect, unless Tod had been kissed, and so taken into the general confidence. "Tod, come and be kissed."

But, being a young gentleman of by no means effusive nature, Tod preferred to remain stationary, holding to the toe of his red shoe and gazing upward with an expression of approbation and indifference commingled, which delighted his feminine admirers beyond expression.

"He knows it is something new," said 'Toinette. "See how he looks at it." Whereupon, of course, there was a chorus of delighted acquiescence, and Aunt Dolly must needs go down upon the hearthrug, too.

"Has Aunt Mollie got a grand new dress on, Beauty?" she said, glowing with such pretty, womanly adoration of this atom of all-ruling baby-dom, as made her seem the very cream and essence of lovableness and sweet nonsense. And then, Master Tod, still remaining unmoved by adulation, and still regarding his small circle of tender sycophants with round, liquid, baby eyes serene, and dewy red lips apart, was so effective in this one of his many entrancing moods, that he was no longer to be resisted, and so was caught up and embraced with ecstasy.

"He notices everything," cries Aunt Dolly; "and I 'm sure he understands every word he hears. He is *so* different from other babies."

Different! Of course he was different. There was not one of them but indignantly scouted at the idea of there ever having before existed such a combination of infantile gifts and graces. The most obtuse of people could not fail to acknowledge his vast superiority, in spite of their obtuseness.

"But," remarked Aimée, with discretion, "you had better stand up, Mollie, or you will crush your front breadths."

Mollie, with a saving recollection of front breadths, arose, and as it chanced just in time to turn toward the door as Ralph Gowan came in.

He was looking his best to-night,—that enviable, thorough-bred best, which was the natural result of culture, money, and ease; and Dolly, catching sight of Mollie's guileless blushes, deplored, while she did not wonder at them, understanding her as she did. It was just like the child to blush, feeling herself the centre of observation, but she could not help wishing that her blush had not been quite so quick and sensitive.

But if she had flushed when he entered, she flushed far more when he came to speak to her. He held in his hand a bouquet of flowers,—white camellia buds and bloom, and dark, shadowy green; a whim of his own, he said.

"I heard about the maroon dress," he added, when he had given it to her, "and my choice of your flowers was guided accordingly. White camellias, worn with maroon sik, are artistic, Mollie, your brother will tell you."

"They are very pretty," said Mollie, looking down at them in grateful confusion; "and I am much obliged. Thank you, Mr. Gowan."

"A great many good wishes go with them," he said, good-naturedly. "If I were an enchanter, you should never grow any older from this day forward." And his speech was something more than an idle compliment. There was something touching to him, too, in the fact of the child's leaving her childhood behind her, and confronting so ignorantly the unconscious dawn of a womanhood which might hold so much of the bitterness of knowledge.

But, of course, Mollie did not understand this.

"Why?" she asked him, forgetting her camellias, in her wonder at his fancy.

"Why?" said he. "Because seventeen is such a charming age, Mollie; and it would be well for so many of us if we did not outlive its faith and freshness."

He crossed over to Dolly then, and made his well-turned speech of friendly greeting to her also, but his most ordinary speech to her had its own subtle warmth. He was growing very fond of Dolly Crewe. But Dolly was a trifle preoccupied; she was looking almost anxiously at Mollie and the camellias.

"He has been paying her a compliment or she would not look so fluttered and happy," she was saying to herself. "I wish he wouldn't. It may please him, but it is dangerous work for Mollie."

And when she raised her eyes to meet Ralph Gowan's, he saw that there was the ghost of a regretful shadow in them.

She had too much to do, however, to be troubled long. Phil's friends began to drop in, one by one, and the business of the evening occupied her attention. There was coffee to be handed round, and she stood at a side-table and poured it out herself into quaint cups of old china, which were a relic of former grandeur; and as she moved to and fro, bringing one of these cups to one, or a plate of fantastic little cakes to another, and flavoring the whole repast with her running fire of spicy speeches, Gowan found himself following her with his eyes and rather extravagantly comparing her to ambrosia-bearing Hebe, at the same time thinking that in Vagabondia these tilings were better done than elsewhere.

The most *outré* of Phil's hirsute and carelessly garbed fellow-Bohemians somehow or other seemed neither vulgar nor ill at ease. They evidently felt at home, and admired faithfully and with complete unison the feminine members of their friend's family; and their readiness to catch at the bright or grotesque side of any situation evinced itself in a manner worthy of imitation. Then, too, there was Tod, taking excursionary rambles about the carpet, and, far from being in the way, rendering himself an innocent centre of attraction. Brown cracked jokes with him, Jones bribed him with cake to the performance of before-unheard-of feats, and one muscular, fiercely mustached and bearded young man, whose artistic forte was battle-pieces of the most sanguinary description, appropriated him bodily and set him on his shoulder, greatly to the detriment of his paper collar.

"The spirit of Vagabondia is strong in Tod," said Dolly, who at the time was standing near Gowan upon the hearth-rug, with her own coffee-cup in hand; "its manifestation being his readiness to accommodate himself to circumstances."

Through the whole of the evening Mollie and the camellias shone forth with resplendence. Those of Phil's masculine friends who had known her since her babyhood felt instinctively that to-night the Rubicon had been passed. Unconscious as she was of herself, she was imposing in the maroon silk, and these free-and-easy, good-natured fellows were the very men to be keenly alive to any subtle power of womanhood. So when they addressed her their manner was a trifle subdued, and their deportment toward her had a faint savor of delicate reverence.

Dolly was in her element. Her songs, her little supper, and her plans of entertainment were a perfect success. Such jokes as she made and such laughter as she managed to elicit through the medium of the smallest of them, and such aptness and tact as she displayed in keeping up the general fusillade of *bon-mots* and repartee. It would have been impossible for a witticism to fall short of its mark under her active superintendence, even if witticisms had been prone to fall short in Vagabondia, which they decidedly were not. She kept Griffith busy, too, from first to last, perhaps because she felt it to be the safest plan; at any rate, she held him near her, and managed to keep him in the best of spirits all the evening, and more than once Gowan, catching a glimpse of her as she addressed some simple remark to the favored one, recognized a certain bright softness in her face which told its own story. But there would have been little use in openly displaying his discomfiture; so, after feeling irritated for a moment or so, Ralph Gowan allowed himself to drift into attendance on Mollie, and, being almost gratefully received by that young lady, he did not find that the time passed slowly.

"I am so glad you came here." she said to him, plaintively, when he first crossed the room to her side. "I do so hate Brown."

"Brown!" he echoed. "Who *is* Brown, Mollie? and what has Brown been doing to incur your resentment?"

Mollie gave her shoulders a petulant shrug.

"Brown is that little man in the big coat," she said, "the one who went away when you came. I wish he would stay away. I can't bear him," with delightful candor.

"But why?" persisted Gowan, casting a glance at the side of the room where Dolly stood talking to her lover. "Is it because his coat is so big, or because he is so little, that he is so objectionable? To be at once moral and instructive, Mollie, a man is not to be judged by his coat."

"I know that," returned Mollie, her unconscious innocence asserting itself; "it is n't that. *You* couldn't be as disagreeable as he is if you were dressed in rags."

Gowan turned quickly to look at her, forgetting even Dolly for the instant,— but she was quite in earnest, and met his questioning eyes with the most pathetic ignorance of having said anything extraordinary. Indeed, her faith in what she had said was so patent that he found it impossible to answer her with a light or jesting speech.

"It is n't that," she went on, pulling at a glossy green leaf on her bouquet. "If he did n't—if he would n't—if he didn't keep saying things—"

"What sort of things?" asked Gowan, to help her out of her dilemma.

"I—don't know," was the shy reply. "Stupid things."

"Stupid things!" he repeated. "Poor Brown!" and his eyes wandered to Dolly again.

But it would not have been natural if he had not been attracted by Mollie, after all, and in the course of time in a measure consoled by her. She was so glad to be protected from the advances of the much despised Brown, that he found it rather pleasant than otherwise to constitute himself her body-guard,—to talk to her as they sat, and to be her partner in the stray dances which accidentally enlivened the evening entertainment. She danced well, too, he discovered, and with such evident enjoyment of her own smooth, swaying movements as was quite magnetic, and made him half reluctant to release her when their first waltz was ended, and she stopped all aflush with new bloom.

"I am *so* fond of dancing," she said, catching her breath in a little sigh of ecstasy. "We all are. It is one of the things we *can* do without spending any money, you know."

It was shortly after this, just as they were standing in twos and threes, chatting and refreshing themselves with Dolly's confections and iced lemonade, that an entirely unexpected advent occurred. There suddenly fell upon the general ear a sound as of rolling wheels, and a carriage stopped before the door.

Dolly, standing in the midst of a small circle of her own, paused in her remarks to listen.

"It is a carriage, that is certain," she said,—"and somebody is getting out. I don't know "—and then a light breaking over her face in a flash of horror and delight in the situation commingled. "Phil," she exclaimed, "the Philistines be upon us,—it is Lady Augusta!"

And it was. In two minutes that majestic lady was ushered in by the excited Belinda, and announced in the following rather remarkable manner,—

"If yer please, Miss Dolly, here's your aunt, Mr. Phil."

For a second her ladyship was speechless, even though Dolly advanced to meet her at once. The festive gathering was too much for her, and the sight of Ralph Gowan leaning over Mollie in all her bravery, holding her flowers for her, and appearing so evidently at home, overpowered her completely. But she recovered herself at length.

"I was not aware," she said to Dolly, "that you were having a"—pause for a word sufficiently significant—"that you were holding a reception,"—a scathing glance at the pensive Brown, who was at once annihilated. "You will possibly excuse my involuntary intrusion. I thought, of *course*" (emphasis), "that I should find you alone, and as I had something to say to you concerning Euphemia, I decided to call tonight on my way from the conversazione at Dr. Bugby's,—perhaps, Dorothea, your friends" (emphasis again) "will excuse you for a moment, and you will take me into another room,"—this last as if she had suddenly found herself in a fever hospital and was rather afraid of contagion.

But apart from Mollie, who pouted and flushed, and was extremely uncomfortable, nobody seemed to be either chilled or overwhelmed. Phil's greeting was so cordial and unmoved that her ladyship could only proffer him the tips of her fingers in imposing silence, and Dolly's air of placid good-humor was so perfect that it was as good as a modest theatrical entertainment.

She led her visitor out of the room with a most untroubled countenance, after her ladyship had honored Gowan with a word or so, kindly signifying her intense surprise at meeting him in the house, and rather intimating, delicately, that she could not comprehend his extraordinary conduct, and hoped he would not live to regret it.

The interview was not a long one, however. In about ten minutes the carriage rolled away, and Dolly came back to the parlor with a touch of new color on her cheek, and a dying-out spark of fire in her eye; and though her spirits did not seem to have failed her, she was certainly a trifle moved by something.

"Let us have another waltz." she said, rather as if she wished to dismiss Lady Augusta from the carpet "I will play this time. Phil, find a partner."

She sat down to the piano at once, and swept off into one of Phil's own compositions, and from that time till the end of the evening she scarcely gave them a moment's pause, and was herself so full of sparkle and resources that she quite enraptured Gowan, and made the shabby room and the queer life seem more novel and entrancing than ever.

But when the guests were gone, and only Griffith, who was always last, remained with Phil and the girls, grouped about the fire, the light died out of her mood, and she looked just a trifle anxious and tired.

"Girls," she said, "I have some bad news to tell you,—at least some news that isn't exactly good. Lady Augusta has given me what Belinda would call 'a warning.' I visit the select precincts of Bilberry House as governess no more."

There is no denying it was a blow to them all. Her salary had been a very necessary part of the family income, and if they had been straitened with it, certainly there would be a struggle without it.

"Oh!" cried Mollie, remorsefully. "And you have just spent nearly all you had on my dress. And you do so want things yourself, Dolly. What shall you do?"

"Begin to take in the daily papers and peruse the advertising column," she answered, courageously. "Never mind, it will all come right before long, and we can keep up our spirits until then."

But, despite her assumed good spirits, when she went to see Griffith out of the front door, she held to his arm with a significantly clinging touch, and was so silent for a moment that he stooped in the dark to kiss her, and found her cheek wet with tears.

It quite upset him, too, poor fellow! Dolly crying and daunted was a state of affairs fraught with anguish to him.

"Why, Dolly!" he exclaimed, tremulously. "Dolly, you are crying!"

And then she did give way, and for a minute or so quite needed the shelter and rest of his arms. She cared for no other shelter or rest; he was quite enough for her in her brightest or darkest day,—just this impecunious young man, whose prospects were so limited, but whose affection for her was so wholly without limit. She might be daunted, but she could not remain long uncomforted while her love and trust were still unchanged. Ah! there was a vast amount of magic in the simple, silent pressure of the arm within that shabby coat-sleeve.

So, as might be expected, she managed to recover herself before many minutes, and receive his tender condolences with renewed spirit; and when she bade him good-night she was almost herself again, and was laughing, even though her eyelashes were wet.

"No," she said, "we are *not* going to destruction, Lady Augusta to the contrary, and the family luck must assert itself some time, since it has kept itself so long in the background. And in the mean time—well," with a little parting wave of her hand, "Vagabondia to the rescue!"

CHAPTER VI.
"WANTED, A YOUNG PERSON."

THEEE was much diligent searching of the advertising columns of the daily papers for several weeks after this. Advertisements, in fact, became the staple literature, and Dolly's zeal in the perusal of them was only to be equalled by her readiness to snatch at the opportunities they presented. No weather was too grewsome for her to confront, and no representation too unpromising for her to be allured by. In the morning she was at Bayswater calling upon the chilling mother of six (four of them boys) whose moral nature needed judicious attention, and who required to be taught the rudiments of French, German, and Latin; in the afternoon she was at the general post-office applying to Q. Y. Z., who had the education of two interesting orphans to negotiate for, and who was naturally desirous of doing it as economically as possible; and at night she was at home, writing modest, business-like epistles to every letter in the alphabet in every conceivable or inconceivable part of the country.

"If I had only been born 'a stout youth,' or 'a likely young man,' or 'a respectable middle-aged person,' I should have been 'wanted' a dozen times a day," she would remark; "but as it is, I suppose I I must wait until something 'presents itself,' as the Rev. Marmaduke puts it."

And in defiance of various discouraging and dispiriting influences, she waited with a tolerable degree of tranquillity until, in the course of time, her patience was rewarded. Sitting by the fire one morning with Tod and a newspaper, her eye was caught by an advertisement which, though it did not hold out any extra inducements, still attracted her attention, so she read it aloud to Aimée and 'Toinette.

"Wanted, a young person to act as companion to an elderly lady. Apply at the printers."

"There, Aimée," she commented, "there is another. I suppose I might call myself 'a young person,' Don't you think I had better 'apply at the printer's'?"

"They don't mention terms," said Aimée.

"You would have to leave home," said 'Toinette.

Dolly folded up the paper and tossed it on to the table with a half sigh. She had thought of that the moment she read the paragraph, and then, very naturally, she had thought of Griffith. It would not be feasible to include him in her arrangements, even if she made any. Elderly ladies who engage "young persons" as companions were not in the habit of taking kindly to miscellaneous young men, consequently the prospect was not a very bright one.

There would only be letter-writing left to them, and letters seemed such cold comfort contrasted with every-day meetings. She remembered, too, a certain six months she had spent with her Bilberry charges in Switzerland, when Griffith had nearly been driven frantic by her absence and his restless dissatisfaction, and when their letters had only seemed new aids to troublous though unintentional games at cross-purposes. There might be just the same thing to undergo again, but, then, how was it to be avoided? It was impossible to remain idle just at this juncture.

"So it cannot be helped," she said, aloud. "I must take it if I can get it, and I must stay in it until I can find something more pleasant, though I cannot help wishing that matters did not look so unpromising. Tod, you will have to go down, Aunt Dolly is going to put on her hat and present herself at the printer's in the character of a young person in search of an elderly lady."

Delays were dangerous, she had been taught by experience, so she ran up-stairs at once for her out-door attire, and came down in a few minutes, drawing on her gloves and looking a trifle ruefully at them.

"They are getting discouragingly white at the seams," she said, "and it seems almost impossible to keep them sewed up. I shall have to borrow Aimée's muff. What a blessing it is that the weather is so cold!"

At the bottom of the staircase she met Mollie.

"Phemie is in the parlor, Dolly," she announced, "and she wants to see you. I don't believe Lady Augusta knows she is here, either, she looks so dreadfully fluttered."

And when she entered the room, surely enough Phemie jumped up with a nervous bound from a chair immediately behind the door, and, dropping her muff and umbrella and two or three other small articles, caught her in a tremulous embrace, and at once proceeded to bedew her with tears.

"Oh, Dolly!" she lamented, pathetically; "I have come to say good-by; and, oh! what shall I do without you?"

"Good-by!" said Dolly. "Why, Phemie?"

"Switzerland!" sobbed Phemie. "The—the select seminary at Geneva, Dolly, where th-that professor of m-music with the lumpy face was."

"Dear me!" Dolly ejaculated. "You don't mean to say you are going there, Phemie?"

"Yes, I do," answered Euphemia. "Next week, too. And, oh dear, Dolly!" trying to recover her handkerchief, "if it had been anywhere else I could have borne it, but that," resignedly, "was the reason mamma settled on it. She found out how I *loathed* the very thought of it, and then she decided immediately. And don't you remember those mournful girls, Dolly, who used to walk out like a funeral procession, and how we used to make fun—at least, how you used to make fun of the lady principal's best bonnet?"

It will be observed by this that Miss Dorothea Crewe's intercourse with her pupils had not been as strictly in accordance with her position as instructress as it had been friendly. She had even gone so far as to set decorum at defiance, by being at once entertaining and jocular, though to her credit it must be said that she had worked hard enough for her modest salary, and had not neglected even the most trivial of her numerous duties.

She began to console poor Euphemia to the best of her ability, but Euphemia refused to be comforted.

"I shall have to take lessons from that lumpy professor, Dolly," she said. "And you know how I used to hate him when he *would* make love to you. And that was mamma's fault, too, because she would patronize him and call him 'a worthy person.' He was the only man who admired you I ever knew her to encourage, and she would n't have encouraged him if he had n't been so detestable."

It was very evident that the eldest Miss Bilberry was in a highly rebellious and desperate state of mind. Dolly's daily visits, educational though they were, had been the brightest gleams of sunlight in her sternly regulated existence. No one had ever dared to joke in the Bilberry mansion but Dolly, and no one but Dolly, had ever made the clan gatherings bearable to Euphemia; and now that Dolly was cut off from them all, and there were to be no more jokes and no more small adventures, life seemed a desert indeed. And then with the calamitous prospect of Switzerland and the lumpy professor before her, Phemie was crushed indeed.

"Mamma doesn't know I came," she confessed, tearfully, at last; "but I could n't help it, Dolly, I could n't go away without asking you to write to me and to let me write to you. You will write to me, won't you?"

Dolly promised at once, feeling a trifle affected herself. She had always been fond of Phemie, and inclined to sympathize with her, and now she exerted herself to her utmost to cheer her. She persuaded her to sit down, and after picking up the muff and umbrella and parcels, took a seat by her, and managed to induce her to dry her tears and enter into particulars.

"It will never do for Lady Augusta to see that you have been crying," she said. "Dry your eyes, and tell me all about it, and—wait a minute, I have a box of chocolates here, and I know you like chocolates."

It was a childish consolation, perhaps, but Dolly knew what she was doing and whom she was dealing with, and this comforting with confections was not without its kindly girlish tact. Chocolates were one of Phemie's numerous school-girl weaknesses, and a weakness so rarely indulged in that she perceptibly brightened when her friend produced the gay-colored, much-gilded box. And thus stimulated, she poured forth her sorrows with more coherence and calmness. She was to go to Switzerland, that was settled, and the others were to be placed in various other highly select educational establishments. They were becoming too old now, Lady Augusta had decided, to remain under Dolly's care.

"And then," added Euphemia, half timidly, "you won't be vexed if I tell you, will you?"

"Certainly not," answered Dolly, who knew very well what was coming, though poor Phemie evidently thought she was going to impart an extremely novel and unexpected piece of intelligence. "What is it, Phemie?"

"Well, somehow or other, I don't believe mamma exactly likes you, Dolly."

Now, considering circumstances, this innocent speech amounted to a rich sort of thing to say, but Dolly did not laugh; she might caricature Lady Augusta for the benefit of her own select circle of friends, but she never made jokes about her before Phemie, however sorely she might be tempted. So, now she helped herself to a chocolate with perfect sobriety of demeanor.

"Perhaps not," she admitted. "I have thought so myself, Phemie." And then, as soon as possible, changed the subject.

At length Phemie rose to go. As Lady Augusta was under the impression that she was merely taking the dismal daily constitutional, which was one of her unavoidable penances, it would not do to stay too long.

"So I *must* go," lamented Phemie; "but, Dolly, if you would n't mind, I should *so* like to see the baby. I have never seen him since the day we called with mamma,—and I am so fond of babies, and he was so pretty."

Dolly laughed, in spite of herself. She remembered the visit so well, and Lady Augusta's loftily resigned air of discovering, in the passively degenerate new arrival, the culminating point of the family depravity.

"It is much to be regretted," she had said, disapprovingly; "but it is exactly what I foresaw from the first, and you will have to make the best of it."

And then, on Dolly's modestly suggesting that they intended to do so, and were not altogether borne down to the earth by the heavy nature of their calamity, she had openly shuddered.

But Phemie had quite clung to the small bundle of lawn and flannel, and though she had never seen Tod since, she had by no means forgotten him.

"He will be quite a big boy when I come back," she added. "And I should so like to see him once again while he is a baby."

"Oh, you shall see him," said Dolly. "Tod is the one individual in this house who always feels himself prepared to receive visitors. He is n't fastidious about his personal appearance. If you will come into the next room, I dare say we shall find him."

And they did find him. Being desirous of employing, to the greatest advantage, the time spent in his retirement within the bosom of his family, he was concentrating his energies upon the mastication of the toe of his slipper, upon which task he was bestowing the strictest and most undivided attention, as he sat in the centre of the hearth-rug.

"He has got another tooth, Aunt Dolly," announced 'Toinette, triumphantly, as soon as the greetings were over. "Show Aunt Dolly his tooth." And, being laid upon his back on the maternal knee, in the most uncomfortable and objectionable of positions, the tooth was exhibited, as a matter calling forth public rejoicings.

Phemie knelt on the carpet before him, the humblest of his devotees.

"He is prettier than ever," she said. "Do you think he would come to me, Mrs. Crewe?"

And, though the object of her admiration at once asserted his prerogatives by openly rejecting her overtures with scorn, she rejoiced over him as ecstatically as if he had shown himself the most amiable of infant prodigies, which he most emphatically had not, probably having been rendered irascible by the rash and inconsiderately displayed interest in his dental developments. Whatever more exacting people might have thought, Phemie was quite satisfied.

"I wish I was in your place, Dolly," she said, as she was going away. "You seem so happy together here, somehow or other. Oh, dear! You don't know how dreadful our house seems by contrast. If things *would* break or upset, or look a little untidy,—or if mamma's caps and dresses just would n't look so solid and heavy—"

"Ah!" laughed Dolly, "you have n't seen our worst side, Phemie,—the shabby side, which means worn shoes and old dresses and bills. We don't get our whistle for nothing in Vagabondia, though, to be sure,"—and I won't say a memory of the shabby coat-sleeve did not suggest the amendment,— "I don't think we pay too dearly for it; and I believe there is not one of us who would not rather pay for it than live without it."

And when she gave the girl her farewell kiss, it was a very warm one, with a touch of pity in it. It was impossible for her to help feeling sympathy for any one who was without the Griffith element in existence.

After this she went out herself to apply at the printer's, and was sent from there to Brabazon Lodge, which was a suburban establishment, in a chilly aristocratic quarter. An imposing edifice, Brabazon Lodge, built of stone, and most uncompromisingly devoid of superfluous ornament. No mock minarets or unstable towers at Brabazon Lodge,—a substantial mansion in a substantial garden behind substantial iron gates, and so solid in its appointments that it was quite a task for Dolly to raise the substantial lion's head which formed the front-door knocker.

"Wanted, a young person," she was saying to herself, meekly, when her summons was answered by a man-servant, and she barely escaped announcing herself as "the young person, sir."

Once inside the house, she was not kept waiting. She was ushered into a well-appointed side-room, where a bright fire burned in the grate. The man retired to make known her arrival to his mistress, and Dolly settled herself in a chair by the hearth.

"I wonder how many 'young persons' have been sent away sorrowing this morning," she said, "and I wonder how Griffith will like the idea of my filling the position of companion to an elderly lady, or any other order of lady, for the matter of that? Poor old fellow!" and she gave vent to an unmistakable sigh.

But the appearance of the elderly lady put an end to her regrets. The door opened and she entered, and Dolly rose to receive her. The next instant, however, she gave a little start. She had seen the elderly lady before, and confronting her now recognized her at once,—Miss Berenice MacDowlas. And that Miss MacDowlas recognized her also was quite evident, for she advanced with the air of one who was not at all at a loss.

"How do you do?" she remarked, succinctly, and gave Dolly her hand.

That young person took it modestly.

"I believe I have had the pleasure—" she was beginning, when Miss MacDowlas interrupted her.

"You met me at the Bilberrys'," she said. "I remember seeing you very well. You are Dorothea Crewe."

Dolly bowed in her most insinuatingly graceful manner.

"Take a seat," said Miss MacDowlas.

Dolly did so at once.

Miss MacDowlas looked at her with the air of an elderly lady who was not displeased.

"I remember you very well," she repeated. "You were governess there. Why did you leave?"

Dolly did not know very definitely, and told her so.

The notice given her had been unexpected. Lady Augusta had said it was because her pupils were old enough to be sent from home.

"Oh!" said Miss MacDowlas, and looked at her again from her hat to her shoes.

"You are fond of reading?" she asked next

"Yes," answered Dolly.

"You read French well?"

"Yes," said Dolly. She knew she need not hesitate to say that, at least.

"You are good company and are fond of society?"

"I am fond of society," said Dolly, "and I hope I am 'good company,'"

"You don't easily lose patience?"

"It depends upon circumstances," said Dolly.

"You can play and sing?"

"I did both the night I met you," returned the young person.

"So you did," said Miss MacDowlas, and examined her again.

It was rather an odd interview, upon the whole, but it did not end unfortunately. Miss MacDowlas wanted a companion who was quick-witted and amusing, and, having seen that Dolly was both on the evening of the Bilberry clan gathering, she had taken a fancy to her. So after a little sharp questioning, she announced her decision. She would employ her to fill the vacant situation at the same rate of salary she had enjoyed in her position of governess to the youthful Bilberrys, and she would employ her at once.

"I want somebody to amuse me," she said, "and I think you can do it. I am often an invalid, and my medical man says the society of a young person will benefit me."

So it was settled that the following week Dolly should take up her abode at Brabazon Lodge and enter upon the fulfilment of her duties. She was to read, play, sing, assist in the entertainment of visitors, and otherwise make herself generally useful, and, above all, she was to be amusing.

She left the house and proceeded homeward in a peculiar frame of mind. She could have laughed, but she was compelled to admit to herself that she could also have cried with equal readiness. She had met with an adventure indeed. She was a young person at large no longer; henceforth she was the property of the elderly dragon she had so often laughed at with Griffith. And yet the dragon had not been so objectionable, after all. She had been abrupt and unceremonious, but she had been better than Lady Augusta, and she had not shown herself illiberal. But there would be no more daily visits from Griffith, no more *téte-à-tétes* in the shabby parlor, no more sitting by the fire when the rest had left the room, no more tender and inconsistently long farewells at the front door. It was not pleasant to think about. She found herself catching her breath quickly, with a sound like a little sob.

"He will miss it awfully," she said to herself, holding her muff closely with her small, cold hands, and shutting her eyes to work away a tear; "but he won't miss it more than I shall. He might live without me perhaps, but I could n't live without him. I wonder if ever two people cared for each other as we do before? And I wonder if the time will ever come—" And there she broke off again, and ended as she so often did. "Poor old fellow!" she said. "Poor, dear, patient, faithful fellow! how I love you!"

She hurried on briskly after this, but she was wondering all the time what he would say when he found out that they were really to be separated. He would rebel, she knew, and anathematize fate vehemently. But she knew the rest of them would regard it as rather a rich joke that chance should have thrown her into the hands of Miss MacDowlas. They had all so often laughed at Griffith's descriptions of her and her letters, given generally when he had been galled into a caustic mood by the arrival of one of the latter.

Beaching Bloomsbury Place, Dolly found her lover there. He had dropped in on his way to his lodgings, and was awaiting her in a fever of expectation, having heard the news from Aimée.

"What is this Aimée has been telling me?" he cried, the moment she entered the room. "You can't be in earnest, Doll! You can't leave home altogether, you know."

She tossed her muff on the table and sat down on one of the low chairs, with her feet on the fender.

"I thought so until this morning," she said, a trifle mournfully; "but it can't be helped. The fact is, it is all settled now. I am an engaged young person."

"Settled!" exclaimed Griffith, indignantly. "Engaged! Dolly, I did n't think you would have done it."

"I could n't help doing it," said Dolly, her spirits by no means rising as she spoke. "How could I?"

But he would not be consoled by any such cold comfort. He had regarded the possibility of her leaving the house altogether as something not likely to be thought of. Very naturally, he was of the opinion that Dolly was as absolute a necessity to every one else as she was to himself. What *should* he do without her? How could he exist? It was an unreasoning insanity to talk about it. He was so roused by his subject indeed, that, neither of them being absolutely angelic in temperament, they wandered off into something very like a little quarrel about it,—he, goaded to lover-like madness by the idea that she could live without him; she, finding her low spirits culminate in a touch of anger at his hotheaded, affectionate obstinacy.

"But it is not to be expected," he broke out at last, without any reason whatever,—"it is not to be expected that you can contend against everything. You are tired of disappointment, and I don't blame you. I should be a selfish dolt if I did. If Gowan had been in my place he could have married you, and have given you a home of your own. I never shall be able to do that. But," with great weakness and evidence of tribulation at the thought, "I didn't think you would be so cool about it, Dolly."

"Cool!" cried Dolly, waxing wroth and penitent both at once, as usual. "Who is cool? Not I, that is certain. I shall miss you every hour of my life, Griffith." And the sad little shadow on her face was so real that he was pacified at once.

"I am an unreasonable simpleton!" was his next remorseful outburst.

"You have said that before," said Dolly, rather hard-heartedly; but in spite of it she did not refuse to let him be as affectionate as he chose when he knelt down by her chair, as he did the next minute.

"It would be a great deal better for me," she half whispered, breaking the suspicious silence that followed,—"it would be a great deal better for *me* if I did not care for you half so much;" and yet at the same time she leaned a trifle more toward him in the most traitorous of half-coaxing, half-reproachful ways.

"It would be the death of *me*," said Griffith; and he at once plunged into an eloquently persuasive dissertation upon the height and depth and breadth and force of his love for her. He was prone to such dissertations, and always ready with one to improve any occasion; and I am compelled to admit that, far from checking him, Dolly rather liked them, and was given to encourage and incite him to their delivery. When this one was ended, he was quite in the frame of mind to listen to reason, and let her enter into particulars concerning her morning's efforts, which she did, at length, only adding a flavor of the mysterious up to the introduction of Miss MacDowlas.

"What!" cried out Griffith, when she let out the secret. "Confound it! No! Not Aunt MacDowlas in the flesh, Dolly? You are joking."

"No," answered Dolly, shaking her head at the amazed faces of the girls, who had come in during the recital, and who had been guilty of the impropriety of all exclaiming at once when the climax was reached. "I am in earnest. I am engaged as companion to no less a person than Miss Berenice MacDowlas."

"Why, it is like something out of a three-volumed novel," said Mollie.

"It is a good joke," said 'Toinette.

"It is very awkward," commented Aimée. "If she finds out you are engaged to Griffith, she will think it so indiscreet of you both that she will cut him off with a shilling."

"Indiscreet!" echoed Dolly. "So we are indiscreet, my sage young friend,— but indiscretion is like variety, it is the spice of life."

And by this brisk speech she managed to sweep away the shadow which had touched Griffith's face, at the unconscious hint at their lack of wisdom.

"Don't say such a thing again," she said to Aimée afterward, when they were talking the matter over, as they always talked things over together, "or he will fancy that you share his own belief that he has something to reproach himself with. Better to be indiscreet than to love one another less."

"A great deal better," commented the wise one of the family, oracularly. She was not nineteen yet, this wise one, but she was a great comfort and help to Dolly, and indeed to all of them. "And it is n't *my* way to blame you, either, Dolly, though things *do* look so entangled. *I* never advised you to give it up, you know."

"Give it up," cried Dolly, a soft, pathetic warmth and color rising to her face and eyes. "Give it up! There would be too much of what has past and what is to come to give up with it. Give it up! I wouldn't if I could, and I could n't if I would."

CHAPTER VII.
IN WHICH A SPARK IS APPLIED.

IT was several days before Bloomsbury Place settled down and became itself again after Dolly's departure. They all missed her as they would have missed any one of their number who had chanced to leave them; but Griffith, coming in to make his daily visits, was naturally almost disconsolate, and for a week or so refused to be comforted.

He could not overcome his habit of dropping in on his way to and from his lodgings, which were near by; it was a habit of too long standing to be overcome easily, and besides this, he was so far a part of the family circle that his absence from it would have been regarded by its other members as something rather like a slight, so he was obliged to pay them the delicate attention of presenting himself at least once a day. And thus his wounds were kept open. To come into the parlor and find them all there but Dolly, to see her favorite chair occupied by Mollie or Aimée or 'Toinette, to hear them talk about her and discuss her prospects,—well, there were times when he was quite crushed by it.

"If there was any hope of a better day coming," he said to Aimée, who, through being the family sage, was, of course, the family confidante, "if there was only something real to look forward to, but we are just where we were three years ago, and this sort of thing cannot go on forever. What right have I to hold her to her word when other men might make her happier?"

Ainice, sitting on a stool at his feet and looking reflective, shook her head.

"That is not a right view to take," she said, "and it is n't fair to Dolly. Dolly would be happier with you on a pound a week than she would be with any one else on ten thousand a year. And you ought to know that by this time, Griffith. It is n't a question of happiness at all."

"I don't mean—" he was beginning, but Aimée interrupted him. Her part of this love affair was to lay plans for the benefit of the lovers and to endeavor to settle their little difficulties in her own way.

"I am very fond of Dolly," she said.

"Fond of her!" echoed Griffith. "So am I. Who isn't?"

"I am very fond of Dolly," Aimée proceeded.

"And *I* know her as other people do not, perhaps. She does not show as much of her real self to outsiders as they think. I have often thought her daring, open way deceived people when it made them fancy she was so easy to read. She has romantic fancies of her own the world never suspects her of,—if I did not know her as I do, she is the last person on earth I should suspect of cherishing such fancies. The fact is, you are a sort of romance to her, and her love for you is one of her dreams, and she clings to it as closely as she would cling to life. It is a dream she has lived on so long that it has become part of herself, and it is my impression that if anything happened to break her belief in it she would die,—yes, *die!*" with another emphatic shake of the pretty head. "And Dolly is n't the sort of girl to die for nothing."

Griffith raised his bowed head from his hands, his soft, dark, womanish eyes lighting up and his sallow young face flushing. "God bless her,—no!" he said. "Her life has not been free from thorns, even so far, and she has not often cried out against them."

"No," answered Aimée. "And when the roses come, no one will see as you will how sweet she finds them. Your Dolly is n't Lady Augusta's Dolly, or Mollie's, or Ralph Gowan's, or even mine; she is the Dolly no one but her lover and her husband has ever seen or ever will see. *You* can get at the spark in the opal."

Griffith was comforted, as he often found himself comforted, under the utterances of this wise one.

His desperation was toned down, and he was readier to hope for the best and to feel warm at heart and grateful,—grateful for Dolly and the tender thoughts that were bound up in his love for her. The tender phantom Aimée's words had conjured up, stirred within his bosom a thrill so loving and impassioned, that for the time the radiance seemed to emanate from the very darkest of his clouds of disappointment and discouragement. He was reminded that but for those very clouds the girl's truth and faith would never have shone out so brightly. But for their poverty and long probation, he could never have learned how much she was ready to face for love's sake. And it was such an innocent phantom, too, this bright little figure smiling upon him through the darkness, with Dolly's own face, and Dolly's own saucy, fanciful ways, and Dolly's own hands outstretched toward him. He quite plucked up spirit.

"If Old Flynn could just be persuaded to give me a raise," he said; "it would n't take much of an income for two people to live on."

"No," answered the wise one, feeling some slight misgivings, more on the subject of the out-go than the income. "You might live on very little—if you had it."

"Yes," said Griffith, apparently struck by the brilliancy of the observation, "Dolly and I have said so often."

"Let me see," considered Aimée, "suppose we were to make a sort of calculation. Give me your lead-pencil and a leaf out of your pocket-book."

Griffith produced both at once. He had done it often enough before when Dolly had been the calculator, and had made a half-serious joke of the performance, counting up her figures on the tips of her fingers, and making great professions of her knowledge of domestic matters; but it was a different affair in Aimée's hands. Aimée was in earnest, and bending over her scrap of paper, with two or three little lines on her white forehead began to set things down with an air at once business-like and vigorous, reading, the various items aloud.

"Rent, coals, taxes, food, wages,—you can't do your own washing, you know,—clothes, etceteras. There it is, Griffith," the odd, tried look settling in her eyes.

Griffith took the paper.

"Thank you," he remarked, resignedly, after he had glanced at it. "Just fifty pounds per annum more than I have any prospect of getting. But you are very kind to take so much interest in it, little woman." "Little woman" was his pet name for her.

She put her hand up to her forehead and gave the wrinkles a little rub, as if she would have liked to rub them away.

"No," she said, in distress. "I am very fond of calculating, so it isn't any trouble to me. I only wish I could calculate until what you want and what you have got would come out even."

Griffith sighed. He had wished the same thing himself upon several occasions.

He had one consolation in the midst of his tribulations, however. He had Dolly's letters, one of which arrived at "the office" every few days. Certainly they were both faithful correspondents. Tied with blue ribbon in a certain strong box, lay an immense collection of small envelopes, all marked with one peculiarity, namely, that the letters inside them had been at once closely written, and so much too tightly packed that it seemed a wonder they had ever arrived safely at their destination. They bore various postmarks, foreign and English, and were of different tints, but they were all directed in the one small, dashing hand, whose *t*"s were crossed with an audacious little flourish, and whose capitals were so prone to run into whimsical little curls. Most of them had been written when Dolly had sojourned with her charges in Switzerland, and some of them were merely notes of appointment from Bloomsbury Place; but each of them held its own magnetic attraction for Griffith, and not one of them would he have parted with for untold gold. He could count these small envelopes by the score, but he had never received one in his life without experiencing a positive throb of delight, which held fresh pleasure every time.

Most of these letters, too, had stories of their own. Some had come when he had been discouraged and down at heart, and they had been so full of sunshine, and pretty, loving conceits, that by the time he had finished reading them he had been positively jubilant; some, I regret to say, were a trifle wilful and coquettish, and had so roused him to jealous fancies that he had instantly dashed off a page or so of insane reproach and distrust which had been the beginning of a lover's quarrel; some of them (always written after he had been specially miserable and unreasoning) were half-pathetic mixtures of reproach and appeal, full of small dashes of high indignation, and outbursts of penitence, and with such a capricious, yet passionate ring in every line, that they had seemed less like letters than actual speech, and had almost forced him to fancy that Dolly herself was at his side, all in the flush and glow of one of her prettiest remorseful outbreaks.

And these letters from Brabazon Lodge were just as real, so they at least helped him to bear his trials more patiently than he could otherwise have done. She was far more comfortable than she had expected to be, she told him. Her duties were light, and Miss MacDowlas not hard to please, and altogether she was not dissatisfied.

"But that I am away from *you*," she wrote, "I should say Brabazon Lodge was better than the Bilberrys'. There is no skirmishing with Lady Augusta, at least; and, though skirmishing with Lady Augusta is not without its mild excitement, it is not necessary to one's happiness, and may be dispensed with. I wonder what Miss MacDowlas would say if she knew why I wear this modest ring on my third finger. When I explained to her casually that we were old friends, she succinctly remarked that you were a reprobate, and, feeling it prudent not to proceed with further disclosures, I bent my head demurely over my embroidery, and subsided into silence. I cannot discover why she disapproves of you unless it is that she has erratic notions about literary people. Perhaps she will alter her opinion in time. As it is, it can scarcely matter whether she knows of our engagement or not. When a fitting opportunity arrives I shall tell her, and I don't say I shall not enjoy the spice of the *denouement*. In the meantime I read aloud to her, talk, work wonders in Berlin wool, and play or sing when she asks me, which is not often. In the morning we drive out, in the afternoon she enjoys her nap, and in the evening I sit decorously intent upon the Berlin wonders, but thinking all the time of you and the parlor in Bloomsbury Place, where Tod disports himself in triumphant indifference to consequences, and where the girls discuss the lingering possibilities of their wardrobes. You may-tell Mollie we are very grand,—we have an immense footman, who accompanies us in our walks or drives, and condescends to open and shut our carriage-door for us, with the air of a gentleman at leisure. I am rather inclined to think that this gentleman has cast an approving eye upon me, as I heard him observe to the housemaid the other day, that I was 'a reether hinterestin' young party,' which mark of friendly notice has naturally cheered me on my lonely way."

Among the people who felt the change in the household keenly, Ralph Gowan may assuredly be included. He missed Dolly as much as any of them did, but he missed her in a different manner. He did not call quite as often as he had been in the habit of doing, and when he did call he was more silent and less entertaining. Dolly had always had an inspiring effect upon him, and, lacking the influence of her presence, even Vagabondia lost something of its charm. So sometimes he was guilty of the impoliteness of slipping into half-unconscious reveries of a few minutes' duration, and, being thus guilty upon one particular occasion, he was roused, after a short lapse of time, through the magnetic influence of a pair of soft eyes fixed upon him, which eyes he encountered the instant he looked up, with a start.

Mollie—the eyes were Mollie's—dropped her brown lashes with a quick motion, turning a little away from him; so he smiled at her with a sense of half-awakened appreciation. It was so natural to smile so at Mollie.

"Why, Mollie," he said, "what ails us? We are not usually so dull. We have not spoken to each other for ten minutes."

The girl did not look at him; her round, childish cheek was flushed, and her eyes were fixed on the fire, half proudly, half with a sort of innocently transparent indifference.

"Perhaps we have nothing worth saying to each other," she said. "Everybody is n't like Dolly."

Dolly! He colored slightly, though he smiled again. How did she know he was thinking of Dolly? Was it so patent a fact that even she could read it in his face? It never occurred to him for an instant that there could exist a reason why the eyes of this grown-up baby should be sharpened. She was such a very baby, with her ready blushes and her pettish, lovely face.

"And so you miss Dolly, too?" he said.

She shrugged her shoulders, as if to imply that she considered the question superfluous.

"Of course I do," she answered; "and of course we all do. Dolly is the sort of person likely to be missed."

She was so petulant about it that, not understanding her, he was both amused and puzzled, and so by degrees was drawn into making divers gallant, almost caressing speeches, such as might have been drawn from him by the changeful mood of a charming, wilful child.

"Something has made you angry," he said. "What is it, Mollie?"

"Nothing has made me angry," she replied. "I am not angry."

"But you look angry," he returned, "and how do you suppose I am to be interesting when you look angry?"

"It cannot matter to you," said Miss Mollie, "whether I am angry or not."

"Not matter!" he echoed, with great gravity. "It amounts to positive cruelty. Just at this particular moment I feel as if I should never smile again."

She reddened to her very throat, and then turned round all at once, flashing upon him such a piteous, indignant, indescribable glance as almost startled him.

"You are making fun of me," she cried out. "You always make fun of *me*. You would n't talk so to Dolly." And that instant she burst into tears.

He was dumbfounded. He could not comprehend it at all. He had thought of her as being so completely a child, that her troubles were never more than a child's troubles, and her moods a child's moods. He had admired her, too, as he would have admired her if she had been six years old, and he had never spoken to her as he would have spoken to a woman, in the whole course of their acquaintance. She was right in telling him that he would not have said such things to Dolly. He was both concerned and touched. What could he do but go to her and be dangerously penitent, and say a great many things easily said, but not soon to be forgotten! Indeed, her soft, nervous, passionate sobs, of which she was so much ashamed, her innocent tremor, and her pretty, wilful disregard of his remorse were such a new sensation to him, that it must be confessed he was not so discreet as he should have been.

"You never speak so to Dolly," she persisted, "nor to Aimée, either, and Aimée is only two years older than I am. It is not my fault," petulantly, "that I am only seventeen."

"Fault!" he repeated after her. "It is a very charming fault, if it is one. Come, Mollie," looking down at her with a tender softness in his eyes, "make friends with me again,—we ought to be friends. See,—let us shake hands!"

Of course she let him take her hand and hold it lightly for a moment as he talked, his really honest remorse at his blunder making him doubly earnest and so doubly dangerous. She had swept even Dolly out of his mind for the time being, and she occupied his attention so fully for the rest of the evening that he had not the time to be absent-minded again. In half an hour all traces of her tears had fled, and she was sitting on her footstool near him, accepting with such evident delight his efforts at amusing her, that she quite repaid him for his trouble.

After this there seemed to be some connecting link between them. In default of other attractions, he made headway with Mollie, and was to some extent consoled. He talked to her when he made his visits, and it gradually became an understood thing that they were very good friends. He won her confidence completely,—so far, indeed, that she used to tell him her troubles, and was ready to accept what meed of praise or friendly blame he might think fit to bestow upon her.

It was a few weeks after the above-recorded episode that Griffith arrived one afternoon, in some haste, with a note from Dolly addressed to Aimée, and containing a few hurried lines. It had been enclosed in a letter to himself.

Somewhat unexpectedly Miss MacDowlas had decided upon giving a dinner-party, and Dolly wanted the white merino, which she had forgotten to put into her trunk when she had packed it. Would they make a parcel of it and send it by Mollie to Brabazon Lodge?

"You will have to go at once, Mollie," said Aimée, after reading the note. "It will be dark in an hour, and you ought not to be out after dark."

"It is a great deal nicer to be out then," said Mollie, whose ideas of propriety were by no means rigid. "I like to see the shop windows lighted up. Where is my hat? Does anybody know?" rising from the carpet and abandoning Tod to his own resources.

Nobody did know, of course. It was not natural that anybody should. Hats and gloves and such small fry were generally left to provide quarters for themselves in Bloomsbury Place.

"What is the use of bothering?" remarked Mrs. Phil, disposing of the difficulty of their non-appearance when required, simply; "they always turn up in time." And in like manner Mollie's hat "turned up," and in a few minutes she returned to the parlor, tying the elastic under her hair.

"Your hair wants doing," said Aimée, having made up her parcel.

"Yes," replied Mollie, contentedly, "Tod has been pulling himself up by it; but it would be such a trouble to do anything to it just now, and I can tuck it back in a bunch. It only looks a little fuzzy, and that 's fashionable. Does this jacket look shabby, Aimée? It is a good thing it has pockets in it. I always *did* like pockets in a jacket, they are so nice to put your hands in when your gloves have holes in them."

"Your gloves oughtn't to have holes in them," commented Aimée.

"But how can you help it if you have n't got the money to buy new ones?" asked Mollie.

"You ought to mend them," said the wise one.

"Mend them!" echoed Mollie, regarding two or three bare pink finger-tips dubiously. "They are not worth mending."

"They were once," said Aimée; "and you ought to have stitched them before it was too late. But that is always our way," wrinkling her forehead with her usual touch of old-young anxiousness. "We are not practical. There! take the parcel and walk quickly, Mollie."

Once on the street, Mollie certainly obeyed her. With the parcel in one arm, and with one hand thrust into the convenient pocket, she hurried on her way briskly, not even stopping once to look at the shop windows. Quite unconscious, too, was she of the notice she excited among the passers-by. People even turned to look after her more than once, as indeed they often did. The scarlet scarf twisted round her throat to hide the frayed jacket collar, and the bit of scarlet mixed with the trimmings of her hat contrasted artistically with her brown eyes, and added brightness to the color on her cheeks. It was no wonder that men and women alike, in spite of their business-like hurry, found time to glance at her and even turn their heads over their shoulders to look backward, as she made her way along the pavement.

It was quite dark when she reached her destination, and Brabazon Lodge was brilliantly lighted up,—so brilliantly, indeed, that when the heavy front door was opened, in answer to her ring, she was a trifle dazzled by the flood of brightness in which Dolly's friend, the "gentleman at leisure," seemed to stand.

On stating her errand, she was handed over to a female servant, who stood in the hall.

"She was to be harsked in," she heard the footman observe, confidentially, to the young woman, "and taken to Miss Crewe's room immediate."

So she was led up-stairs, and ushered into a pretty bedroom, where she found Dolly sitting by the fire in a dressing-gown, with her hair about her shoulders.

She jumped up the moment Mollie entered, and ran to her, brush in hand, to kiss her.

"You are a good child," she said. "Come to the fire and sit down. Did you have any trouble in finding the house? I was afraid you would. It was just like me to forget the dress, and I never missed it until I began to look for it, wanting to wear it to-night. How is Tod?"

"He has got another tooth," said Mollie. "I found it to-day. Dolly," glancing round, "how nice your room is!"

"Yes," answered Dolly, checking a sigh, "but don't sigh after the fleshpots of Egypt, Mollie. One does n't see the dullest side of life at Bloomsbury Place, at least."

"Is it dull here?" asked Mollie.

Dolly shrugged her expressive shoulders.

"Berlin-wool work is n't exciting," she said. "How did you leave Griffith?"

"Low-spirited," replied Mollie. "I heard him tell Aimée this afternoon that he could n't stand it much longer."

Dolly began to brush her hair, and brushed it very much over her face, perhaps because she wished to take advantage of its shadow; for most assuredly Mollie caught sight of something sparkling amongst the abundant waves almost like a drop of dew.

"Dolly," she said at last, breaking the awkward little sympathetic silence which naturally followed, "do you remember our reading the 'Vicar of Wakefield'?"

"Yes," said Dolly, in a mournful half-whisper; she could not trust herself to say more.

"And about the family being 'up,' and then being 'down'? I always think we are like they were. First it is 'the family up,' and then 'the family down.' It is down just now."

"Yes," said Dolly.

"It will be 'up' again, in time," proceeded Mollie, sagaciously. "It always is."

Dolly tried to laugh, but her laugh was a nervous little effort which broke off in another sound altogether. Berlin-wool work and Brabazon Lodge had tried her somewhat and—she wanted Griffith. It seemed to her just then such a far distant unreal Paradise,—that dream of the modest parlor with the door shut against the world, and the green sofa drawn near the fire. Were they ever to attain it, or were they to grow old and tired out waiting, and hoping against hope?

She managed to rally, however, in a few minutes. Feeling discouraged and rebellious was not of much use,—that was one of Vagabondia's earliest learned lessons. And what good was there in making Mollie miserable? So she plucked up spirit and began to talk, and, to her credit be it said, succeeded in being fairly amusing, and made Mollie laugh outright half a dozen times during the remainder of her short stay. It was only a short stay, however. She remembered Aimée's warning at last, and rose rather in a hurry.

"I shall have to walk quickly if I want to get home in time for tea," she said, "so good-night, Dolly. You had better finish dressing."

"So I had," answered Dolly. "I am behind time already, but I shall not be many minutes, and Miss MacDowlas is not like Lady Augusta. Listen; I believe I hear wheels at the door now. It must be later than I fancied."

It was later than she fancied. As Mollie passed through the hall two gentlemen who were ascending the steps crossed her path, and, seeing the face of one who had not appeared to notice her presence, she started so nervously that she dropped her glove. His companion—a handsome, foreign-looking man—bent down and, picking it up, returned it to her, with a glance of admiring scrutiny which made her more excited than ever. She scarcely had the presence of mind to thank him, but rushed past him and out into the night in a passionate flutter of pain and sudden childish anger, inconsistent enough.

"He never saw me!" she said to herself, catching her breath piteously. "He is going to see Dolly. It is n't the party he cares for, and it is n't Miss MacDowlas,—it is nobody but Dolly. He has tried to get an invitation just because—because he cares for Dolly."

She reached home in time for tea, arriving with so little breath and so much burning color that they all stared at her, and Aimée asked her if she had been frightened.

"No," she answered, "but I ran half the way because I wanted to be in time."

She did not talk at tea, and scarcely ate anything, and when Griffith came in, at about nine o'clock, he found her lying on the sofa, flushed and silent. She said she had a headache.

"I took Dolly her dress," she said. "They are having a grand party and— Does Miss MacDowlas know Mr. Gowan, Griffith?"

Griffith started and changed countenance at once.

"No," he answered. "Why?"

"He was there," she said, listlessly. "I met him in the hall as I came out, but he did not see me. He must have tried to get an invitation because—well, you know how he likes Dolly."

And thus, the train having been already laid, was the spark applied.

CHAPTER VIII.
THE BEGINNING OF THE ENDING.

IT was some time before Griffith recovered from the effects of this simple announcement of Mollie's.

Though he scarcely confessed as much to himself, he thought of it very much oftener than was conducive to his own peace of mind, and in thinking of it he found it assuming a greater importance and significance than he had at first recognized in it, and was influenced accordingly. He went home to his lodgings, depressed and heavy of spirit; in fact, he left Bloomsbury Place earlier than usual, because he longed to be alone. He could think of nothing but Dolly,—Dolly in the white merino, shining like a stray star among her employer's guests, and gladdening the eyes of Ralph Gowan. He knew so well how she would look, and how this fellow would follow her in his easy fashion, without rendering himself noticeable, and manage to be near her through the evening and hold his place as if he had a right to it, and he knew, too, how natural it would be for Dolly's eyes to light up in her pleasure at being saved from boredom, and how her innocent gladness would show itself in a score of pretty ways. And it was as Mollie said,—it was for Dolly's sake that Ralph Gowan was there to-night.

"She must know that it is so herself," he groaned, dropping his head upon the table; "but she cannot help it. She would if she could. Yes, I'll believe that. She could never be false to me. I must hold fast to that in spite of everything. I should go mad if I did n't. I could never lose you, Dolly,—I could never lose you!"

But he groaned again the next moment from the bottom of his desperate heart. He had become tangled in yet another web of misery.

"It is only another proof of what I have said a thousand times," he cried out. "My claim upon her is so weak, that this fellow does not think it worth regarding. He thinks it may be set aside,—they all think it may be set aside. I should not wonder," clenching his hand and speaking through his teeth,— "I should not wonder if he has laughed many a time at his fancy of how it will end, and how easy it will be to thrust the old love to the wall!"

At this moment, in the first rankling sting of humiliation and despair, he could almost have struck a murderous blow at the man whom fortune had set on such a pinnacle of pride and insolence, as it seemed to his galled fancy. He was not in the mood to be either just or generous, and he saw in Ralph Gowan nothing but a man who had both the power and will to rival him, and rob him of peace and hope forever. If Dolly had been with him, in all probability his wretchedness would have evaporated in a harmless outburst, which would have touched the girl's heart so tenderly that she would have withheld nothing of love and consolation which could reassure him, and so in the end the tempest would have left no wound behind. But as it was left to himself and his imaginings, every thought held its bitter sting. He was, as it were, upon the brink of an abyss.

And while this danger was threatening her, Dolly was setting herself steadfastly to her task of entertaining her employer's guests, though it must be confessed that she found it necessary to summon all her energies. She was thinking of Griffith, but not as Griffith was thinking of her. She was picturing him looking desolate among the group round the fire at Bloomsbury Place, or else working desperately and with unnecessary energy amidst the dust and gloom of the dimly lighted office; and the result was that her spirit almost failed. It was quite a relief to encounter Ralph Gowan, as she did, on entering the room: he had seen them all latterly, and could enter into particulars; and so, in her pleasure, it must be owned that her face brightened, just as Griffith had fancied it would, when she shook hands with him.

"I did not hear that you were coming," she said. "How glad I am!" which was the most dangerous speech she could have made under the circumstances, since it was purely on her account that he had diplomatized to obtain the invitation.

He did not find it easy to release her hand all at once, and certainly he lighted up also.

"Will you let me tell you that it was not Miss MacDowlas who brought me here?" he said, in a low voice; "though I appreciate her kindness, as a grateful man ought. Vagabondia is desolate without you."

She tried to laugh, but could not; her attempt broke off in the unconscious sigh, which always touched him, he scarcely knew why.

"Is it?" she said, looking up at him without a bit of the old brightness. "Don't tell them, Mr. Gowan, but the fact is I am desolate without it. I want to go home."

He felt his heart leap suddenly, and before he could check himself he spoke.

"I wish—I *wish*," he said, "that you would let me take you home." And the simply sounding words embodied a great deal more of tender fancy than a careless observer would have imagined; and Dolly, recognizing the thrill in his voice, was half startled.

But she shook her head, and managed to smile.

"That is not wisdom," she said. "It savors of the lilies of the field. We cannot quarrel with our bread and butter for sentiment's sake in Vagabondia. Did you know that Mollie had paid me a visit this evening?—or perhaps you saw her; I think she went out as you came in."

"Mollie!" he said, surprisedly; and then looking half annoyed, or at least a trifle disturbed, he added, as if a sudden thought had occurred to him, "then it was Mollie, Chandos spoke of."

"Chandos!" echoed Dolly. "Who is Chandos—and what did Chandos say about Mollie?"

He glanced across the room to where a tall, handsome man was bending over a fussy little woman in pink.

"That is Chandos," he said; "and since you spoke of Mollie's visit, I recollect that, as we came into the house, Chandos was behind me and lingered a moment or so, and when he came to me afterward he asked if I had seen the face that passed us as we entered. It had roused his enthusiasm as far as it can be roused by anything."

"It must have been Mollie," commented Dolly, and she looked at the man on the opposite side of the room, uneasily. "Is he a friend of yours?" she asked, after scrutinizing him for a few seconds.

Gowan shrugged his shoulders.'

"Not a friend," he answered, dryly. "An acquaintance. We have not much in common."

"I am glad to hear it," was Dolly's return. "I don't like Chandos."

She could not have explained why she did not like him, but certainly she was vaguely repelled and could not help hoping that he would never see Mollie again. He was just the man to be dangerous to Mollie; handsome, polished, ready of speech and perfect in manner, he was the sort of man to dazzle and flatter any ignorant, believing child.

"Oh!" she exclaimed, half aloud, "I could not bear to think that he would see her again."

She uttered the words quite involuntarily, but Gowan heard them, and looked at her in some surprise, and so awakened her from her reverie.

"Are you speaking of Mollie?" he asked.

"Yes," she answered, candidly, "though I did not mean to speak aloud. My thoughts were only a mental echo of the remark I made a moment ago,— that I don't like Chandos. I do not like him at all, even at this distance, and I cannot resist feeling that I do not want him to see anything more of Mollie.

We are not very discreet, we Vagabonds, but we must learn wisdom enough to shield Mollie." And she sighed again.

"I understand that," he said, almost tenderly, so sympathetically, in fact, that she turned toward him as if moved by a sudden impulse.

"I have sometimes thought since I came here," she said, "that perhaps *you* might help me a little, if you would. She is so pretty, you see, and so young, and, through knowing so little of the world and longing to know so much, in a childish, half-dazzled way, is so innocently wilful that she would succumb to a novel influence more readily than to an old one. So I have thought once or twice of asking you to watch her a little, and guard her if— if you should ever see her in danger."

"I can promise to do that much, at least," he returned, smiling.

She held out her hand impetuously, just as she would have held it out to Griffith, and, oh, the hazard of it,—the hazard of so throwing aside her mock airs and graces, and showing herself to him just as she showed herself to the man she loved,—the Dolly whose heart was on her lips and whose soul was in her eyes.

"Then we will make a 'paction' of it," she said. "You will help me to take care of her."

"For your sake," he said, "there are few things I would not do."

So from that time forward he fell into the habit of regarding unsuspecting Mollie as his own special charge. He was so faithful to his agreement, indeed, that once or twice Griffith was almost ready to console himself with the thought that perhaps, after all, the child's beauty and tractability would win its way, and Gowan would find himself seriously touched at heart. Just now he could see that his manner was scarcely that of a lover, but there most assuredly was a probability that it might alter and become more warm and less friendly and platonic. As to Mollie herself, she was growing a trifle incomprehensible; she paid more attention to her lovely hair than she had been in the habit of doing, and was even known to mend her gloves; she began to be more conscious of the dignity of her seventeen years. She complained less petulantly of the attentions of Phil's friends, and accepted them with a better grace. The wise one even observed that she tolerated Brown, the obnoxious, and permitted him to admire her—at a distance. In her intercourse with Gowan she was capricious and had her moods. Sometimes she indulged in the weakness of tiring herself in all her small bravery when he was coming, and presented herself in the parlor beauteous and flushed and conscious, and was so delectably shy and sweet that she betrayed him into numerous trifling follies not at all consistent with his high position of mentor; and then, again, she was obstinate, rather incomprehensible, and did not adorn herself at all, and, indeed, was hard enough to manage.

"You are growing very queer, Mollie," said Miss Aimée, wonderingly.

To which sage remark Mollie retorted with a tremulous, sensitive flush, and most unnecessary warmth of manner.

"I 'm not queer at all I wish you would n't bother so, Aimée!"

That very afternoon she came into the room with a card in her hand, after going out to answer a summons at the door-bell.

"Phil," she said, "a gentleman wants you. Chandos, the card says."

"Chandos!" read Phil, rising from the comfort of his couch, and taking his pipe out of his mouth. "Who knows Chandos?—I don't. It must be some fellow on business."

And so it proved. He found the gentleman awaiting him in the next room, and in a very short time learned his errand. Chandos introduced himself— Gerald Chandos, of The Pools, Bedfordshire, who, hearing of Mr. Crewe through numerous friends, not specified, and having a fancy—quite the fancy of an uncultured amateur, modestly—for pictures and an absorbing passion for art in all its forms, had taken the liberty of calling, etc. It was very smoothly said, and Chandos, of The Pools, being an imposing patrician sort of individual, and free from all fopperies or affectations, Phil met his advances complacently enough. It was no unusual thing for an occasional patron to drop in after this manner. He had no fault to find with a man who, having the good fortune to possess money, had the good taste to know how to spend it. So he made friends with Chandos, pretty much as he had made friends with Gowan,—pretty much as he would have made friends with any other sufficiently amiable and well-bred visitor to his modest studio. He showed him his pictures, and talked art to him, and managed to spend an hour very pleasantly, ending by selling him a couple of tiny spirited sketches, which had taken his fancy. It was when he was taking down these sketches from the wall that he heard a sort of smothered exclamation from the man, who stood a few feet apart from him, and, turning to see what it meant, he saw that he had just discovered the fresh, lovely, black-hooded head, with the trail of autumn leaves clinging to the loose trail of hair,—the picture for which Mollie had sat as model. It was very evident that Chandos, of The Pools, was admiring it.

"Ah!" said he, the next minute. "I know this face. There can scarcely be two faces like it."

Phil left his sketches and came to him, the pleasure he felt on the success of his creation warming him up. This picture, with Mollie's face and head, was a great favorite of his.

"Yes," he said, standing opposite to it, with his hands in his pockets, and critical appreciation in his eyes. "You could not very well mistake it. Heads are not my exact forte, you know; but that is Mollie to a tint and a curve, and I am rather proud of it."

Chandos regarded it steadfastly.

"And well you may be," he answered. "Your sister, I believe?"

"Mollie!" exclaimed Phil, stepping a trifle aside, to get into a better light, and speaking almost abstractedly. "Oh, yes, to be sure! She is my sister,—the youngest. There are three of them. That flesh tint is one of the best points."

And in the meantime, while this apparently trivial conversation was being carried on in the studio, Mollie, in the parlor, had settled herself upon a stool close to the fire, and, resting her chin on her hand and her elbow on her knee, was looking reflective.

"That Chandos is somebody new," 'Toinette remarked. "I hope he has come to buy something. I want some gold sleeve-loops for Tod. I saw some beauties the other day, when I was out."

"But you could n't afford them if Phil sold two pictures instead of one," said Aimée. "There are so many other useful things you need."

"He is n't a stranger to me," put in Mollie, suddenly. "I have seen him before."

"Who?" said 'Toinette. She was thinking more of Tod's gold sleeve-loops than of anything else.

"This Mr. Chandos," answered Mollie, without looking up from the fire. "I saw him at Brabazon Lodge the night I went to take Dolly her dress. He was with Mr. Gowan, and I dropped my glove, and he picked it up for me. I was coming out as they were going in."

"I wonder," said Aimée, "whether Mr. Gowan goes to Brabazon Lodge often?"

"I don't know, I 'm sure," answered Mollie, shrugging her shoulder. "How is one to learn? He would n't be likely to tell us. I should think, though, that he does. He is too fond of Dolly"—with a slight choke in her voice—"to stay away, if he can help it."

"It's queer," commented 'Toinette, "how men like Dolly. She is n't a beauty, I 'm sure; and for the matter of that, when her hair is n't done up right, she is n't even pretty."

"It isn't queer, at all," said Mollie, rather crossly; "it's her way. She can make such a deal out of nothing, and she does n't stand at trouble when she wants to *make* people like her. *She* says any one can do it, and it is only a question of patience; but I don't believe her. See how frantic Griffith is about her. He is more desperately in love with her to-day than he was at the very first, seven years ago."

"And she cares more for him, I'm sure," said Aimée.

Mollie's shoulder went up again. "She flirts with people enough, if she does," she commented.

"Ah!" returned Aimée, "that is 'her way,' as you call it, again. Somehow, it seems as if she can't help it. It is as natural to her as the color of her hair and eyes. She can't help doing odd things and making speeches that rouse people and tempt them into liking her. She has done such things all her life, and sometimes I think she will do them even when she is an old woman; though, of course, she will do them in a different way. Dolly would n't be Dolly without her whimsicalness, any more than Dick there, in his cage, would be a canary if he did n't twitter and sing."

"Does she ever do such things to women?" asked Miss Mollie, shrewdly. She seemed to be in a singular mood this afternoon.

"Yes," Aimée protested, "she does; and what is more, she is not different even with children. I have seen her take just as much trouble to please Phemie and the little Bilberrys as she would take to please Griffith or—or Mr. Gowan. And see how fond they were of her. If she had cared for nothing but masculine admiration, do you think Phemie would have adored her as she did, and those dull children would have been so desolate when she left them? No, I tell you. Dolly's weakness—and it isn't such a very terrible weakness, after all—lies in wanting *everybody* to like her,—men, women, and children; yes, down to babies and dogs and cats. And see here, Mollie, ain't we rather fond of her ourselves?"

"Yes," owned Mollie, staring at the fire, "we are. Fond enough."

"And is n't she rather fond of us?"

"Yes, she is—for the matter of that," acquiesced Mollie.

"Yes," began 'Toinette, and then, the sound of footsteps upon the staircase interrupting her, she broke off abruptly to listen. "It is Phil's visitor," she said.

Mollie got up from her seat, roused into a lazy sort of interest.

"I am going to look at him," she said, and went to the window.

The next minute she drew back, blushing.

"He saw me," she said. "I did n't think he could, if I stood here in the corner."

But he had; and more than that, in his admiration of her dimples and round fire-flushed cheeks, had smiled into her face, openly and without stint, as he passed.

After tea Gowan came in. Mollie opened the door for him; and Mollie, in a soft blue dress, and with her hair dressed to a marvel, was a vision to have touched any man's fancy. She was in one of her sweet acquiescent moods, too, having recovered herself since the afternoon; and when she led him into the parlor, she blushed without any reason whatever, as usual, and as a consequence looked enchanting.

"Phil has gone out," she said. "'Toinette is putting Tod to bed, and Aimée is helping her; so there is no one here but me."

Gowan sat down—in Dolly's favorite chair.

"You are quite enough," he said; "quite enough—for me."

She turned away, making a transparent little pretence of requiring a hand-screen from the mantelpiece, and, having got it, she too sat down, and fell to examining a wretched little daub of a picture upon it most minutely.

"This is very badly done," she observed, irrelevantly. "Dolly did it, and made it up elaborately into this screen because it was such a sight. It is just like Dolly, to make fun and joke at her own mistakes. She has n't a particle of talent for drawing. She did this once when Griffith thought he was going to get into something that would bring him money enough to allow of their being married. She made a whole lot of little mats and things to put in their house when they got it, but Griffith did n't get the position, so they had to settle down again."

"Good Heavens!" ejaculated Gowan.

"What is the matter?" she asked.

He moved a trifle uneasily in his chair. He had not meant to speak aloud.

"An unintentional outburst, Mollie," he said. "A cheerful state of affairs, that."

"What state of affairs?" she inquired. "Oh, you mean Dolly's engagement. Well, of course, it *has* been a long one; but then, you see, they like each other very much. Aimée was only saying this afternoon that they cared for each other more now than they did at first."

"Do they?" said Gowan, and for the time being lapsed into silence.

"It's a cross-grained sort of fortune that seems to control us in this world, Mollie," he said, at length.

Mollie stared at the poor little daub on her hand-screen and met his philosophy indifferently enough.

"*You* ought n't to say so," she answered. "And I don't know anything about it."

He laughed—quite savagely for so amiable a young man.

"I!" he repeated. "I ought not to say so, ought n't I? I think I ought. It *is* a cross-grained fortune, Mollie. We are always falling in love with people who do not care for us, or with people who care for some one else, or with people who are too poor to marry us, or—"

"Speak for yourself," said Mollie, with a vigor quite wonderful and new in her. "*I* am not."

And she held her screen up between her face and his, so that he could not see her. She could have burst into a passionate gush of tears. It was Dolly he was thinking about,—it was Dolly who had the power to make him unhappy and sardonic,—always Dolly.

"Then you are a wise child, Mollie," he said. "But you are a very young child yet,—only seventeen, is n't it? Well, it may all come in good time."

"It will not come at all," she asserted, stubbornly.

Dolly's little wretch of a hand-screen was quite trembling in her hand, it made her so desperate to feel, as she did, that she was of such small consequence to him that he could treat her as a child, and make a sort of joke of his confidence. But he did not see it.

"Ah! well, you see," he went on, "I thought so once, but it has come to me nevertheless. The fact is, I am crying for the moon, Mollie, as many a wiser and better man has done before me."

She did not answer, so he rose and walked once or twice across the room. When he came back to the fire, she had risen too, and was standing up, biting the edge of her screen, all flushed, and with a brightness in her eyes he did not understand. Poor little soul! she was suffering very sharply in her childish way.

He laid a hand on either of her shoulders, and spoke to her gently enough.

"Mollie," he said, "let us sit down together and condole with each other. You are not in a good humor to-night, something has rasped you again; and as for me, I am about as miserable, my dear, as it is possible for a man with a few thousand a year to be."

She tried to answer him steadily, and, finding she could not, rushed into novel subterfuge. Subterfuge was a novelty to Mollie.

"Yes," she said, lifting the most beauteous of tear-wet eyes to his quite eagerly. "Yes, I am crossed, and—and something has vexed me. I am getting bad-tempered, I think. Suppose we do sit down."

And then when they did sit down—she on the hearth-rug at his feet, he in Dolly's chair again—she broke out upon him in a voice like a sharp little sob.

"I know what *you* are miserable about," she said. "You are miserable about Dolly."

They had never spoken about the matter openly before, though he had always felt that if he could speak openly to any one, he could to this charming charge of his. Such is the keenness of masculine penetration. And now he felt almost relieved already. The natural craving for sympathy of some kind or other was to satisfy itself through the medium of pretty, much-tried Mollie.

"Yes," he answered, half desperately, half reluctantly. "Dolly is the moon I am crying for,—or rather, as I might put it more poetically, 'the bright particular star.' What a good little thing you are to guess at it so soon!"

"It did n't need much guessing at," she said, curving her innocent mouth in a piteous effort to smile.

He, leaning against the round, padded back of his chair, sighed, and as he sighed almost forgot the poor child altogether, even while she spoke to him. Having all things else, he must still cry for this one other gift, and really he felt very dolorous.

Mollie, pulling her screen to pieces, looked at him with a heavy yet adoring heart. She was young enough to be greatly moved by his physical beauty, and just now she could not turn away from him. His long-limbed, slender figure (which, while still graceful and lithe enough, was *not* a model of perfection, as she fondly imagined), his pale, dark face, his dark eyes, even his rather impolite and uncomplimentary abstraction, held fascination for her. Not having been greatly smiled upon by fortune, she had fallen to longing eagerly and fearfully for this one gift which had been so freely vouchsafed to Dolly, who had neither asked nor cared for it. Surely there was some cross-grained fate at work.

She was very quiet indeed when he at length recollected himself and roused from his reverie. He looked up to find her resting her warm, rose-leaf colored cheek on her hand, and concentrating all her attention upon the fire again. She was not inclined to talk when he spoke to her, and indeed had so far shrunk within herself that he found it necessary to exert his powers to their utmost before he could move her to anything like interest in their usual topics of conversation. In fact, her reserve entailed the necessity of a little hazardous warmth of manner being exhibited on his part, and in the end a few more dangerous, though half-jocular, speeches were made, and in spite of the temporary dissatisfaction of his previous mood, he felt a trifle reluctant to leave the fire and the sweet, unwise face when the time came to go.

"Good-night," he said to her, a few minutes before he went out. And then, noticing for the twentieth time how becoming the soft blue of her dress was and how picturesque she was herself even in the unconsciousness of her posture, he was tempted to try to bring that little, half-resentful glow into her upraised eyes again.

"I have often heard your sister make indiscreetly amiable speeches to you, Mollie," he said. "Did she ever tell you that you ought to have been born a sultana?"

She shook her head and pouted a little.

"I should n't like to be a sultana," she said.

"What!" he exclaimed. "Not a sultana in spangled slippers and gorgeous robes!"

"No," she answered, with a spice of Dolly in her speech. "The slippers are great flat things that turn up at the toes, and the sultan might buy me for so much a pound, and—and I care for other things besides dress."

"Nevertheless," he returned, "you would have made a dazzling sultana."

Then he went away and left her, and she sat down upon her stool before the fire again and began to pull her hair down and let it hang in grand disorder about her shoulders and over her face.

"If I am so—so pretty," she said slowly, to herself, "people ought to like me, and," sagaciously, "I must be pretty or he would not say so."

And when she went to her room it must be confessed that she crept to the glass and stared at the reflection of the face framed in the abundant, falling hair, until Aimée, wondering at her quietness, raised her head from her pillow, and, seeing her, called her to her senses.

"Mollie," she said, in her quietest way, "you look very nice, my dear and very picturesque, and I don't wonder at your admiring yourself; but if you stand there much longer in your bare feet you will have influenza, and then you will have to wear a flannel round your throat, and your nose will be red, and you won't derive much satisfaction from your looking-glass for a week to come."

CHAPTER IX.
IN WHICH WE ARE UNORTHODOX.

"SOMETHING," announced Phil, painting away industriously at his picture,—"something is up with Grif. Can any of you explain what it is?"

Mollie, resting her elbows on the window-ledge, turned her head over her shoulder; 'Toinette, tying Tod's sleeves with red ribbon, looked up; Aimée went on with her sewing, the two little straight lines making themselves visible on her forehead between her eyebrows. The fact of something being "up" with any one of their circle was enough to create a wondering interest.

"There is no denying," Phil proceeded, "that he is changed somehow or other. He is not the same fellow that he was a few months ago,—before Dolly went away."

"It is Dolly he is bothering about," said Mollie, concisely.

Then Aimée was roused.

"I wish they were married," she said. "I wish they were married and—safe!"

"Safe!" put in Mrs. Phil. "That is a queer thing to say. They are not in any danger, let us devoutly hope."

The two wrinkles deepened, and the wise one sighed.

"I hope not," she answered, bending her small, round, anxious face over her sewing, and attacking it vigorously.

"They never struck me, you know," returned Mrs. Phil, "as being a particularly dangerous couple, though now I think of it I do remember that it has once or twice occurred to me that Griffith has been rather stupid lately."

"It has occurred to me," remarked Phil, dryly, "that he has taken a most unaccountable dislike to Gowan."

Mollie turned round to her window again.

"Not to put it too strongly," continued the head of the family, "he hates him like the deuce."

And he was not far wrong in making the assertion. The time had been coming for some time when the course of this unimposing story of true love was no longer to run smooth, and in these days Griffith was in a dangerous frame of mind. Now and then he heard of Gowan dropping in to spend a few hours at Brabazon Lodge, and now and then he heard of his good fortune in having found in Miss MacDowlas a positive champion. He was even a favorite with her, just as he was a favorite with many other people. Griffith did not visit Brabazon Lodge himself, he had given that up long ago, indeed had only once paid his respects to his relative since her arrival in London. That one visit, short and ceremonious as it was, had been enough for him. Like many estimable ladies, Miss MacDowlas had prejudices of her own which were hard to remove, and appearances had been against her nephew.

"If he is living a respectable life, and so engaged in a respectable profession, my dear," commented Dolly's proprietress, in one of her after conversations on the subject, "why does he look shabby and out at elbows? It is my opinion that he is a very disreputable young man."

"She thinks," wrote Dolly to the victim, "that you waste your substance in riotous living." And it was such an exquisite satire on the true state of affairs, that even Griffith forgot his woes for the moment, and laughed when he read the letter.

Dolly herself was not prone to complain of Miss MacDowlas. She was not so bad as she looked, after all. She was obstinate and rigid enough on some points, but she had her fairer side, and Dolly found it. In a fashion of her own Miss MacDowlas was rather fond of her companion. A girl who was shrewd, industrious, and often amusing, was not to be despised in her opinion; so she showed her fair young handmaiden a certain amount of respect. She had engaged companions before, who being entertaining were not trustworthy, or being trustworthy were insufferably dull. She could trust Dolly with the most onerous of her domestic or social charges, she found, and there was no fear of her small change disappearing or her visitors being bored. So the position of that "young person" became an assured and decently comfortable one.

But, day by day, Griffith was drifting nearer and nearer the old shoals of difficulty. He rasped himself with miserable imaginings, and was often unjust even toward Dolly. Hers was the brighter side of the matter, he told himself.

She was sure to find friends,—she always did, these people would make a sort of favorite of her, and she would be pleased because she was so popular among them. He could not bear the thought of her ephemeral happiness over trifles sometimes. He even fell so low as that at his worst moments, though to his credit, be it spoken, he was always thoroughly ashamed of himself afterward. There were times, too, when he half resented her little jokes at their poverty, and answered them bitterly when he wrote his replies to her letters. His chief consolation he found in Aimée, and the sage of the family found her hands fuller than ever. Quiet little body as she was, she was far-sighted enough to see danger in the distance, and surely she did her best to alter its course.

"If you are not cooler," she would say, "you will work yourself into such a fever of unhappiness, that you will be doing something you will regret."

"That is what I am afraid of," he would sometimes burst forth; "but you must admit, Aimée, that it is a pretty hard case."

"Yes," confessed the young oracle, "I will admit that, but being unreasonable won't make it any easier."

And then the fine little lines would show themselves, and she would set herself industriously to the task of administering comfort and practical advice, and she never failed to cheer him a little, however temporarily.

And she did not fail Dolly, either. Sage axioms and praiseworthy counsel reached Brabazon Lodge in divers small envelopes, addressed to Miss Crewe, and invariably beginning, "My dearest Dolly;" and more than once difficulty had been averted, and Dolly's heart warmed again toward her lover, when she had been half inclined to rebel and exhibit some slight sharpness of temper. Only a few days after the conversation with which the present chapter opens occurred, one of these modestly powerful missives was forwarded, and that evening Griffith met with an agreeable surprise. Chance had taken him into the vicinity of Miss MacDowlas's establishment, and as he walked down the deserted road in a somewhat gloomy frame of mind, he became conscious suddenly of the sound of small, light feet, running rapidly down the footpath behind him.

"Griffith!" cried a clear, softly pitched voice, "Griffith, wait for me."

And, turning, he saw in the dusk of the winter day a little figure almost flying toward him, and in a few seconds more Dolly was standing by him, laughing and panting, and holding to his arm with both hands.

"I thought I should never catch you," she said. "You never walked so fast in your life, I believe, you stupid old fellow. I could n't call out loud, though it is a quiet place, and so I had to begin to run. Goodness! what *would* Lady Augusta have said if she had seen me flying after you!"

And then, stopping all at once, she looked up at him with a wicked little air of saucy daring.

"Don't you want to kiss me?" she said. "You may, if you will endeavor to effect it with despatch before somebody comes."

She was obliged to resign herself to her fate then. For nearly two minutes she found herself rendered almost invisible, and neither of them spoke. Then half released, she lifted her face to look at him, and there were tears on her eyelashes, and in her voice, too, though she was trying very hard to smile.

"Poor old fellow," she half whispered. "Has it seemed long since you kissed me last?"

He caught her to his breast again in his old, impetuous fashion.

"Long!" he groaned. "It has seemed so long that there have been times when it has almost driven me mad. O Dolly! Dolly!"

She let him crush her in his arms and kiss her again, and she nestled against his shoulder for a minute, and, putting her warm little gloved hand up to his face, gave it a tiny, loving squeeze. But of course that could not last long. Miss Macdowlas's companion might be kissed in the dusk two or three times, but, genteelly sequestered as was the road leading to Brabazon Lodge, some stray footman or housemaid might appear on the scene, from some of the neighboring establishments, at any moment, so she was obliged to draw herself away at last.

"There!" she said, "you must let me take your arm and walk on now, and you must tell me all about things. I have a few minutes to spare, and I have *so* wanted you," heaving a weary little sigh, and holding his arm very tightly indeed.

"Dolly," he asked, abruptly, "are you sure of that?"

The other small hand clasped itself across his sleeve in an instant.

"Sure?" she answered. "Sure that I have wanted you? I have been nearly *dying* for you!" with some affectionate extravagance.

"Are you sure," he put it to her, "quite sure that you have not sometimes forgotten me for an hour or so?"

"No," she answered, indignantly, "not for a single second;" which was a wide assertion.

"Not," he prompted her, somewhat bitterly, "when the MacDowlas gives dinner-parties, and you find yourself a prominent feature, 'young person,' as you are? Not when you wear the white merino, and 'heavy swells' admire you openly?"

"No," shaking her head in stout denial of the imputation. "Never. I think about you from morning until night; and the fact is," in a charming burst of candor, "I actually wake in the night and think about you. There! are you satisfied now?"

It would have been impossible to remain altogether unconsoled and unmoved under such circumstances, but he could not help trying her again.

"Dolly," he said, "does Gowan never make you forget me?"

Then she saw what he meant, and flushed up to her forehead, drawing her hand away and speaking hotly.

"Oh!" she said, "it is *that*, is it?"

"Yes," he answered her, "it is that."

Then they stopped in their walk, and each looked at the other,—Griffith at Dolly, with a pale face and much of desperate, passionate appeal in his eyes; Dolly at Griffith, with her small head thrown back in sudden defiance.

"I am making you angry and rousing you, Dolly," he said; "but I cannot help it. There is scarcely a week passes in which I do not hear that he—that fellow—has managed to see you in one way or another. He can always see you," savagely. "*I* don't see you once a month."

"Ah!" said Dolly, with cruel deliberation, "*this* is what Aimée meant when she told me to be careful, and think twice before I did things. I see now."

I have never yet painted Dolly Crewe as being a young person of angelic temperament. I have owned that she flirted and had a temper in spite of her Vagabondian good spirits, good-nature, and popularity; so my readers will not be surprised at her resenting rather sharply what she considered as being her lover's lack of faith.

"I think," she proceeded, opening her eyes wide and addressing him with her grandest air,—"I think I will walk the rest of my way alone, if you please."

It was very absurd and very tragical in a small way, of course, and assuredly she ought to have known better, and perhaps she did know better, but just now she was very fierce and very sharply disappointed. She positively turned away as if to leave him, but he caught hold of her arm and held her.

"Dolly," he cried, huskily, "you are not going away in that fashion. We never parted so in our lives."

She half relented,—not quite, but nearly, so very nearly that she did not try very hard to get away. It was Griffith, after all, who was trying her patience— if Gowan or any other man on earth had dared to imply a doubt in her, she would have routed him magnificently—in two minutes; but Griffith—ah, well, Griffith was different.

"Whose fault is it?" she asked, breaking down ignominiously. "Who is to blame? I never ask you if other people make you forget me. I wanted to—to see you so much that I—I ran madly after you for a quarter of a mile, at the risk of being looked upon as a lunatic by any one who might have chanced to see me. But you don't care for that. I had better have bowed to you and passed on if we had met. Let me go!"

"No," said Griffith, "you shall not go. God knows if I could keep you, you should never leave my arms again."

"You would tire of me in a week, if I belonged to you in real earnest," she said, not trying to get away at all now, however.

"Tire of you!" he exclaimed, in a shaken voice. "Of *you!*" And all at once he drew her round so that the light of the nearest lamp could fall on her face. "Look here!" he whispered, sharply; "Dolly, I swear to you, that if there lives a man on earth base and heartless enough to rob me of you, I will kill him as sure as I breathe the breath of life!"

She had seen him impassioned enough often before, but she had never seen him in as wild a mood as he was when he uttered these words. She was so frightened that she broke into a little cry, and put her hand up to his lips.

"Griffith!" she said, "Grif!—dear old fellow. You don't know what you are saying. Oh! don't—don't!"

Her horror brought him to his senses again; but he had terrified her so that she was trembling all over, and clung to him nervously when he tried to console her.

"It is n't like *you* to speak in such a way," she faltered, in the midst of her tears. "Oh, how dreadfully wrong things must be getting, to make you so cruel!"

It took so long a time to reassure and restore her to her calmness, that he repented his rashness a dozen times. But he managed to comfort her at length, though to the last she was tearful and dejected, and her voice was broken with soft, sorrowful little catchings of the breath.

"Don't let us talk about Ralph Gowan," she pleaded, when he had persuaded her to walk on with him again. "Let us talk about ourselves,—we are always safe when we talk about ourselves," with an innocent, mournful smile.

And so they talked about themselves. He would have talked of anything on earth to please her then. Talking of themselves, of course, implied talking nonsense,—affectionate, sympathetic nonsense, but still nonsense; and so, for a while, they strolled on together, and were as tenderly foolish and disconnected as two people could possibly be.

But, in spite of her resolution to avoid the subject, Dolly could not help drifting back to Ralph Gowan. "Griffith," she said, plaintively, "you are very jealous of him."

"I know that," he answered.

"But don't you *know*," in desperate appeal, "that there is n't the slightest need for you to be jealous of anybody?"

"I know," he returned, dejectedly, "that I am a very wretched fellow sometimes."

"Oh, dear!" sighed Dolly.

"I know," he went on, "that seven years is a long probation, and that the prospect of another seven, or another two, for the matter of that, would drive me mad. I know I am growing envious and distrustful; I know that there are times when I hate that fellow so savagely that I am ashamed of myself. Dolly, what has he ever done that he should saunter on the sunny side, clad in purple and fine linen all his life? The money he throws away in a year would furnish the house at Putney."

"Oh, dear!" burst forth Dolly. "You *are* going wrong. It is all because I am not there to take care of you, too. Those are not the sentiments of Vagabondia, Grif."

"No," dryly; "they are of the earth, earthy."

Dolly shook her head dolefully.

"Yes," she acquiesced; "and they are a bit shabby, too. You are going down, Grif. You never used to be shabby. None of us were ever exactly that, though we used to grumble sometimes. We used to grumble, not because other people had things, but because we had n't them."

"I am getting hardened, I suppose," bitterly. "And it is hardly to be wondered at."

"Hardened!" She stopped him that moment, and stood before him, holding his arm and looking up at him. "Hardened!" she repeated. "Grif, if you say that again, I will never forgive you. What is the good of our love for each other if it won't keep our hearts soft? When we get hardened we shall love each other no longer. What have we told each other all these years? Have n't we said that so long as we had one another we could bear anything, and not envy other people? It was n't all talk and sentiment, was it? It was n't on *my* part, Grif. I meant it then, and I mean it now, though I know there are many good, kind-hearted people in the world who would not understand it, and would say I was talking unpractical rubbish, if they heard me. Hardened! Grif, while you have me, and I have you, and there is nothing on our two consciences? Why, it sounds,"—with another most dubious shake of her small head,—"it sounds as if you would n't care about the house at Putney!"

He was conquered, of course; before she had spoken a dozen words he had been conquered; but this figure of his not caring for the house at Putney broke him utterly. He did not look very hardened when he answered her.

"Dolly," he said, "you are an angel! I have told you so before, and it may be a proof of the barrenness of my resources to tell you so again, but it is true. God forgive me, my precious! I should like to see the man whose heart could harden while such a woman loved him."

It was a pretty sight to see her put her hands on his shoulders, and stand on tiptoe to kiss him, in her honest, earnest way, without waiting for him to ask her.

"Ah!" she said, "I knew it wasn't true," and then, still letting her hands rest on his shoulders, she burst forth in her tender, impulsive way again. "Grif," she said, "I don't think I am very wise, and I know I am not very thoughtful. I do things often that it would be better to leave undone,—I am fond of making the Philistines admire me, and I sometimes tease you; but, dear old fellow, right deep down at the bottom of my heart," faltering slightly, "I do— *do* want to be a good woman; and there is never a night passes—though I never told you so before—that I do not pray to God to let me help you and let you help me to be tender and faithful and true."

It was the old story,—love was king. Wisdom to the winds! Practicality to the corners of the earth! Prudence, power, and grandeur, hide your diminished heads! Here were two people who cared nothing for you, and who flung you aside without a fear as they stood together under the trees in the raw evening air,—one a penniless little hired entertainer of elderly ladies, the other an equally impecunious bondsman in a dingy office.

They were quite happy,—even happy when time warned them that they must bid each other goodnight. They walked together to the gates of Barbazon Lodge, and parted in a state of bliss.

"Good-night," said Dolly. "Be good,—as somebody wise once said,—'Be good, and you will be happy.'"

"Good-night," answered Griffith; "but might n't he have put it the other way, Dolly, 'Be happy, and you will be good—because you can't help it'?"

He had his hand on *her* shoulder, this time, and as she laughed she put her face down so that her soft, warm cheek nestled against it.

"But he didn't put it that way," she objected. "And we must take wisdom as it comes. There! I must go now," rather in a hurry. "Some one is coming— see!"

"Confound it!" he observed, devoutly. "Who is it?"

"I don't know," answered Dolly; "but you must let me go. Good-night, again."

He released her, and she ran in through the gate, and up the gravel walk, and so he was left to turn away and pass the intruder with an appearance of nonchalance. And pass him he did, though whether with successful indifference or not, one can hardly say; but in passing him he looked up, and in looking up he recognized Ralph Gowan.

"Going to see her," he said, to himself, just as poor Mollie had said the same thing, and just with the same heartburn. "The dev—But, no," he broke off sharply, "I won't begin again. It is as she says,—the blessed little darling!—it is shabby to be down on him because he has the best of it." And he went on his way, not rejoicing, it is true, but still trying to crush down a by no means unnatural feeling of rebellion.

CHAPTER X.
IN SLIPPERY PLACES.

THE wise one sat at the window and looked out. The view commanded by Bloomsbury Place was not a specially imposing or attractive one. Four or five tall, dingy houses with solitary scrubby shrubs in their small front slips of low-spirited looking gardens, four or five dingy and tall houses without the scrubby shrubs in their small front slips of low-spirited looking gardens, rows of Venetian blinds of various shades, and one or two lamp-posts,—not much to enliven the prospect.

The inhabitants of the houses in Bloomsbury Place were not prone to sitting at their front windows, accordingly; but this special afternoon, the weather being foggy, Aimée finding herself alone in the parlor, had left the fire just to look at this same fog, though it was by no means a novelty. The house was very quiet. 'Toinette was out, and so was Mollie, and Tod was asleep, lying upon a collection of cushions on the hearth-rug, with two fingers in his mouth, his round baby face turned up luxuriously to catch the warmth.

The wise one was waiting for Mollie, who had gone out a few hours before to execute divers commissions of a domestic nature.

"She might have been back in half the time," murmured the family sage, who sat on the carpet, flattening her small features against the glass. "She might have done what she has to do in *less* than half the time, but I knew how it would be when she went out. She is looking in at the shop windows and wishing for things. I wish she would n't. People stare at her so, and I don't wonder. I am sure I cannot help watching her myself, sometimes. She grows prettier every day of her life, and she is beginning to know that she does, too."

Five minutes after this the small face was drawn away from the window-pane with a sigh of relief.

"There she is now. What a time she has been! Who is with her, I wonder? I cannot see whether it is Phil or Mr. Gowan, it is getting so dark. It must be Mr. Gowan. 'Toinette would be with them if it was Phil."

"Why, Mollie," she exclaimed, when the door opened, "I saw somebody with you, and I thought it was Mr. Gowan. Why did n't he come in? Don't waken Tod."

Mollie came in rather hurriedly, and going to the fire knelt down before it, holding out her hands to warm them. Her cheeks were brilliant with color and her eyes were bright; altogether, she looked a trifle excited.

"It was n't Mr. Gowan," she answered. "Ugh! how cold it is,—not frosty, you know, but that raw sort of cold, Aimée. I would rather have the frost myself, would n't you?"

But Aimée was not thinking of the weather.

"Not Mr. Gowan!" she ejaculated. "Who was it, then?"

Mollie crept nearer to the fire and gave another little shudder.

"It was—somebody else," she returned, with a triumphant little half-laugh. "Guess who!"

"Who!" repeated Aimée. "Somebody else! It was not any one I know."

"It was somebody Phil knows."

The wise one arose and came to the fire herself.

"It was some one taller than Brown!"

"Brown!" echoed Mollie, with an air of supreme contempt. "He is *twice* as tall. Brown is only about five feet high, and he wears an overcoat ten times too big for him, and it flaps—yes, it *flaps* about his odious little heels. I should think it wasn't Brown. It was a gentleman."

The wise one regarded her pretty, scornful face dubiously.

"Brown is n't so bad as all that implies, Mollie," she said. "His coat is the worst part of him. But if it was n't Brown and it was n't Mr. Gowan, who was it?"

Mollie laughed and shrugged her shoulders again, and then looked up at her small inquisitor charmingly defiant.

"It was—Mr. Chandos!" she confessed.

Aimée gazed at her for a moment in blank amazement.

"But," she objected, "you don't know him any more than I do. You have only seen him once through the window, and you have never been introduced to him."

"I have seen him twice," said Mollie. "Don't you recollect my telling you that he picked up my glove for me the night I carried Dolly's dress to Bra-bazon Lodge, and," faltering a little and dropping her eyes, "he introduced himself to me. He met me in town. I was passing through the Arcade, and he stopped to ask about Phil. He apologized, of course, you know, for doing it, but he said he was very anxious to know when Phil would be at home, and—and perhaps I would be so kind as to tell him. He wants to see him about a picture. And—then, you know, somehow or other, he said something else, and—and I answered him—and he walked to the gate with me."

"He took a great liberty," said Aimée. "And it was very imprudent in you to let him come. I don't know what you could be thinking of. The idea of picking up people in the street like that, Mollie; you must be crazy."

"I could n't help it," returned Mollie, not appearing at all disturbed. "He knows Phil and he knows Dolly—a little. And he is very nice. He wants to know us all. And he says Mr. Gowan is one of his best friends. I liked him myself."

"I dare say you did," despairingly. "You are such a child. You would like the man in the moon or a Kaffre chief—"

"That is not true," interposed the delinquent. "I don't know about the man in the moon. He might be well enough—at any rate, he would be travelled and a novelty, but Kaffre chiefs are odious. Don't you remember those we saw last winter?"

"Mollie," said Aimée, "you are only jesting because you are ashamed of yourself. You *know* you were wrong to let that man come home with you."

Then Mollie hung her head and made a lovely rebellious move.

"I don't care," she said; "if it was n't exactly correct, it was nice. But that is always the way," indignantly, "nice things are always improper."

Here was a defection for you. The oracle quite shuddered in her discreet disapproval.

"If you go on in that way," she said, "you will be ending by saying that improper things are always nice."

"Never mind how I end," observed the prisoner at the bar. "You have ended by wakening Tod;" which remark terminated the conversation somewhat abruptly.

A day or so later came Chandos—upon business, so he said, but he remained much longer than his errand rendered necessary, and by some chance or other it came to pass that Phil brought him into the parlor, and introduced him to their small circle, in his usual amiable, informal manner. Then he was to be seen fairly, and prepossessing enough he was. Mollie, sitting in her corner in the blue dress, and looking exquisite and guileless, was very demurely silent at first; but in due time Aimée began to see that she was being gradually drawn out, and at last the drawing out was such a success, subtle as it was, that she became quite a prominent feature in the party, and made so many brilliant speeches without blushing, that the family eyes began to be opened to the fact that she was really a trifle older than she had been a few years ago, after all. The idea had suggested itself to them faintly on one or two occasions of late, and they were just beginning to grasp it, though they were fully as much startled as they would have been if Tod had unexpectedly roused himself from his infantile slumbers, and mildly but firmly announced his intention of studying for the ministry or entering a political contest.

Aimée was dumbfounded. She had not expected this. She was going to have her hands full, it was plain. She scarcely wondered now at her discovery of two evenings before. And then she glanced slyly across the room again, and took it all in once more,—Mollie, bewitching in all the novelty of her small effort at coquetry; Chandos, leading her on, and evidently enjoying the task he had set himself intensely.

It was quite a new Mollie who was left to them after their visitor was gone. There was a touch of triumph and excitement in the pretty flushed face, and a ghost of defiance in the brown eyes. She was not quite sure that young Dame Prudence would not improve the occasion with a short homily.

So she was a trifle restless. First she stood at the window humming an air, then she came to the table and turned over a few sketches, then she knelt down on pretence of teasing Tod.

But impulse was too much for her. She forgot Tod in a few minutes and fell into a sitting position, folding her hands idly on the blue garment.

"I knew he would come," she said, abstractedly. Then Dame Prudence addressed her.

"Did you?" she remarked. "How did you?"

She started and blushed up to her ears.

"How?" she repeated. "Oh, I knew!"

"Perhaps he told you he would," put in Dame P. "Did he?"

"Aimée," was the rather irrelevant reply, rather suddenly made, "do you like him?"

"I never judge people," primly enunciated, "upon first acquaintance. First impressions are rarely to be relied upon."

"That 's a nice speech," in her elder sister's most shockingly flippant manner, "and it sounds well, but I have heard it before—thousands of times. People always say it when they want to be specially disagreeable, and would like to cool you down. There is the least grain of Lady Augusta in you, Aimée."

"And considering that Lady Augusta is the most unpleasant person we know, *that* is a nice speech," returned the oracle.

"Oh, well, I only said 'a grain,' and a grain is not much."

"It is quite enough."

"Well," amiably, "suppose we say half a grain."

"Suppose we say you are talking nonsense."

Mollie's air was Dolly's own as she answered her,—people always said she was like Dolly, despite the fact that Dolly was not a beauty at all.

"There may be something in that," she said.

"Suppose we admit it and return to the subject. Do you think he is nice, Aimée?"

"Do you?"

"Yes, I do," but without getting rose-colored this time.

Aimée looked at her calmly, but with some quiet scrutiny in her glance.

"As nice," she put it to her,—"as nice as Ralph Gowan?"

She grew rose-colored then in an instant up to her ears again and over them, and she turned her face aside and plucked at the hearth-rug with nervous fingers.

"Well?" suggested Aimée.

"He is as handsome and—as tall, and he dresses as well."

"Do you like him as well?" said Aimée.

"Ye-es—no. I have not known him long enough to tell you."

"Well," returned Aimée, "let me tell you. As I said before, I do not think it wise to judge people from first impressions, but this I do know, *I* don't like him as I like Mr. Gowan, and I never shall. He is not to be relied upon, that Gerald Chandos; I saw it in his eyes."

And she set her chin upon her hand, and her small, round, fair face covered itself all at once with an anxious cloud.

She kept a quiet watch upon Mollie after this, and in the weeks that followed she was puzzled, and not only puzzled, but baffled outright many a time. This first visit of Mr. Gerald Chandos was not his last. His business brought him again and again, and when the time came that he had no pretence of business, he was on sufficiently familiar terms with them all to make calls of pleasure. So he did just as Ralph Gowan had done, slipped into his groove of friend and acquaintance unobtrusively, and was made welcome as other people were,—just as any sufficiently harmless individual would have been under the same circumstances. There was no dragon of high renown to create social disturbances in Vagabondia.

"As long as a man behaves himself, where's the odds?" said Phil; and no one ever disagreed with him.

But Mr. Gerald Chandos had not been to the house more than three times before Aimée found cause to wonder. She discovered that Ralph Gowan was not so enthusiastically attached to him, after all; and furthermore she had her reasons for thinking that Gowan was rather disturbed at his advent, and would have preferred that he had not been adopted so complacently.

"If Dolly was at home," she said to herself, "I should be inclined to fancy he was a trifle jealous; and if he cared just a little more for Mollie, I might think he was jealous; but Dolly is away, and though he is fond of Mollie, and thinks her pretty, he does n't care for her in that way exactly, so there must be some other reason. He is not the sort of person to have likes or dislikes without reason."

In her own sage style she approved of Ralph Gowan just as she approved of Griffith. And then, as I have said, Mollie puzzled her. It was astonishing how the child altered, and how she began to bloom out, and adopt independent, womanly airs and graces. She took a new and important position in the household. From her post of observation the wise one found herself looking on with a smile sometimes, there was such a freshness in her style of enacting the *rôle* of beauty. She struck Phil's friends dumb now and then with her conscious power, and the unhappy Brown suffered himself to be led captive without a struggle.

"Her 'prentice han' she tried on Brown," Dolly had said, months before, in a wretched attempt at parody; and certainly the tortures of Brown were prolonged and varied. But it was her manner toward Chandos that puzzled Aimée. Perhaps she was a trifle proud of his evident admiration; at all events, she seemed far from averse to it, and the incomprehensible part of the affair was that sometimes she allowed him to rival even Ralph Gowan.

"And yet," commented Aimée, "she likes Ralph Gowan better. She never can help blushing and looking conscious when he comes or when he talks to her, and she is as cool as Dolly when she finds herself with Chandos. It is very odd."

It was not so easy to manage her as it used to be, Ralph Gowan discovered. She was growing capricious and fanciful, and ready to take offence. If they were left alone together, she would change her mood every two minutes. Sometimes she would submit to his old jesting, gallant speeches quite humbly and shyly for a while, and then she would flame out all at once in anger, half a woman's and half a child's. He was inclined to fancy now and then that she had never forgiven him for his first interference on the subject of Gerald Chandos, for at the early part of the acquaintance he did interfere, as he had promised Dolly he would.

"I am not glad to see that fellow here, Mollie," he had said, the first night he met him at the house.

She stood erect before him, with her white throat straight, and a spark in her eyes.

"What fellow?" she asked.

"Chandos," he answered, coolly and briefly.

"Oh!" she returned. "How is it that when one man dislikes another he always speaks of him as 'that fellow'? I know some one who always refers to you as 'that fellow.'"

"Do you?" dryly, as before. He knew very well whom she meant.

"*I* am glad to see 'that fellow' here," she went on. "He is a gentleman, and he is n't stupid. No one else comes here who is so amusing. I am tired of Brown & Company."

"Ah!" he answered, biting his lip. He felt the rebuff, if it was only Mollie who gave it. "Very well then, if you are tired of Brown & Company, and would prefer to enter into partnership with Chandos, it is none of my business, I suppose. I will give you one warning, however, because I promised your sister to take care of you." Her skin flamed scarlet at that. "That fellow is not a gentleman exactly, and he is a very dangerous acquaintance for any woman to make."

"He is a friend of yours," she interrupted.

"That is a natural mistake on your part," he replied,—"natural, but still a mistake. He is *not* a friend of mine. As I before observed, he is not exactly a gentleman—not to put too fine a point upon it—from a moral point of view. We won't discuss the matter further."

They had parted bad friends that night. Mollie was restive under his cool decisiveness for various reasons; he was irritated because he felt he had failed, and had lost ground instead of gaining it. So sometimes since, he had fancied that she had not wholly forgiven him, and yet there were times when she was so softly submissive that he felt himself in some slight danger of being as much touched and as fairly bewitched as he was when Dolly turned her attention to him. Still she was frequently far from amiable, and upon more than one occasion he found her not precisely as polite as she might have been.

"You are not as amiable, Mollie," he said to her once, "as you used to be. We were very good friends in the old days. I suppose you are outgrowing me. I should be afraid to offer you a bunch of camellias now as a token of my affection."

He smiled down at her indolently as he said it, and before he had finished he began to feel uncomfortable. Her eyelids drooped and her head drooped, and she looked sweetly troubled.

"I know I am not as good as I used to be," she admitted. "I know it without being told. Sometimes," very suddenly, "I think I must be growing awfully wicked."

"Well," he commented, "at least one must admit that is a promising state of mind, and augurs well for future repentance."

She shook her head.

"No, it doesn't," she answered him, "and that is the bad side of it. I am getting worse every day of my life."

"Is it safe," he suggested, cynically,—"is it safe for an innocent individual to cultivate your acquaintance? Would it not be a good plan to isolate yourself from society until you feel that the guileless ones may approach you without fear of contamination? You alarm me."

She lifted up her head, her eyes flashing.

"*You* are safe," she said; "so it is rather premature to cry 'wolf' so soon."

"It is very plain that you are outgrowing me," he returned. "Dolly herself could not have made a more scathing remark."

But, fond as he was of tormenting her, he did not want to try her too far, and so he endeavored to make friends. But his efforts at reconciliation were not a success. She was not to be coaxed into her sweet mood again; indeed she almost led him to fear that he had wounded her irreparably by his jests. And yet, when he at last consulted his watch, and went to the side-table for his hat and gloves, he turned round to find her large eyes following him in a wistful sort of way.

"Are you going?" she asked him at length, a half-reluctant appeal in her voice.

"I am due at Brabazon Lodge now," he answered.

She said no more after that, but relapsed into silence, and let him go without making an effort to detain him, receiving his adieus in her most indifferent style.

But she was cross and low-spirited when he was gone, and Aimée, coming into the room with her work, found her somewhat hard to deal with, and indeed was moved to tell her so.

"You are a most inexplicable girl, Mollie," she said. "What crotchet is troubling you now?"

"No crotchet at all," she answered, and then all at once she got up and stood before the mantel-glass, looking at herself fixedly. "Aimée," she said, "if you were a man, would you admire me?"

Aimée gave her a glance, and then answered her with sharp frankness. "Yes, I should," she said.

She remained standing for a few minutes, taking a survey of herself, front view, side view, and even craning her pretty throat to get a glimpse of her back; and then a pettish sigh burst from her, and she sat down again at her sister's feet, clasping her hands about her knees in a most unorthodox position.

"I should like to have a great deal of money," she said after a while, and she frowned as she said it.

"That is a startling observation," commented Aimée, "and shows great singularity of taste."

Mollie frowned again, and shrugged one shoulder, but otherwise gave the remark small notice.

"I should like," she proceeded, "to have a carriage, and to live in a grand house, and go to places. I should like to marry somebody rich." And having blurted out this last confession, she looked half ashamed of herself.

"Mollie," said Aimée, solemnly dropping her hands and her work upon her lap, "I am beginning to feel as Dolly does; I am beginning to be afraid you are going to get yourself into serious trouble."

Then this overgrown baby of theirs, who had so suddenly astonished them all by dropping her babyhood and asserting herself a woman, said something so startling that the wise one fairly lost her breath.

"If I cannot get what I want," she said, deliberately, "I will take what I can get."

"You are going out of your mind," ejaculated Aimée.

"It does n't matter if I am," cried the romantic little goose, positively crushing the oracle by breaking down all at once, and flinging herself upon the hearthrug in a burst of tears,—"it does n't matter if I am. Who cares for *me*?"

CHAPTER XI.
IN WHICH COMES A WIND WHICH BLOWS NOBODY GOOD.

THEEE weeks waited the wise one, keeping her eyes on the alert and her small brain busy, but preserving an owl-like silence upon the subject revolving in her mind. But at the end of that time she marched into the parlor one day, attired for a walk, and astonished them all by gravely announcing her intention of going to see Dolly.

"What are you going for?" said Mrs. Phil.

"Rather sudden, is n't it?" commented Mollie.

"I 'm going on business," returned Aimée, and she buttoned her gloves and took her departure, without enlightening them further.

Arriving at Brabazon Lodge, she found Miss MacDowlas out and Dolly sitting alone in the parlor, with a letter from Griffith in her hand and tears in her eyes.

Her visitor walked to the hearth, her face wrinkling portentously, and kissed her with an air of affectionate severity.

"I don't know," she began, comprehending matters at a glance, "I am sure I don't know what I am to do with you all. *You* are in trouble now."

"Take off your things," said Dolly, with a helpless little sob, "and—and then I will tell you all about it. You must stay and have tea with me. Miss MacDowlas is away, and I—am all alone, and—and, O Aimée!"

The hat and jacket were laid aside in two minutes, and Aimée came back to her and knelt down.

"Is there anything in your letter you do not want me to see?" she asked.

"No," answered Dolly, in despair, and tossed it into her lap.

It was no new story, but this time the Fates seemed to have conspired against her more maliciously than usual. A few days before Grif had found himself terribly dashed in spirit, and under the influence of impulse had written to her. Two or three times in one day he had heard accidental comments upon Gowan's attentions to her, and on his return to his lodgings at night he had appealed to her in a passionate epistle.

He was not going to doubt her again, he said, and he was struggling to face the matter coolly, but he wanted to see her. It would be worse than useless to call upon her at the Lodge, and have an interview under the disapproving eyes of Miss MacDowlas, and so he had thought they might meet again by appointment, as they had done before by chance. And Dolly had acquiesced at once. But Fortune was against her. Just as she had been ready to leave the house, Ralph Gowan had made his appearance, and Miss MacDowlas had called her down-stairs to entertain him.

"I would not have cared about telling," cried Dolly, in tears, "but I could not tell her, and so I had to stay, and—actually—*sing*—Aimée. Yes, sing detestable love-sick songs, while my own darling, whom I was *dying* to go to, was waiting outside in the cold. And that was not the worst, either. He was just outside in the road, and when the servants lighted the gas he saw me through the window. And I was at the piano"—in a burst—"and Ralph Gowan was standing by me. And so he went home and wrote *that*," signifying with a gesture the letter Aimée held. "And everything is wrong again."

It was very plain that everything *was* wrong again. The epistle in question was an impetuous, impassioned effusion enough. He was furious against Gowan, and bitter against everybody else. She had cheated and slighted and trifled with him when he most needed her love and pity; but he would not blame her, he could only blame himself for being such an insane, presumptuous fool as to fancy that anything he had to offer could be worthy of any woman.

What had he to offer, etc., for half a dozen almost illegible pages, dashed and crossed, and all on fire with his bitterness and pain.

Having taken it from Aimée, and read it for the twentieth time, Dolly fairly wrung her hands over it.

"If we were only just *together!*" she cried. "If we only just had the tiniest, shabbiest house in the world, and could be married and help each other! He does n't mean to be unjust or unkind, you know, Aimée; he would be more wretched than I am if he knew how unhappy he has made me."

"Ah!" sighed Aimée. "He should think of that before he begins."

Then she regained possession of the letter, and smoothed out its creases on her knee, finishing by folding it carefully and returning it to its envelope, looking very grave all the time.

"Will you lend me this?" she said at last, holding the epistle up.

"What are you going to do with it?" asked Dolly, disconsolately.

"I am going to ask Griffith to read it again. I shall be sure to see him to-morrow night."

"Very well," answered Dolly; "but don't be too hard upon him, Aimée. He has a great deal to bear."

"I know that," said Aimée. "And sometimes he bears it very well; but just now he needs a little advice."

Troubled as she was, Dolly laughed at the staid expression on her small, discreet face; but even as she laughed she caught the child in her arms and kissed her.

"What should we do without you!" she exclaimed. "We need some one to keep us all straight, we Vagabonds; but it seems queer that such a small wiseacre as you should be our controlling power."

The mere sight of the small wiseacre had a comforting effect upon her. Her spirits began to rise, and she so far recovered herself as to be able to look matters in the face more cheerfully. There was so much to talk about, and so many questions to ask, that it would have been impossible to remain dejected and uninterested. It was not until after tea, however, that Aimée brought her "business" upon the carpet. She had thought it best not to introduce the subject during the earlier part of the evening; but when the tea-tray was removed, and they found themselves alone again, she settled down, and applied herself at once to the work before her.

"I have not told you yet what I came here for this afternoon," she said.

"You don't mean to intimate that you did not come to see me!" said Dolly.

"I came to see you, of course," decidedly; "but I came to see you for a purpose. I came to talk to you about Mollie."

Dolly almost turned pale.

"Mollie!" she exclaimed. "What is the trouble about Mollie?"

"Something that puzzles me," was the answer. "Dolly, do you know anything about Gerald Chandos?"

"What!" said Dolly. "It is Gerald Chandos, is it? He is not a fit companion for her, I know that much."

And then she repeated, word for word, the conversation she had had with Ralph Gowan.

Having listened to the end, Aimée shook her head.

"I like Mr. Gowan well enough," she said, "but he has been the cause of a great deal of trouble among us, without meaning to be, and I am afraid it is not at an end yet."

They were both silent for a few moments after this, and then Dolly, looking up, spoke with a touch of reluctance.

"I dare say you can answer me a question I should like to ask you?" she said.

"If it is about Mollie, I think I can," Aimée returned.

"You have been with her so long," Dolly went on, two tiny lines showing themselves upon *her* forehead this time, "and you are so quick at seeing things, that you must know what there is to know. And yet it hardly seems fair to ask. Ralph Gowan goes to Bloomsbury Place often, does he not?"

"He goes very often, and he seems to care more for Mollie than for any of the rest of us."

"Aimée," Dolly said next, "does—this is my question—does Mollie care for him?"

"Yes, she does," answered Aimée. "She cares for him so much that she is making herself miserable about him."

"Oh, dear!" cried Dolly. "What—"

Aimée interrupted her.

"And that is not the worst. The fact is, Dolly, I don't know what to make of her. If it was any one but Mollie, or if Mollie was a bit less innocent and impetuous, I should not be so much afraid; but sometimes she is angry with herself, and sometimes she is angry with him, and sometimes she is both, and then I should not be surprised at her doing anything innocent and frantic. Poor child! It is my impression she has about half made up her mind to the desperate resolve of making a grand marriage. She said as much the other night, and I think that is why she encourages Mr. Chandos."

"Oh, dear," cried Dolly, again. "And does she think he wants to marry her?"

"She knows he makes violent love to her, and she is not worldly-wise enough to know that Lord Burleighs are out of date."

"Out of date!" said Dolly; "I doubt if they ever were in date. Men like Mr. Gerald Chandos would hesitate at marrying Venus from Bloomsbury Place."

"If it was Ralph Gowan," suggested Aimée.

"But Ralph Gowan is n't like Chandos," Dolly returned, astutely. "He is worth ten thousand of him. I wish he would fall in love with Mollie and marry her. Poor Mollie! Poor, pretty, headlong little goose! What are we to do with her?"

"Mr. Gowan is very fond of her, in a way," said Aimée. "If he did not care a little for you—"

"I wish he did not!" sighed Dolly. "But it serves me right," with candor. "He would never have thought of me again if I—well, if I had n't found things so dreadfully dull at that Bilberry clan gathering."

"'If,'" moralized Aimée, significantly. "'If' is n't a wise word, and it often gets you into trouble, Dolly. If you hadn't, it would have been better for Grif, as well; but what cannot be cured must be endured."

Their long talk ended, however, in Dolly's great encouragement. It was agreed that the family oracle was to bring Griffith to his senses by means of some slight sisterly reproof, and that she was to take Mollie in hand discreetly at once and persuade her to enter the confessional.

"She has altered a great deal, and has grown much older and more self-willed lately," said Aimée; "but if I am very straightforward and take her by surprise, I scarcely think she will be able to conceal much from me, and, at least, I shall be able to show her that her fancies are romantic and unpractical."

She did not waste any time before applying herself to her work, when she went home. Instead of going to Bloomsbury Place at once, she stopped at Griffith's lodgings on her way, and rather scandalized his landlady by requesting to be shown into his parlor. Only the grave simplicity of the small, slight figure in its gray cloak, and the steadfast seriousness in the pretty face reconciled the worthy matron to the idea of admitting her without investigation. But Aimée bore her scrutiny very calmly. The whole family of them had taken tea in the little sitting-room with Griffith, upon one or two occasions, so she was not at all at a loss, although she did not find herself recognized.

"I am one of Mr. Crewe's sisters," she said; and that, of course, was quite enough. Mrs. Cripps knew Mr. Crewe as well as she knew Grif himself, so she stepped back into the narrow passage at once, and even opened the parlor door, and announced the visitor in a way that made poor Grif s heart beat.

"One of Mr. Crewe's sisters," she said.

He had been sitting glowering over the fire, with his head on his hands and his elbows on his knees, and when he started up he looked quite haggard and dishevelled. Was it—*could* it be Dolly? He knew it could not be, but he turned pale at the thought. It would have been such rapture, in his present frame of mind, to have poured out his misery and distrust, and then to have clasped her to his heart before she had time to explain. He was just in that wretched, passionate, relenting, remorseful stage.

But it was only Aimée, in her gray cloak; and as the door closed behind her, that small person advanced toward him, crumpling her white forehead and looking quite disturbed at the mere sight of him. She held up a reproachful finger at him warningly.

"I knew it would be just this way," she said. "And you are paler and more miserable than ever. If you and Dolly would just be more practical and reason more for each other, instead of falling headlong into quarrels and making everything up headlong every ten minutes, how much better it would be for you! If I was not so fond of you both, you would be the greatest trials I have."

He was so glad to see the thoughtful, womanly little creature, that he could have caught her up in his arms, gray cloak and all, and have kissed her only a tithe less impetuously than he would have kissed Dolly. He was one of the most faithful worshippers at her shrine, and her pretty wisdom and unselfishness had won her many. He drew the easiest chair up to the fire for her, and made her sit down and warm her feet on the fender, while she talked to him, and he listened to her every word, as he always did.

"I have been to see Dolly," she said, "and I found her crying,—all by herself and crying." And she paused to note the effect of her words.

His heart gave a great thump. It always did give a hard thump when he thought of Dolly as she looked when she cried,—a soft, limp little bundle of pathetic prettiness, covering her dear little face in her hands, shedding such piteous, impassioned tears, and refusing to be kissed or comforted. Dolly sobbing on his shoulder was so different from the coquettish, shrewd, mock-worldly Dolly other people saw.

Aimée put her hand into her dress-pocket under the gray cloak and produced her letter,—took it out of its envelope, laid it on her knee, and smoothed out its creases again.

"She was crying over this letter," she proceeded,—"your letter; the one you wrote to her when I think you cannot have been quite calm enough to write anything. I think you cannot have read it over before sending it away. It is always best to read a letter *twice* before posting it. So I have brought it to you to read again, and there it is," giving it to him.

He burst forth with the story of his wrongs, of course, then. He could not keep it in any longer. Things had gone wrong with him in every way before this had happened, he said, and he had longed so for just one hour in which Dolly could comfort him and try to help him to pluck up spirits again, and she had written to him a tender little letter, and promised to give him that hour, and he had been so full of impatience and love, and he had gone to the very gates and waited like a beggar outside, lest he should miss her by any chance, and the end of his waiting had been that he had caught a glimpse of the bright, warm room, and the piano, and Dolly with Gowan bending over her as if she had no other lover in the world. He told it all in a burst, clenching his hand and scarcely stopping for breath; but when he ended he dashed the letter down, pushed his chair round, and dropped his head on his folded arms on the table, with a wild, tearing sob.

"It is no fault of hers," he cried, "and it was only the first sting that made me reproach her. I shall never do it again. She is only in the right, and that fellow is in the right when he tells himself that he can take better care of her and make her happier than I can. I will be a coward no longer,—not an hour longer. I will give her up to-night. She will learn to love him—he is a gentleman at least—if I were in his place I should never fear that she would not learn in time, and forget—and forget the poor, selfish beggar who would have died for her, and yet was not man enough to control the jealous rage that tortured her. I 'll give her up. I'll give it all up—but, oh! my God! Dolly, the—the little house, and—and the dreams I have had about it!"

Aimée was almost in despair. This was not one of his ordinary moods; this was the culminating point,—the culmination of all his old sufferings and pangs. He had been working slowly toward this through all the old unhappiness and self-reproach. The constant droppings of the bygone years had worn away the stone at last, and he could not bear much more. Aimée was frightened now. Her habit of forethought showed her all this in a very few seconds. His nervous, highly strung, impassioned temperament had broken down at last. Another blow would be too much for him. If she could not manage to set him right now and calm him, and if things went wrong again, she was secretly conscious of feeling that the consequences could not be foreseen. There was nothing wild and rash and wretched he might not do.

She got up and went to him, and leaned upon the table, clasping her cool, firm little hand upon his hot, desperate one. A woman of fifty could not have had the power over him that this slight, inexperienced little creature had. Her childish face caught color and life and strength in her determination to do her best for these two whom she loved so well. Her small-boned, fragile figure deceived people into undervaluing her reserve forces; but there was mature feeling and purpose enough in her to have put many a woman three times her age to shame. The light, cool touch of her hand soothed and controlled Griffith from the first, and when she put forth all her powers of reasoning, and set his trouble before him in a more practical and less headlong way, not a word was lost upon him. She pictured Dolly to him just as she had found her holding his letter in her hand, and she pictured her too as she had really been the night he watched her through the window,—not staying because she cared for Gowan, but because circumstances had forced her to remain when she was longing in her own impetuous pretty way to fly to him, and give him the comfort he needed. And she gave Dolly's story in Dolly's own words, with the little sobs between, and the usual plentiful sprinkling of sweet, foolish, loving epithets, and—with innocent artfulness—made her seem so charming and affectionate, a little centre-figure in the picture she drew, that no man with a heart in his breast could have resisted her, and by the time Aimée had finished, Grif was so far moved that it seemed a sheer impossibility to speak again of relinquishing his claims.

But he could not regain his spirits sufficiently to feel able to say very much. He quieted down, but he was still down at heart and crushed in feeling, and could do little else but listen in a hopeless sort of way.

"I will tell you what you shall do," Aimée said at last. "You shall see Dolly yourself,—not on the street, but just as you used to see her when she was at home. She shall come home some afternoon. I know Miss MacDowlas will let her,—and you shall sit in the parlor together, Grif, and make everything straight, and begin afresh."

He could not help being roused somewhat by such a prospect. The cloud was lifted for one instant, even if it fell upon him again the next.

"I shall have to wait a week," he said. "Old Flynn has asked me to go to Dartmouth, to attend to some business for him, and I leave here to-morrow morning."

"Very well!" she answered. "If we must wait a week, we must; but you can write to Dolly in the interval, and settle upon the day, and then she can speak to Miss MacDowlas."

He agreed to the plan at once, and promised to write to Dolly that very night. So the young peacemaker's mind was set at rest upon this subject, at least, and after giving him a trifle more advice, and favoring him with a few more sage axioms, she prepared to take her departure.

"You may put on your hat and take me to the door; but you had better not come in if you are going to finish your letter before the post closes," she said; "but the short walk will do you good, and the night-air will cool you."

She bade him good-night at the gate when they reached Bloomsbury Place, and she entered the house with her thoughts turning to Mollie. Mollie had been out, too, it seemed. When she went up-stairs to their bedroom, she found her there, standing before the dressing-table, still with her hat on, and looking in evident preoccupation at something she held in her hand. Hearing Aimée, she started and turned round, dropping her hand at her side, but not in time to hide a suspicious glitter which caught her sister's eye. Here was a worse state of affairs than ever. She had something to hide, and she had made up her mind to hide it. She stood up as Aimée approached, looking excited and guilty, but still half-defiant, her lovely head tossed back a little and an obstinate curve on her red lips. But the oracle was not to be daunted. She confronted her with quite a stern little air.

"Mollie," she began at once, without the least hesitation,—"Mollie, you have just this minute hidden something from me, and I should n't have thought you could do it."

Mollie put her closed hand behind her.

"*If* I am hiding something," she answered, "I am not hiding it without reason."

"No," returned Dame Prudence, severely, "you are not. You have a very good reason, I am afraid. You are ashamed of yourself, and you know you are doing wrong. You have got a secret, which you are keeping from *me*, Mollie," bridling a little in the prettiest way. "I didn't think you would keep a secret from *me*."

Mollie, very naturally, was overpowered. She looked a trifle ashamed of herself, and the tears came into her eyes. She drew her hand from behind her back, and held it out with a half-pettish, half-timid gesture.

"There!" she said; "if you must see it."

And there, on her pink palm, lay a shining opal ring.

"And," said Aimée, looking at it without offering to touch it, and then looking at her,—"and Mr. Gerald Chandos gave it to you?"

"Yes, Mr. Gerald Chandos did," trying to brave it out, but still appearing the reverse of comfortable. "And you think it proper," proceeded her inquisitor, "to accept such presents from a gentleman who cares nothing for you?"

Care nothing for her! Mollie drew herself upright, with the air of a Zenobia. She had had too few real love affairs not to take arms at once at such an imputation cast upon her prowess.

"He cares enough for me to want me to marry him," she said, and then stopped and looked as if she could have bitten her tongue off for betraying her.

Aimée sat down in the nearest chair and stared at her, as if she doubted the evidence of her senses.

"To do what?" she demanded.

There was no use in trying to conceal the truth any longer. Mollie saw that much; and besides this, her feelings were becoming too strong for her from various causes. The afternoon had been an exciting one to her, too. So, all at once, so suddenly that Aimée was altogether unprepared for the outbreak, she gave way. The ring fell unheeded on to the carpet, slipped from her hand and rolled away, and the next instant she went down upon her knees, hiding her face on her arms on Aimée's lap, and began to cry hysterically.

"It—it is to be quite a secret," she sobbed. "I would not tell anybody but you, and I dare not tell you quite all, but he *has* asked me to marry him, Aimée, and I have—I have said yes." And then she cried more than ever, and caught Aimée's hand, and clung to it with a desperate, childish grasp, as if she was frightened.

It was very evident that she was frightened, too. All the newly assumed womanliness was gone. It was the handsome, inexperienced, ignorant child Mollie she had known all her life who was clinging to her, Aimée felt,—the pretty, simple, thoughtless Mollie they had all admired and laughed at, and teased and been fond of. She seemed to have become a child again all at once, and she was in trouble and desperate, it was plain.

"But the very idea!" exclaimed Aimée, inwardly; "the bare idea of her having the courage to engage herself to him!"

"I never heard such a thing in my life," she said, aloud. "Oh, Mollie! Mollie! what induced you to give him such a mad answer? You don't care for him."

"He—he would not take any other answer, and he is as nice as any one else," shamefacedly. "He is nicer than Brown and the others, and—I do like him— a little," but a tiny shudder crept over her, and she held her listener's hand more tightly.

"As nice as any one else!" echoed Aimée, indignantly. "Nicer than Brown! You ought to be in leading-strings!" with pathetic hopelessness. "That was n't your only reason, Mollie."

The hat with the short crimson feather had been unceremoniously pushed off, and hung by its elastic upon Mollie's neck; the pretty curly hair was all crushed into a heap, and the flushed, tear-wet face was hidden in the folds of Aimée's dress. There was a charming, foolish, fanciful side to Mollie's desperation, as there was to all her moods.

"That was not your only reason," repeated Aimée.

One impetuous, unhappy little sob, and the poor simple child confessed against her will.

"Nobody—nobody else cared for me!" she cried.

"Nobody?" said Aimée; and then, making up her mind to go to the point at once, she said, "Does 'nobody' mean that Ralph Gowan did not, Mollie?"

The clinging hand was snatched away, and the child quite writhed.

"I hate Ralph Gowan!" she cried. "I detest him! I wish—I wish—I *wish* I had never seen him! Why could n't he stay away among his own people? Nobody wanted him. Dolly doesn't care for him, and Grif hates him. Why could n't he stay where he was?"

There was no need to doubt after this, of course. Her love for Ralph Gowan had rendered her restless and despairing, and so she had worked out this innocent romance, intending to defend herself against him. The heroines of her favorite novels married for money when they could not marry for love, and why should not she? Remember, she was only seventeen, and had been brought up in Vagabondia among people who did not often regard consequences. Mr. Gerald Chandos was rich, made violent love to her, and was ready to promise anything, it appeared,—not that she demanded much; the Lord Burleighs of her experience invariably showered jewels and equipages and fine raiment upon their brides without being asked. She would have thought it positive bliss to be tied to Ralph Gowan for six or seven years without any earthly prospect of ever being married; to have belonged to him as Dolly belonged to Grif, to sit in the parlor and listen to him while he made love to her as Grif made love to Dolly, would have been quite enough steady-going rapture for her; but since that was out of the question, Mr. Gerald Chandos and diamonds and a carriage would have to fill up the blank.

But, of course, she did not say this to Aimée. In fact, after her first burst of excitement subsided, Aimée could not gain much from her. She cried a little more, and then seemed vexed with herself, and tried to cool down, and at last so far succeeded that she sat up and pushed her tangled hair from her wet, hot face, and began to search for the ring.

"It has got a diamond in the centre," she said, trying to speak indifferently. "I don't believe you looked at it. The opals are splendid, too."

"Are you going to wear it?" asked Aimée.

She colored up to her forehead. "No, I am not," she answered. "I should have worn it before if I had intended to let people see it. I told you it was a secret. I have had this ring three or four days."

"Why is it a secret?" demanded Dame Prudence. "I don't believe in secrets,—particularly in secret engagements. Is n't Phil to know?"

She turned away to put the ring into its case.

"Not yet," she replied, pettishly. "Time enough when it can't be helped. It is a secret, I tell you, and I don't care about everybody's talking it over."

And she would say no more.

CHAPTER XII.
IN WHICH THERE IS AN EXPLOSION.

"It is my impression," said Dolly, "that something is going to happen."

She was not in the best of spirits. She could not have explained why. Griffith was safe, at least, though he had been detained a week longer than he had anticipated, and consequently their meeting would have to be deferred; but though this had been a disappointment, Dolly was used to such disappointments, and besides the most formidable part of the waiting was over, for it was settled now that he would be home in two days. It was Tuesday now, and on Thursday he was to return, and she was going to Bloomsbury Place in the afternoon, and he was to join the family tea as he had used to do in the old times. But still she did not feel quite easy. She was restless and uncomfortable in spite of herself, and was conscious of being troubled by a vague presentiment of evil.

"It is not like me to be blue," she said to herself; "but I am blue to-day. I wonder what is going on at home."

Then, as was quite natural, her thoughts wandered to Mollie, and she began to ponder upon what Aimée had told her. How were matters progressing, and what was going to be the end of it all? The child's danger was plainer to her than it was to Aimée; and, fond as she was of Mollie, she had determined to improve the occasion of her visit home, by taking the fair delinquent aside and administering a sound lecture to her. She would tell her the truth, at least, and try to open her innocent eyes to the fact that Mr. Gerald Chandos was not a man of the King Cophetua stamp, and that there was neither romance nor poetry in allowing such a man to amuse himself at her expense.

Poor Mollie! It would be a humiliating view to take of a first conquest, but it would be the best thing for her in the end. Dolly sighed over the mere prospect of the task before her. She remembered what her first conquest had been, and how implicitly she had believed in her new power, and how trustingly she had swallowed every sugared nothing, and how she had revelled in the field of possible romance which had seemed spread before her, until she had awakened one fine day to find the first flush of her triumph fading, and her adorer losing his attractions and becoming rather tame. That had been long ago, even before Griffith's time, but she had not forgotten the experience, and she knew it would have been a severe shock to *her* innocent self-love and self-gratulation, if any one had hinted to her that there was a doubt of her captive's honesty. She was roused from her reverie by a message from Miss MacDowlas. It was only a commonplace sort of message. There were some orders to be left at the poulterer's and fruiterer's, and some bills to be paid in town, and, these affairs being her business, Miss MacDowlas had good-naturedly ordered the carriage for her, as she had a long round to make.

Dolly got up and laid her work aside. She was not sorry for the opportunity of going out, so she ran up-stairs with some alacrity to put on her hat, and, having dressed, went to Miss MacDowlas for more particular instructions.

"You are looking rather pale and the drive will do you good," said that lady. "Call at Pullet's and pay his bill, and order the things on his list first. By the way, it was when I drove round to give orders to Pullet the other day, that I saw your pretty sister with Gerald Chandos. She is too pretty, far too pretty, and far too young and inexperienced, to be giving private interviews to such people as Gerald Chandos," sharply.

"Private!" repeated Dolly, with some indignation. "I think that is a mistake. Mr. Gerald Chandos has no need to make his interview private. The doors are open to him at Bloomsbury Place so long as he behaves himself."

"The more is the pity," answered Miss MacDowlas; "but that this was a private interview I am certain. My pretty Miss Innocence came up the street slowly with her handsome baby-face on fire, and two minutes later Gerald Chandos followed her in a wondrous hurry, and joined her and carried her off, looking very guilty and charming, and a trifle reluctant, I must admit."

Dolly's cheeks flushed, and her heart began to beat hotly. If this was the case it was simply disgraceful, and Miss Mollie was allowing herself to be led too far.

"I am sorry to hear this," she said to Miss Mac-Dowlas, "but I am indebted to you for telling me. I will attend to it when I go home on Thursday, and," with a flash of fire, "if it is needful I will attend to Mr. Gerald Chandos himself."

She entered the carriage, feeling hot with anger and distress. She had not expected such a blow, even though she had told herself that she was prepared to hear of any romantic imprudence. And then in the midst of her anger she began to pity Mollie, as it seemed natural to pity her always when she was indiscreet. Who had ever taught her to be discreet, poor child? Had she herself? No, she had not. She had been fond of her and proud of her beauty, but she had laughed at her unsophisticated, thoughtless way with the rest, and somehow they had all looked upon her as they looked upon Tod,—as rather a good joke. Dolly quite hated herself as she remembered how she had related her own little escapades for the edification of the family circle, and how Mollie had enjoyed them more than any one else. She had never overstepped the actual bounds of propriety herself, but she had been coquettish and fond of admiration, and had delighted to hold her own against the world.

"I was n't a good example to her!" she cried, remorsefully. "She ought to have had a good, wise mother. I wish she had. I wish I had one myself."

And she burst into tears, and leaned her head against the cushioned carriage, feeling quite overcome by her self-reproach and consciousness. Their mother had died when Mollie was born, and they had been left to fight their own battles ever since.

She was obliged to control herself, however. It would never do to present herself to Pullet in tears. So she sat up and dried her eyes with her handkerchief, and turned to the carriage window to let the fresh air blow upon her face. But she had not been looking out two minutes when her attention was attracted by something down the street,—a bit of color,—a little tuft of scarlet feathers in a hat, and then her eyes, wandering lower, recognized a well-remembered jacket and a well-remembered dress, and then the next instant she uttered an exclamation in spite of herself.

"It is Mollie!" she cried. "It is Mollie, and here is Gerald Chandos!"

For at the door of a bookseller's she was just nearing stood the gentleman in question, holding a periodical in his hand, and evidently awaiting an arrival.

He caught sight of Mollie almost as soon as she did herself, and the instant he saw her he hurried toward her, and by the time Miss MacDowlas's carriage rolled slowly up to them, in its usual stately fashion, he was holding the small disreputable glove Mollie had just taken out of the convenient jacket pocket, and the fair culprit herself was listening to his eager greeting with the old, bright, uncontrollable blushes, and the old dangerous trick of drooping brown-fringed eyelids, and half-shy, half-wilful air. Dolly instinctively called to her almost aloud. She could not resist the impulse.

"Mollie!" she said. "Mollie!"

But, of course, Mollie did not hear her, and the carriage passed her, and Dolly sank back into her corner catching her breath.

"It was not a mistake," she said; "it was true. It is worse than I thought. Miss MacDowlas was right. It was no accident which brought them both here. He is a cowardly scoundrel and is playing upon her ignorance. If I had believed in him before, I should know that he is not to be trusted now. She is walking on the edge of a precipice, and she thinks she is safe and never dreams of its existence. Oh, Mollie! Mollie! the world means nothing to you yet, and it is we who have to show you all the thorns!"

She finished her errands and drove homeward as quickly as possible. She could think of nothing but Mollie, and by the time she reached Barbrazon Lodge her head ached with the unpleasant excitement. The servant who opened the door met her with a piece of information. Mr. Gowan had called to see her on some special business, and was awaiting her arrival in the drawing-room. He had been there almost an hour.

She did not go to her room at all, but ran up-stairs to the drawing-room quickly, feeling still more anxious. It was just possible that somebody was ill, and Ralph Gowan had come to break the news to her because no one else had been at liberty. With this idea uppermost, she opened the door and advanced toward him, looking pale and troubled.

He met her half-way, and took her outstretched hand, looking troubled himself.

"You are not very well," he said at once. "I am sorry to see that." And his voice told her immediately that he had not come with good news.

She smiled faintly, but when she sat down she put her hand to her forehead.

"Am I pale, then?" she answered. "I suppose I must be. It is nothing but a trifle of headache, and," with a hesitant laugh, "that I half fancied you had come to tell me something unpleasant."

He was silent for a moment,—so silent that she looked up at him with a startled face.

"It *is* something unpleasant!" she exclaimed. "You have come with ill news, and you are afraid to begin."

"Not so bad as that,—not afraid, but rather reluctant," he answered. "It is *not* pleasant news; and but that I felt it would be wisest to warn you at once, I would rather any one else had brought it. I have stumbled upon a disagreeable report."

"Report!" Dolly echoed, and her thoughts flew to Mollie again.

"Don't be alarmed," he said. "It is only a disagreeable one because the subject of it has managed to connect himself with some one whose happiness we value."

Dolly rose from her chair and stood up, turning even paler than before.

"This some one whose happiness we value is Mollie," she said. "And the report you have heard is about Mr. Gerald Chandos. Am I not right?"

"Yes," he returned, "you are right. The hero of the report is Gerald Chandos."

"What has he been doing?" she asked, sharply. "Don't hesitate, please. I want to know."

He was evidently both distressed and perplexed. He took two or three hurried steps across the room, as if to give himself a little extra time to settle his words into the best form. But Dolly could not wait.

"Mr. Gowan," she said, "what has that man been doing?"

He turned round and answered her.

"He has been passing himself off to your brother as an unmarried man," he said.

She slipped back into her chair again, and wrung her hands passionately.

"And he is married?" she demanded. "Oh! how was it you did not know this?"

"Not one in ten of Mr. Gerald Chandos's friends know it," he returned. "And I am only a chance acquaintance. It is not an agreeable story to tell, if what report says is true. Remember, it is only report as yet, and I will not vouch for it. It is said that the marriage was the end of a boyish folly, and that the happy couple separated by mutual consent six months after its consummation. The woman went to California, and Chandos has not seen her since, though he hears of her whereabouts occasionally."

"And you are not quite sure yet that the report is true?" said Dolly.

"Not quite sure," he replied; "but I wish I had greater reason to doubt it."

Recurring mentally to the little scene she had witnessed on the street only an hour or so previously, and remembering Mollie's blushes and drooping eyes, and the look they had won from Mr. Gerald Chandos as he took her half-reluctant hand in his, Dolly bit her lips hard, feeling her blood grow hot within her. She waited just a minute to cool herself, and then spoke.

"Mr. Gowan," she said, "in the first place I ought to thank you."

"Nay," he said, "I promised to help you to care for Mollie."

"I ought to thank you," she repeated. "And I do. But in the second place I am going to ask you to do something for me which may be disagreeable."

"You may be sure," he replied, "that I shall not hesitate."

"Yes," she said, "I think I am sure of that, or I should not ask you. I am so eager about the matter, that I could not bear to waste the time. I want you to help me. On Thursday afternoon I am going home. Can you trace this report to its source before then, and let me know whether it is a true or a false one?"

"I can try."

She clasped both her gloved hands together on the small table before her, and lifted to his such a determined young face and such steadfast eyes, that he was quite impressed. She would rise in arms against the world for poor, unwise Mollie, it was plain. It was not so safe a matter to trifle in Vagabondia, it would seem,—that Gerald Chandos would find to his cost.

"If you bring word to me that what you have heard is a truth," she said, "I can go to Mollie with my weapon in my hand, and I can end all at one blow. However wilful and incredulous she may have been heretofore, she will not attempt to resist me when I tell her that. It is a humiliating thing to think he has insulted her by keeping his secret so far; but we meet with such covert stings now and then in Vagabondia, and perhaps it will prove a blessing in disguise. If we had used our authority to make her dismiss him without having a decided reason to give her, she might only have resented our intervention as being nothing but prejudice. As it is, she will be frightened and angry."

So it was agreed upon that he should take in hand the task of sifting the affair to the bottom. His time was his own, and chance had thrown him among men who would be likely to know the truth. As soon as he had gained the necessary information, Dolly would hear from him, or he would call upon her and give her all particulars.

"You have a whole day before you,—nearly two whole days, I may say, for I shall not be likely to leave here until five or six o'clock on Thursday," Dolly said, when their rather lengthened interview terminated.

"I will make the most of my time," he replied.

Dolly stood at the window and watched him go down the walk to the gates.

"This is the something which was going to happen," she commented. "Having set matters straight with Grif, I suppose it is necessary, for the maintenance of my self-control, that I should have a difficulty about Mollie; but I think I could have retained my equilibrium without it."

The two days passed quietly enough up to Thursday afternoon. Whatever Ralph Gowan had discovered, he was keeping to himself for the present. He had not written, and he had not called. Naturally, Dolly was impatient. She began to be very impatient indeed, as the afternoon waned, and it became dusk. Worse still, her old restlessness came upon her. She could not make up her mind to leave Brabazon Lodge until she had either seen or heard from Gowan, and she was afraid that if she lingered late Griffith would arrive before her, and would be troubled by her non-appearance. Since the night they had met in the street she had not seen him, and she had much to say to him. She had looked forward anxiously to this evening, and the few quiet hours they were to spend together in the dear old disreputable parlor at Bloomsbury Place. They had spent so many blissful evenings in that parlor, that the very thought of it made her heart beat happily. Nobody would be there to interfere with them. The rest of the family would, good-naturedly, vacate and leave them alone, and she would take her old chair by the fire, and Grif would sit near her, and in ten minutes after they had sat so together, they would have left all their troubles behind them, and wandered off into a realm of tender dreams and sweet unrealities. But, impatient as she was to be gone, Dolly could not forget Mollie's interest. It was too near her heart to be forgotten. She must attend to Mollie's affairs first, and then she could fly to Grif and the parlor with an easy conscience. So she waited until five o'clock before dressing to go out, and then, after watching at the window for a while, she decided to go to her room and put on her hat and make all her small preparations, so that when her visitor arrived she might be ready to leave the house as soon as he did.

"It won't do to keep Grif waiting too long, even for Mollie's sake," she said. "I must consider him, too. If Mr. Gowan does not come by six or half-past, I shall be obliged to go."

She purposely prolonged her toilet, even though it had occupied a greater length of time than usual in the first instance. There had been a new acquisition in the shape of a dress to don, and one or two coquettish aids to appearance, which were also novelties. But before six o'clock she was quite ready, and, having nothing else to do, was reduced to the necessity of standing before the glass and taking stock of herself and her attire.

"It fits," she soliloquized, curving her neck in her anxiety to obtain a back view of herself. "It fits like a glove, and so Grif will be sure to like it. His admiration for clothes that fit amounts to a monomania. He will make his usual ecstatic remarks on the subject of figure, too. And I must confess," with modest self-satisfaction,—"I must confess that those frills are not unbecoming. If we were only rich—and married—how I would dress, to please him! Being possessed of a figure, one's results are never uncertain. Figure is a weakness of mine, also. With the avoirdupois of Miss Jolliboy, life would appear a desert. Ten thousand per annum would not console me. And yet she wears sables and seal-skin, and is happy. It is a singular fact, worthy of the notice of the philosopher, that it is such women who invariably possess the sable and seal-skin. Ah, well!" charitably, "I suppose it is a dispensation of Providence. When they attain that size they need some compensation."

Often in after time she remembered the complacent little touch of vanity, and wondered how it had been possible that she could stand there, making so thoughtless and foolish a speech when danger was so near, and so much of sharp, passionate suffering was approaching her.

She had waited until the last minute, and finding, on consulting her watch, that it was past six, she decided to wait no longer. She took up her gloves from the dressing-table and drew them on; she settled the little drooping plume in her hat and picked up her muff, and then, giving a last glance and a saucy nod to the piquant reflection in the glass, she opened her bedroom door to go out.

And then it was, just at this last moment, that there came a ring at the hall-door bell,—evidently a hurried ring, and withal a ring which made her heart beat, she knew not why.

She stood at the head of the staircase and listened. A moment later, and the visitor was speaking to the servant who had admitted him.

"Mr. Gowan," she heard. "Miss Crewe—wish to see her at once—at once."

She knew by his voice that something was wrong, and she did not wait for the up-coming of the servant. She almost flew down the staircase, and entered the parlor an instant after him; and when he saw her he met her with an exclamation of thankfulness.

"Thank God!" he said, "that you are ready!" He was pale with excitement, and fairly out of breath. He did not give her time to answer him. "You must come with me," he said. "There is not a moment to lose. I have a cab at the door. I have driven here at full speed. The report is true, and I have found out that to-night Chandos leaves London. But that is not the worst,—for God's sake, be calm, and remember how much depends upon your courage,—he intends taking your sister with him."

Terrible as the shock was to her, she was calm, and did remember how much might depend upon her. She forgot Grif and the happy evening she had promised herself; she forgot all the world but Mollie,—handsome, lovable, innocent Mollie, who was rushing headlong and unconsciously to misery and ruin. A great, sharp change seemed to come upon her as she turned to Ralph Gowan. She was not the same girl who, a minute or so before, had nodded at her pretty self in the glass; the excited blood tingled in her veins; she was full of desperate, eager bravery,—she could not wait a breath's space.

"Come!" she exclaimed, "I am ready. You can tell me the rest when we are in the cab."

She did not even know where they were going until she heard Gowan give the driver the directions. But, as they drove through the streets, she learned all.

In spite of his efforts, it was not until the eleventh hour that he had succeeded in obtaining positive proof of the truth of the report, though he had found less cause to doubt it each time he made fresh inquiries. In the end he had been driven to the necessity of appealing to a man who had been Chandos's confidential valet, and who, rascal though he was, still was able to produce proofs to be relied on. Then he had been roused to such indignation that he had driven to the fellow's lodgings with the intention of confronting him with his impudent guilt, and there he had made the fearful discovery that he had just left the place with "a pretty, childish-looking girl,—tall, and with a lovely color," as the landlady described her; and he had known it was Mollie at once.

The good woman had given him all particulars. They had come to the house together in a cab, and the young lady had not got out, but had remained seated in it while her companion had given his orders to his servant indoors. She—his housekeeper—had heard him say something about Brussels, and, having caught a glimpse of the charming face in the vehicle outside, she had watched it from behind the blinds, suspecting something out of the common order of things.

"Not that he did not treat her polite and respectful enough," she added; "for he did and she—pretty young thing—seemed quite to expect it, and not to be at all ashamed of herself, though she were a trifle shy and timid. I even heard him ask her if she would rather he rode outside, and she said she 'thought so, if he pleased,' And he bowed to her and went, quite obedient. That was what puzzled me so; if he 'd ha' been freer, I could have understood it."

"It does not puzzle me!" cried Dolly, clenching her hands and fairly panting for breath when she heard it. "He knows how innocent she is, and he is too crafty to alarm her by his manner. Oh, cannot we make this man drive faster?—cannot we make him drive faster?"

Gowan drew out his watch and referred to it.

"There is no danger of our losing their train," he said. "It does not leave the station until nearly seven, and it is not yet half-past six. If they leave London to-night, we shall meet them; if they do not, I think I can guess where we shall find them. Remember, you must not allow yourself to become excited. We have only our coolness and readiness of action to rely upon. If we lose our presence of mind, we lose all."

He did not lose his presence of mind, at least.

Even in the midst of her distress, Dolly found time to feel grateful to him beyond measure, and to admire his forethought. He never seemed to hesitate for a moment. He had evidently decided upon his course beforehand, and there was no delay. Reaching the station, he assisted Dolly to descend from the cab and led her at once to a seat where she could command a view of all who made their appearance upon the platform. Then he left her and went to make inquiries from the officials. He was not absent long. In a few minutes he returned with the necessary information. The train was not due for twenty minutes, and as yet no lady and gentleman answering to his description had been seen by any one in the place.

He came to Dolly and took a seat by her, looking down at her upturned, appealing face pityingly, but reassuringly.

"We are safe yet," he said. "They have not arrived, and they can have taken passage in no other train. We will watch this train leave the station, and then we will drive at full speed to the hotel Chandos is in the habit of visiting when he makes a flying journey. I know the place well enough."

The next half-hour was an anxious one to both. The train was behind time, and consequently they were compelled to wait longer than they had expected. A great many people crowded into the station and took tickets for various points,—workingmen and their wives, old women with bundles, and young ones without, comfortable people who travelled first-class and seemed satisfied with themselves, shabbily attired little dressmakers and milliners with bandboxes, a party of tourists, and a few nice girls; in fact, the usual samples of people hurrying or taking it easy, losing their temper or preserving it; but there was no Mollie. The last moment arrived, the guards closed the carriage doors with the customary bang, and the customary cry of "All right;" there were a few puffs and a whistle, and then the train moved slowly out of the station. Mollie was not on her way to Brussels yet; that was a fact to be depended upon.

Dolly rose from her seat with a sigh which was half relief.

"Now for trying the hotel," said Gowan. "Take my arm and summon up your spirits. In less than a quarter of an hour, I think I may say, we shall have found our runaway, and we shall have to do our best to reduce her romantic escapade to a commonplace level. We may even carry her back to Bloomsbury Place before they have had time to become anxious about her. Thank Heaven, we were so fortunate as to discover all before it was too late!"

Bloomsbury Place! A sudden pang shot through Dolly's heart. She recollected then for the first time that at Bloomsbury Place Griffith was waiting for her, and that it might be a couple of hours before she could see him and explain. She got into the cab and leaned back in one corner, with the anxious tears forcing themselves into her eyes. It seemed as if fate itself was against her.

"What will he think?" she exclaimed, unconsciously. "Oh, what will he think?" Then, seeing that Gowan had heard her, she looked at him piteously.

"I did not mean to speak aloud," she said. "I had forgotten in my trouble that Grif will be waiting for me all this time. He has gone to the house to meet me, and—I am not there."

Perhaps he felt a slight pang, too. For some time he had been slowly awakening, to the fact that this otherwise unfortunate Grif was all in all to her, and shut out the rest of the world completely. He had no chance against him, and no other man would have any. Still, even in the face of this knowledge, the evident keenness of her disappointment cut him a little.

"You must not let that trouble you," he said, generously. "Donne will easily understand your absence when you tell him where you have been. In the meantime, I have a few suggestions to make before we reach the hotel."

It was Mollie he was thinking of. He was wondrously tender of her in his man's pity for her childish folly and simplicity. If possible, they must keep her secret to themselves. If she had left no explanation behind her, she must have given some reason for leaving the house, and if they found her at the hotel it would not be a difficult matter to carry her back home without exciting suspicion, and thus she would be saved the embarrassment and comment her position would otherwise call down upon her. Griffith might be told in confidence, but the rest of them might be left to imagine that nothing remarkable had occurred. These were his suggestions.

Dolly agreed to adopt them at once, it is hardly necessary to say. The idea that it would be possible to adopt them made the case look less formidable. She had been terribly troubled at first by the thought of the excitement the explanation of the escapade would cause at Bloomsbury Place. Phil would have been simply furious,—not so much against Mollie as against Chandos. His good-natured indifference to circumstances would not have been proof against the base betrayal of confidence involved in the affair. And then even in the after-time, when the worst was over and forgotten, the innumerable jokes and thoughtless sarcasms she would have had to encounter would have been Mollie's severest punishment. When the remembrance of her past danger had faded out of the family mind, and the whimsical side of the matter presented itself, they would have teased her, and Dolly felt that such a course would be far from safe. So she caught at Ralph Gowan's plan eagerly.

Still she felt an excited thrill when the cab drew up before the door of the hotel. Suppose they should not find her? Suppose Chandos had taken precautions against their being followed?

But Gowan did not seem to share her misgivings, though the expression upon his face was a decidedly disturbed one as he descended from the vehicle.

"You must remain seated until I come back," he said. "I shall not be many minutes, I am sure. I am convinced they are here." And then he closed the cab door and left her.

She drew out her watch and sat looking at it to steady herself. Her mind was not very clear as to how she intended to confront Mr. Gerald Chandos and convince Mollie. The convincing of Mollie would not be difficult, she was almost sure, but the confronting of Gerald Chandos was not a pleasant thing to think of.

She was just turning over in her mind a stirring, scathing speech, when the cab door opened again, and Gowan stood before her. He had not been absent five minutes.

"It is as I said it would be," he said. "They are here,—at least Mollie is here. Chandos has gone out, and she is alone in the private parlor he has engaged for her. They have evidently missed their train. They intended to leave by the first in the morning. I have managed to give the impression that we are expected, and so we shall be shown on to the scene at once without any trouble."

And so they were. A waiter met them at the entrance and led them up-stairs without the slightest hesitation.

"It is not necessary to announce us," said Gowan. And the man threw open the door of No. 2 with a bow.

They crossed the threshold together without speaking, and when the door closed behind them they turned and looked at each other with a simultaneous but half-smothered exclamation.

It was a pretty room, bright with a delicate gay-hued carpet and thick white rugs, numerous mirrors and upholstering of silver-gray and blue. There was a clear-burning fire in the highly polished steel-grate, and one of the blue and silver-gray sofas had been drawn up to it, and there, upon this sofa, lay Mollie with her hand under her cheek, sleeping like a baby.

They were both touched to the heart by the mere sight of her. There was something in the perfect repose of her posture and expression that was childish and restful. It was a difficult matter to realize that she was sleeping on the brink of ruin and desolation. Something bright gathered on Dolly's lashes and slipped down her cheek as she looked at her.

"Thank God, we have found her!" she said. "Just to think that she should be sleeping like that,—as if she was at home. If she was two years old she might wear just such a look."

Gowan hardly liked to stand by as she went toward the sofa. The girl's face, under the coquettish hat, seemed to grow womanly, her whole figure seemed to soften as she knelt down upon the carpet by the couch and laid her hand upon Mollie's shoulder, speaking to her gently.

"Mollie," she said, "dear, waken."

Just that, and Mollie started up with a faint cry, dazzled by the light, and rubbing her eyes and her soft, flushed cheeks, just as she had done the night Gowan surprised her asleep in the parlor.

"Dolly," she cried out, when she saw who was with her,—"Dolly," in a half-frightened voice, "why did you come here?"

"I came to take you home," answered Dolly, tremulously, but firmly. "Thank God! I am not too late! Oh, Mollie, Mollie, how could you?"

Mollie sat up among her blue and gray cushions and stared at her for a moment, as if she was not wide enough awake to realize what she meant. But the next instant she caught sight of Ralph Gowan, and that roused her fully, and she flushed scarlet.

"I don't know what you mean," she said. "I don't know what you mean by coming here in this way. And I don't know what Mr. Gowan means by bringing you,—for I feel sure he has brought you. I am not a baby, to be followed as if I could not take care of myself. I am going to be married to Mr. Gerald Chandos to-morrow, and we are going on the Continent for our wedding tour."

She was in a high state of rebellion. It was Gowan's presence she was resenting, not Dolly's. To tell the truth, she was rather glad to see Dolly. She had begun to feel the loneliness of her position, and it had half intimidated her. But the sight of Gowan roused her spirit. What right had he to come and interfere with her, since he did not care for her and thought she was nothing but a child? It made her feel like a child. She turned her back to him openly as she spoke to Dolly.

"I am going to be married in the morning," she repeated; "and we are going to Brussels."

Then, in her indignation against Mr. Gerald Chandos, Dolly fired a little herself.

"And has it never occurred to you," she said, "that it is rather a humiliating thing this running away, as if you knew you were doing something disgraceful? May I ask what reason Mr. Gerald Chandos gives for asking you to submit to such an insult, for it is an insult?"

"He has very good reasons," answered Mollie, beginning to falter all at once, as the matter was presented to her in this new and trying light. "He has very good reasons,—something about business and—and his family, and he does not intend to insult me. He is very fond of me and very proud of me, and he is going to try to make me very happy. He—he has bought me a beautiful trousseau—" And then, seeing the two exchange indignant yet pitying glances, she broke off suddenly and burst forth as if she was trying to hide in anger the subtle, mysterious fear which was beginning to creep upon her. "How dare you look at each other so!" she cried. "How dare you look at me so! I have done nothing wrong. He says many other people do the same thing and—and I won't be looked at so. I shall not tell you another word. You—you look as if I was going to do something wicked and dreadful." And she flung herself face downward upon the sofa cushions and broke into a passionate, excited sob.

Then Dolly could control herself no longer. She flashed out into a storm of wrath and scorn against this cool, systematic scoundrel, who would have wrought such harm against such simple ignorance of the world. What had they not saved her from, poor, foolish child? She clenched her little, gloved hand and struck it against the sofa arm, the hot color flaming up on her cheeks and the fire lighting in her eyes.

"Mollie!" she exclaimed, "that is what is true! You are going to do something that is dreadful to think of, though you do not think so because you do not know the truth. And we have come to tell you the truth and save you. That man is a villain,—he is the worst of villains. He does not intend to marry you,—he cannot marry you, and, knowing he cannot, he has been laying traps for months to drag you down into a horrible pit of shame. Yes, of the bitterest grief and shame,—poor, simple child as you are,—for I must tell you the whole dreadful truth, though I would far rather hide it from you, if I could. There are some wicked, wicked men in the world, Mollie, and Gerald Chandos is one of the worst, for he has got a wife already."

It did not seem to be Mollie who sprang up from her cushions and confronted them with wide-opened eyes. Every bit of color had died out of her cheeks and lips, and she turned from one to the other with a wild, appealing look.

"It is n't true," she insisted, desperately; but her voice was broken, and she sobbed out her words in her fright. "It is n't true! It is n't true! You want to frighten me." And all at once she ran to Ralph Gowan like a child, and caught hold of his arm with her pretty, shaking hands. "Mr. Gowan," she said, "you know, don't you? and you won't—you won't—Oh, where is Aimée? I want

Aimée! Aimée is n't like the rest of you! *She* would have made me go home without being so cruel as this." And the next minute she turned so white and staggered so, that Dolly ran to her, and Gowan was obliged to take her in his arms.

"Tell her that what I have said is true," said Dolly, crying. "She will begin to understand then."

And so, while he held her, panting and sobbing and clinging to him, Gowan told her all that he had learned. He was as brief as possible and as tender as a woman. His heart so warmed toward the pretty, lovable, passionately frightened creature, that his voice was far from steady as he told his story.

She did not rebel an instant longer, then. Her terror, under the shock, rendered her only helpless and hysterical. She had so far lost control over herself that she would have believed anything they had chosen to tell her.

"Take me away," she cried, whitening and shivering, all her bright, pretty color gone, all her wilful petulance struck down at a blow. "Take me home,— take me home to Aimée. I want to go away from here before he comes. I want to go home and die."

How they got her down-stairs and into the carriage, Dolly scarcely knows. It was enough that they got her there and knew she was safe. Upon the table in the room above they had left a note directed to Mr. Gerald Chandos,— Dolly had directed it and Dolly had written it.

"Is there pen and ink here?" she had asked Gowan; and when he had produced the articles, she had bent over the table and dashed a few lines off with an unsteady yet determined hand.

"There!" she had said, when she closed the envelope. "Mr. Chandos will go to Brussels, I think, and he will understand why he goes alone, and, for my part, I incline to the belief that he will not trouble us again."

And in five minutes more they were driving toward Bloomsbury Place.

But now the first excitement was over, Dolly's nerve began to fail her. Now that Mollie was safe, she began to think of Griffith. It seemed a cruel trick of fortune's to try his patience so sharply just at this very point. She knew so well what effect his hours of waiting would have upon him. But it was useless to rebel now; so she must bear it as well as she could, and trust to the result of her explanation. Yet despite her hope, every minute of the long drive seemed an age, and she grew feverish and restless and wretched. What if he had not waited, and was not there to listen to what she had to say? Then there would be all the old trouble to face again,—perhaps something worse.

"It is nine o'clock," she said, desperately, as they passed a lighted church tower. "It is nine o'clock." And she leaned back in her corner again, with her heart beating strongly. Her disappointment was so keen that she could have burst into a passion of tears. Her happy evening was gone, and her dream of simple pleasure had fled with its sacrificed hours. She could not help remembering this, and being quite conquered by the thought, even though Mollie was safe.

They had settled what to do beforehand. At the corner of the street Gowan was to leave them, and the two girls were to go in together, Mollie making her way at once to her room upon pretext of headache. A night's rest would restore her self-control, and by the next morning she would be calm enough to face the rest, and so her wild escapade would end without risk of comment if she was sufficiently discreet to keep her own counsel. At present she was too thoroughly upset and frightened even to feel humiliation.

"Nearly half-past nine," said Gowan, as he assisted them to descend to the pavement at their journey's end.

The light from an adjacent lamp showed him that the face under Dolly's hat was very pale and excited, and her eyes were shining and large with repressed tears as she gave him her hand.

"I cannot find words to thank you just yet," she said, low and hurriedly. "I wish I could; but—you know what you have helped me to save Mollie from to-night, and so you know what my gratitude must be. The next time I see you, perhaps, I shall be able to say what I wish, but now I can only say goodnight, and—oh, God bless you!" And the little hand fairly wrung his.

Mollie shook hands with him, trembling and almost reluctantly. She was pale, too, and her head drooped as if it would nevermore regain the old trick of wilful, regal carriage.

"You have been very kind to take so much trouble," she said. "You were kinder than I deserved,—both of you."

"Now," said Dolly, when he sprang into the cab, and they turned away together,—"now for getting into the house as quietly as possible. No," trying to speak cheerily, and as if their position was no great matter, "you must n't tremble, Mollie, and you mustn't cry. It is all over now, and everything is as commonplace and easy to manage as can be. You have been out, and have got the headache, and are going to bed. That is all. All the rest we must forget. Nothing but a headache, Mollie, and a headache is not much, so we won't fret about it. If it had been a heartache, and sin and shame and sorrow—but it isn't. But, Mollie," they had already reached the house then, and stood upon the steps, and she turned to the girl and put a hand on each of her shoulders, speaking tremulously, "when you go up-stairs, kneel down by your bedside and say your prayers, and thank God that it is n't,—thank God that it is n't, with all your heart and soul." And she kissed her cheek softly just as they heard Aimée coming down the hall to open the door.

"Dolly!" she exclaimed when she saw them, "where have you been? Griffith has been here since five, and now he is out looking for you. I had given you up entirely, but he would not. He fancied you had been delayed by something."

"I have been delayed by something," said Dolly, her heart failing her again. "And here is Mollie, with the headache. You had better go to bed, Mollie. How long is it since Grif left the house?"

"Scarcely ten minutes," was the answer. "It is a wonder you did not meet him. Oh, Dolly!" ominously, "how unlucky you are!"

Dolly quite choked in her effort to be decently composed in manner.

"I *am* unlucky," she said; and without saying more, she made her way into the parlor.

She took her hat off there and tossed it on the sofa, utterly regardless of consequences, and then dropped into her chair and looked round the room. It did not look as she had pictured it earlier in the day. Its cheerfulness was gone, and it looked simply desolate. The fire had sunk low in the grate, and the hearth was strewn with dead ashes;—somehow or other, everything seemed chilled and comfortless. She was too late for the brightness and warmth,—a few hours before it had been bright and warm, and Grif had been there waiting for her. Where was he now? She dropped her face on the arm of her chair with a sob of disappointed feeling and foreboding. What if he had seen them leave Ralph Gowan, and had gone home!

"It's too bad!" she cried. "It is cruel! I can't bear it! Oh, Grif, *do* come!" And her tears fell thick and fast.

Ten minutes later she started up with a little cry of joy and relief. That was his footstep upon the pavement, and before he had time to ring she was at the door. She could scarcely speak to him in her excitement.

"Oh, Grif!" she said; "Grif—darling!"

But he did not offer to touch her, and strode past her outstretched hands.

"Come into this room with me," he said, hoarsely; and the simple sound of his voice struck her to the heart like a blow.

She followed him, trembling, and when they stood in the light, and she saw his deathly, passion-wrung face, her hand crept up to her side and pressed against it.

He had a package in his hand,—a package of letters,—and he laid them down on the table.

"I have been home for these," he said. "Your letters,—I have brought them back to you."

"Grif!" she cried out.

He waved her back.

"No," he said, "never mind that. It is too late for that now, that is all over. Good God! all over!" and he panted for breath. "I have been in this room waiting for you," he struggled on, "since five o'clock. I came with my heart full to the brim. I have dreamt about what this evening was to be to us every night for a week. I was ready to kneel and kiss your feet. I waited hour after hour. I was ready to pray—yes, to *pray*, like a fool—that I might hold you in my arms before the night ended. Not half an hour ago I went out to see if you were coming. And you were coming. At the corner of the street you were bidding good-night to—to Ralph Gowan—"

"Listen!" she burst forth. "Mollie was with me—

"Ralph Gowan was with you," he answered her; "it does not matter who else was there. You had spent those hours in which I wanted you with him. That was enough,—nothing can alter that." And then all at once he came and stood near her, and looked down at her with such anguish in his eyes that she could have shrieked aloud. "It was a poor trick to play, Dolly," he said; "so poor a one, that it was scarcely like you. Your coquetries had always a fairer look. The commonest jilt might have done such a thing as that, and almost have done it better. It is an old trick, too, this playing the poor fool against the rich one. The only merit of your play has been that you have kept it up so long."

He was almost mad, but he might have seen that he was trying her too far, and that she would break down all at once. The long strain of the whole evening; his strange, unnatural mood; her struggle against wretchedness—all were too much for her to bear. She tried to speak, and, failing, fought for strength, sobbed thrice, a terrible, hysterical sob, like a child's, and then turned white and shivered, without uttering a word.

"Yes," he said, "a long time, Dolly"—but his sentence was never ended, for that instant she went down as if she had been shot, and lay near his feet quivering for a second, and then lying still.

He was not stayed even then. He bent down and lifted her in his arms and carried her to the sofa, pale himself, but not relenting. He seemed to have lived past the time when the pretty, helpless figure, in all its simple finery, would have stirred him to such ecstasy of pain. He was mad enough to have believed even her helplessness a lie, only that the cruel, ivory pallor was so real. He did not even stoop to kiss her when he turned away. But all the treasure of faith and truth and love had died out of his face, the veriest dullard could have seen; his very youth had dropped away from him, and he left the old, innocent dreams behind, with something like self-scorn.

"Good-by," he said; "we have lost a great deal, Dolly—or I have lost it, I might say. And even you—I believe it pleased even you until better fortune came; so, perhaps, you have lost something, too."

Then he went to the bell and touched it, and, having done so, strode out into the narrow hall, opened the front door and was gone; and when, a few minutes later, Aimée came running down to answer the strange summons, she found only the silent room, Dolly's white, piteous face upon the sofa-cushion, and the great package of those old, sweet, foolish letters upon the table.

CHAPTER XIII
A DEAD LETTER.

IT was all over,—all over at last. Dolly's first words had said this much when she opened her eyes, and found Aimée bending over her.

"Has he gone?" she had asked. "Did he go away and leave me?"

"Do you mean Grif?" said Aimée.

She made a weak gesture of assent.

"Yes," Aimée answered. "He must have gone. I heard the bell ring, and found you lying here when I came to see what it meant."

"Then," said Dolly, "all is over,—all is over at last." And she turned her face upon the cushion and lay so still that she scarcely seemed to breathe.

"Take another drink of water, Dolly," said Aimée, keeping back her questions with her usual discretion. "You must, dear."

But Dolly did not stir.

"I don't want any more," she said. "I am not going to faint again. You have no need to be afraid. I don't easily faint, you know, and I should not have fainted just now only—that the day has been a very hard one for me, and somehow I lost strength all at once. I am not ill,—only worn out."

"You must be very much worn out, then," said Aimée; "more worn out than I ever saw you before. You had better let me help you up-stairs to bed."

"I don't want to go to bed yet!" in a strange, choked voice, and the next moment Aimée saw her hands clench themselves and her whole frame begin to shake. "Shut the door and lock it," she said, wildly. "I can't stop myself. Give me some sal volatile. I can't breathe." And such a fit of suffocating sobbing came upon her that she writhed and battled for air.

Aimée flung herself upon her knees by her side, shedding tears herself.

"Oh, Dolly," she pleaded, "Dolly, darling, don't. Try to help yourself against it. I know what the trouble is. He went away angry and disappointed, and it has frightened you. Oh, please don't, darling. He will come back to-morrow; he will, indeed. He always does, you know, and he will be so sorry."

"He has gone forever," Dolly panted, when she could speak. "He will never come back. To-night has been different from any other time. No," gasping and sobbing, "it is fate. Fate is against us,—it always was against us. I think God is against us; and oh, how can He be? He might pity us,—we tried so hard and loved each other so much. We did n't ask for anything but each other,—we did n't want anything but that we might be allowed to cling together all our lives and work and help each other. Oh, Grif, my darling,—oh, Grif, my dear, my dear!" And the sobs rising again and conquering her were such an agony that Aimée caught her in her arms.

"Dolly," she said, "you must not, you must not, indeed. You will die, you can't bear it."

"No," she wailed, "I can't bear it,—that is what it is. I can't bear it. It is too hard to bear. But there is no one to help me,—God won't. He does not care for us, or He would have given us just one little crumb out of all He has to give. What can a poor helpless girl be to Him? He is too high and great to care for our poor little powerless griefs. Oh, how wicked I am!" in a fresh burst. "See how I rebel at the first real blow. It is because I am so wicked, perhaps, that all has been taken from me,—all I had in the world. It is because I loved Grif best. I have read in books that it was always so. Oh, why is it? I can't understand it. It seems cruel,—yes, it does seem cruel,—as cruel as death, to give him to me only that I might suffer when he was taken away. Oh, Grif, my darling! Grif, my love, my dear!"

This over again and again, with wild, heart-broken weeping, until she was so worn out that she could cry no more, and lay upon Aimée's arm upon the cushion, white and exhausted, with heavy purple rings about her wearied, sunken eyes. It was not until then that Aimée heard the whole truth. She had only been able to guess at it before, and now, hearing the particulars, she could not help fearing the worst.

It was just as she had feared it would be; another blow had come upon him at the very time when he was least able to bear it, and it had been too much for him. But she could not reveal her forebodings to Dolly. She must comfort her and persuade her to hope for the best.

"You must go to bed, Dolly," she said, "and try to sleep, and in the morning everything will look different. He may come, you know,—it would be just like him to come before breakfast. But if he does not come—suppose," hesitatingly,—"suppose I was to write to him, or—suppose you were to?"

She was half afraid that pride would rise against this plan, but she was mistaken. Seven years of love had mastered pride. Somehow or other, pride had never seemed to come between them in their little quarrels, each had always been too passionately eager to concede, and too sure of being met with tenderest penitence. Dolly had always known too confidently that her first relenting word would touch Grifs heart, and Grif had always been sure that his first half-softened reproach would bring the girl to his arms in an impetuous burst of loving repentance. No, it was scarcely likely that other people's scruples would keep them apart. So Dolly caught at the proposal almost eagerly.

"Yes," she said, "I will write and tell him how it was. It was not his fault, was it, Aimée? How could I have borne such a thing myself? It would have driven me wild, as it did him. It was not unreasonable at all that he should refuse to listen, in his first excitement, after he had waited all those hours and suffered such a disappointment. And then to see what he did. My poor boy! he was not to blame at all. Yes, yes," feverishly, "I will write to him and tell him. Suppose I write now—don't you think I had better do it now, and then he will get the letter in the morning, and he will be sure to come before dinner,—he will be sure to come, won't he?"

"He always did," said Aimée.

"Always," said Dolly. "Indeed, I never had to write to him before to bring him. He always came without being written to. There never was any one like him for being tender and penitent. You always said so, Aimée. And just think how often I have tried his patience! I sometimes wish I could help doing things,—flirting, you know, and making a joke of it. He never flirted in his life, poor darling, and what right had I to do it? When he comes to-morrow I will tell him how sorry I am for everything, and I will promise to be better. I have not been half so good as he has. I wish I had. I should not have hurt him so often if I had."

"You have been a little thoughtless sometimes," said Aimée. "Perhaps it *would* have been better if you could have helped it."

"A little thoughtless," said Dolly, restlessly. "I have been wickedly thoughtless sometimes. And I have made so many resolutions and broken them all. And I ought to have been doubly thoughtful, because he had so much to bear. If he had been prosperous and happy it would not have mattered half so much. But it was all my vanity. You don't know how vain I am, Aimée. I quite hate myself when I think of it. It is the wanting people to admire me,—everybody, men and women, and even children,—particularly among Lady Augusta's set, where there is a sort of fun in it. And then I flirt before I know; and then, of course, Grif cannot help seeing it. I wonder that he has borne with me so long."

She was quite feverish in her anxiety to condemn herself and exculpate her lover. She did not droop her face against the pillow, but roused herself, turning toward Aimée, and talking fast and eagerly. A bright spot of color came out on either cheek, though for the rest she was pale enough. But to Aimée's far-seeing eyes there was something so forced and unnaturally strung in her sudden change of mood that she felt a touch of dread Suppose something should crush her newly formed hopes,—something terrible and unforeseen! She felt a chill strike her to the heart at the mere thought of such a possibility. She knew Dolly better than the rest of them did,—knew her highly strung temperament, and feared it, too. She might be spirited and audacious and thoughtless, but a blow coming through Grif would crush her to the earth.

"You—you mustn't set your heart too much upon his getting the letter in the morning, Dolly," she said. "He might be away when it came, or—or twenty things, and he might not see it until night, but—"

"Well," said Dolly, "I will write it at once if you will give me the pen and ink. The earlier it is posted the earlier he will get it."

She tried to rise then; but when she stood up her strength seemed to fail her, and she staggered and caught at Aimee's arm. But the next minute she laughed.

"How queer that one little faint should make me so weak!" she said. "I am weak,—actually. I shall feel right enough when I sit down, though."

She sat down at the table with her writing materials, and Aimée remained upon the sofa watching her. Her hand trembled when she wrote the first few lines, but she seemed to become steadier afterward, and her pen dashed over the paper without a pause for a few minutes. The spot of color on her cheeks faded and burned by turns,—sometimes it was gone, and again it was scarlet, and before the second page was finished tears were falling soft and fast. Once she even stopped to wipe them away, because they blinded her; but when she closed the envelope she did not look exactly unhappy, though her whole face was tremulous.

"He will come back," she said, softly. "He will come back when he reads this, I know. I wish it was to-morrow. To-morrow night he will be here, and we shall have our happy evening after all. I can excuse myself to Miss MacDowlas for another day."

"Yes," said Aimée, a trifle slowly, as she took *it* from her hand. "I will send Belinda out with it now." And she carried it out of the room.

In a few minutes she returned. "She has taken it," she said. "And now you had better go to bed, Dolly."

But Dolly's color had faded again, and she was resting her forehead upon her hands, with a heavy, anxious, worn look, which spoke of sudden reaction. She lifted her face with a half-absent air.

"I hope it will be in time for to-night's post," she said. "Do you think it will?"

"I am not quite sure, but I hope so. You must come to bed, Dolly."

She got up without saying more, and followed her out into the hall, but at the foot of the staircase she stopped. "I have not seen Tod," she said. "Let us go into 'Toinette's room and ask her to let us have him to-night. We can carry him up-stairs without wakening him. I have done it many a time. I should like to have him in my arms to-night."

So they turned into Mrs. Phil's room, and found that handsome young matron sitting in her dressing-gown before the fire, brushing out her great dark mantle of hair.

"Don't waken Tod," she cried out, as usual; and then when she saw Dolly she broke into a whispered volley of wondering questions. Where in the world had she been? What had she been doing with herself until such an hour? Where was Grif? Was n't he awfully vexed? What had he said when she came in? All of which inquiries the two parried as best they might.

As to Tod—well, Tod turned her thoughts in another direction. He was a beauty, and a king, and a darling, and he was growing sweeter and brighter every day,—which comments, by the way, were always the first made upon the subject of the immortal Tod. He was so amiable, too, and so clever and so little trouble. He went to sleep in his crib every night at seven, and never awakened until morning. Aunt Dolly might look at him now with those two precious middle fingers in his little mouth. And Aunt Dolly did look at him, lifting the cover slightly, and bending over him as he lay there making a deep dent in his small, plump pillow,—a very king of babies, soft and round and warm, the white lids drooped and fast closed over his dark eyes, their long fringes making a faint shadow on his fair, smooth baby cheeks, the two fingers in his sweet mouth, the round, cleft chin turned up, the firm, tiny white pillar of a throat bare.

"Oh, my bonny baby!" cried Dolly, the words rising from the bottom of her heart, "how fair and sweet you are!"

They managed to persuade Mrs. Phil to allow them to take possession of him for the night; and when they went up-stairs Dolly carried him, folded warmly in his downy blanket, and held close and tenderly in her arms.

"Aunt Dolly's precious!" Aimée heard her whispering to him as she gave him a last soft good-night kiss before they fell asleep. "Aunt Dolly's comfort! Everything is not gone so long as he is left."

But she evidently passed a restless night. When Aimée awakened in the morning she found her standing by the bedside, dressed and looking colorless and heavy-eyed.

"I never was so glad to see morning in my life," she said. "I thought the day would never break. I—I wonder how long it will be before Grif will be reading his letter?"

"He may get it before nine o'clock," answered Aimée; "but don't trouble about it, or the day will seem twice as long. Take Tod down-stairs and wash and dress him. It will give you something else to think of."

The wise one herself had not slept well. Truth to say, she was troubled about more matters than one. She was troubled to account for the meaning of Dolly's absence with Gowan. Even in her excitement, Dolly had not felt the secret quite her own, and had only given a skeleton explanation of the true state of affairs.

"It was something about Mollie and Gerald Chan-dos," she had said; "and if I had not gone it would have been worse than death to Mollie. Don't ask me to tell you exactly what it was, because I can't. Perhaps Mollie will explain herself before many days are over. She always tells you everything, you know. But it was no real fault of here; she was silly, but not wicked, and she is safe from Gerald Chandos now forever. And *I* saved her, Aimée."

And so the wise one had lain awake and thought of all sorts of possible and impossible escapades. But as she was dressing herself this morning, the truth flashed upon her, though it was scarcely the whole truth.

"She was going to elope with him," she exclaimed all at once; "*that* was what she was going to do. Oh, Mollie, Mollie, what a romantic goose you are!"

And having reached this solution, she closed her small, determined mouth in discreet silence, resolving to wait for Mollie's confession, which she knew was sure to come sooner or later. As to Mollie herself, she came down subdued and silent. She had slept off the effects of her first shock, but had by no means forgotten it. She would never forget it, poor child, as long as she lived, and she was so grateful to find herself safe in the shabby rooms again, that she had very little to say; and since she was in so novel a mood, the members of the family who were not in the secret decided that her headache must have been a very severe one indeed.

"Don't say anything to her about Grif," Dolly cautioned Aimée, "it would only trouble her." And so the morning passed; but even at twelve o'clock there was no Grif, and Dolly began to grow restless and walk to and fro from the window to the hearth at very short intervals. Dinner-hour arrived, too, but still no arrival; and Dolly sat at the table, among them, eating nothing and saying little enough. How could she talk when every step upon the pavement set her heart bounding? When dinner was over and Phil had gone back to the studio, she looked so helpless and woe-begone that Aimée felt constrained to comfort her.

"It may have been delayed," she whispered to her, "or he may have left the house earlier than usual, and so won't see it until to-night. He will be here to-night, Dolly, depend upon it."

And so they waited. Ah, how that window was watched that afternoon! How often Dolly started from her chair and ran to look out, half suffocated by her heart-beatings! But it was of no avail. As twilight came on she took her station before it, and knelt upon the carpet for an hour watching; but in the end she turned away all at once, and, running to the fire again, caught Tod up in her arms, and startled Aimée by bursting into a passion of tears.

"Oh, Tod!" she sobbed, "he is not coming! He will never come again,—he has left us forever! Oh, Tod, love poor Aunt Dolly, darling." And she hid her face on the little fellow's shoulder, crying piteously.

She did not go to the window again. When she was calmer, she remained on her chair, colorless and exhausted, but clinging to Tod still in a queer pathetic way, and letting him pull at her collar and her ribbons and her hair. The touch of his relentless baby hands and his pretty, tyrannical, restless ways seemed to help her a little and half distract her thoughts.

She became quieter and quieter as the evening waned; indeed, she was so quiet that Aimée wondered. She was strangely pale; but she did not start when footsteps were heard on the street, and she ceased turning toward the door when it opened.

"He—he may come in the morning," Aimée faltered as they went up-stairs to bed.

"No, he will not," she answered her, quite steadily. "It will be as I said it would,—he will never come again."

But when they reached their room, the unnatural, strained quiet gave way, and she flung herself upon the bed, sobbing and fighting against just the hysterical suffering which had conquered her the night before.

It was the very ghost of the old indomitable Dolly who rose the next morning. Her hands shook as she dressed her hair, and there were shadows under her eyes. But she must go back to Brabazon Lodge, notwithstanding.

"I can say I have a nervous headache," she said to Aimée. "Nervous headaches are useful things."

"If a letter comes," said Aimée, "I will bring it to you myself."

The girl turned toward her suddenly, her eyes hard and bright and her mouth working.

"I have had my last letter," she said. "My last letters came to me when Grif laid that package upon the table. He has done with me."

"Done with you?" cried Aimée, frightened by her manner. "With *you*, Dolly?"

Then for the first time Dolly flushed scarlet to the very roots of her hair.

"Yes," she said, "he has done with me. If there had been half a chance that he would ever come near me again, the letter I wrote to him that night would have brought him. A word of it would have brought him,—the first word. But he is having his revenge by treating it with contempt. He is showing me that it is too late, and that no humility on my part can touch him. I scarcely could have thought that of him," dropping into a chair by the toilet-table and hiding her face in her hands.

"It is not like Grif to let me humble myself for nothing. And I did humble myself,—ah, how I did humble myself! That letter,—if you could have seen it, Aimée,—it was all on fire with love for him. I laid myself under his feet,—and he has trodden me down! Grif—Grif, it was n't like you,—it was n't worthy of you,—it was n't indeed!"

Her worst enemy would have felt herself avenged if she had heard the anguish in her voice. She was crushed to the earth under this last great blow of feeling that he had altered so far. Grif,—her whilom greatest help and comfort,—the best gift God had given her! Dear, old, tender, patient fellow! as she had been wont to call him in her fits of penitence.

Grif, whose arms had always been open to her at her best and at her worst, who had loved her and borne with her, and waited upon her and done her bidding since they were both little more than children. When had Grif ever turned from her before? Never. When had Grif ever been cold or unfaithful in word or deed? Never. When had he ever failed her? Never—never—never—until now! And now that he had failed her at last, she felt that the bitter end had come. The end to everything,—to all the old hopes and dreams, to all the old sweet lovers' quarrels and meetings and partings, to all their clinging together, to all the volumes and volumes of love and trust that lay in the past, to all the world of simple bliss that lay still unrevealed in their lost future, to all the blessed old days when they had pictured to each other what that future was to be. It had all gone for nothing in the end. It must all have gone for nothing, when Grif—a new Grif—not her own true, stanch, patient darling—not her own old lover—could read her burning, tender, suffering words and pass them by without a word of answer. And with this weight of despair and pain upon her heart, she went back to the wearisome routine of Brabazon Lodge,—went back heavy with humiliation and misery which she scarcely realized,—went back suffering as no one who knew her—not even Grif himself—could ever have understood that it was possible for her to suffer. No innocent coquetries now, no spirit, no jests; for the present at least she had done with them, too.

"You are not in your usual spirits, my dear," said Miss MacDowlas.

"No," she answered, quietly, "I am not."

This state of affairs continued for four days, and then one morning, sitting at her sewing in the breakfast-room, she was startled almost beyond self-control by a servant's announcement that a visitor had arrived.

"One of your sisters, ma'am," said the parlor-maid. "Not the youngest, I think."

She was in the room in two seconds, and flew to Aimée, trembling all over with excitement.

"Not a letter!" she cried, hysterically. "It is n't a letter,—it can't be!" And she put her hand to her side and fairly panted.

The poor little wise one confronted her with something like fear. She could not bear to tell her the ill news she had come to break.

"Dolly, dear!" she said, "please sit down; and—please don't look at me so. It isn't good news. I must tell you the truth; it is bad news, cruel news. Oh, don't look so!"

They were standing near the sofa, and Dolly gave one little moan, and sank down beside it.

"Cruel news!" she cried, throwing up her hand. "Yes, I might have known that,—I might have known that it would be cruel, if it was news at all Every one is cruel,—the whole world is cruel; even Grif,—even Grif!"

Aimée burst into tears.

"Oh, Dolly, I did my best for you!" she said. "I did, indeed; but you must try to bear it, dear,—it is your own letter back again."

Then the kneeling figure seemed to stiffen and grow rigid in a second. Dolly turned her deathly face, with her eyes aflame and dilated.

"Did *he* send it back to me?" she asked, in a slow, fearful whisper.

Her expression was so hard and dreadful a one that Aimée sprang to her side and caught hold of her.

"No,—no!" she said; "not so bad as that! He would never have done that. He has never had it. He has gone away; we don't know where. It came from the dead-letter office."

Dolly took the letter from her and opened it slowly, and there, as she knelt, read it, word for word, as if it had been something she had never seen before. Then she put it back into the envelope and laid it down.

"A dead letter!" she said. "A dead letter! If *he* had sent it back to me, I think it would have cured me; but *now* there is no cure for me at all. If he had read it, he would have come,—if he had *only* read it; but it is a dead letter, and he is gone."

There were no tears, the blow had been too heavy. It was only Aimée who had tears to shed, and it was Dolly who tried to console her in a strained, weary sort of way.

"Don't cry," she said, "it is all over now. Perhaps the worst part of the pain is past. There will be no house at Putney, and the solitary rose-bush will bloom for some one else; they may sell the green sofa, now, as cheap as they will, we shall never buy it. Our seven years of waiting have all ended in a dead letter."

CHAPTER XIV.
SEVEN LONG YEARS, BELOVED, SEVEN LONG YEARS.

AND so Grif disappeared from the haunts of Vagabondia, and was seen no more. And to Aimée was left the delicate task of explaining the cause of his absence, which, it must be said, she did in a manner at once creditable to her tact and affection for both Dolly and the unconscious cause of all her misery.

"There has been a misunderstanding," she said, "which was no fault of Dolly's, and scarcely a fault of Grif's; and it has ended very unhappily, and Grif has gone away, and just at present it seems as if everything was over,— but I can't help hoping it is not so bad as that."

"Oh, he will come back again—safe enough," commented Phil, philosophically, holding paint-brush No. 1 in his mouth, while he manipulated with No. 2. "He will come back in sackcloth and ashes; he is just that sort, you know,—thunder and lightning, fire and tow. And they will make it up ecstatically in secret, and pretend that nothing has been the matter, and there will be no going into the parlor for weeks without whistling all the way across the hall."

"I always go in backward after they have had a quarrel," said Mollie, looking up from a half-made pinafore of Tod's, which, in the zeal of her repentance, she had decided on finishing.

"Not a bad plan, either," said Phil "We all know how *their* differences of opinion terminate. As to matters being at an end between them, that is all nonsense; they could n't live without each other six months. Dolly would take to unbecoming bonnets, and begin to neglect her back hair, and Grif would take to prussic acid or absinthe."

"Well, I hope he *will* come back," said Aimée; "but, in the meantime, I want to ask you to let the affair rest altogether, and not say a word to Dolly when she comes. It will be the kindest thing you can do. Just let things go on as they have always done, and ignore every thing new you may see."

Phil looked up from his easel in sudden surprise; something in her voice startled him, serenely as he was apt to view all unexpected intelligence.

"I say," he broke out, "you don't mean that Dolly is very much cut up about it?"

The fair little oracle hesitated; remembering Dolly's passionate despair and grief over that "dead letter," she could scarcely trust herself to speak.

"Yes," she answered at last, feeling it would be best only to commit herself in Phil's own words, "she is very much cut up."

"Whew!" whistled Phil; "that is worse than I thought!" And the matter ended in his going back to his picture and painting furiously for a few minutes, with an almost reflective air.

They did not see anything of Dolly for weeks. She wrote to them now and then, but she did not pay another visit to Bloomsbury Place. It was not the old home to her now, and she dreaded seeing it in its new aspect,—the aspect which was desolate of Grif. Most of her letters came to Aimée; but she rarely referred to her trouble, rather seeming to avoid it than otherwise. And the letters themselves were bright enough, seeming, too. She had plenty to say about Miss MacDowlas and their visitors and her own duties; indeed, any one but Aimée would have been puzzled by her courage and apparent good spirits. But Aimée saw below the surface, and understood, and, understanding, was fonder of her than ever.

As both Dolly and herself had expected, Mollie did not keep her secret from the oracle many weeks. It was too much for her to bear alone, and one night, in a fit of candor and remorse, she poured out everything from first to last, all her simple and unsophisticated dreams of grandeur, all her gullibility, all her danger,—everything, indeed, but the story of her pitiful little fancy for Ralph Gowan. She could not give that up, even to Aimée, though at the close of her confidence she was unable to help referring to him.

"And as to Mr. Gowan," she said, "how can I ever speak to him again! but, perhaps, he would not speak to me. He must think I am wicked and bold and hardened—and bad," with a fresh sob at every adjective. "Oh, dear! oh, dear!" burying her face in Aimée's lap, "if I had only stayed at home and been good, like you. He could have respected me, at least, couldn't he? And now— oh, what am I to do!"

Aimée could not help sighing. If she only *had* stayed at home, how much happier they all might have been! But she had promised Dolly not to add to her unhappiness by hinting at the truth, so she kept her own counsel.

It was fully three months before they saw Ralph Gowan again. He had gone on the Continent, they heard. A feeling of delicacy had prompted the journey. As long as he remained in London, he could scarcely drop out of his old friendly position at Bloomsbury Place, and he felt that for a while at least Mollie would scarcely find it easy to face him. So he went away and rambled about until he thought she would have time to get over her first embarrassment.

But at the end of the three months he came back, and one afternoon surprised them all by appearing amongst them again. Mollie, sitting perseveringly at work over her penitential sewing, shrank a little, and dropped her eyelids when he came in, but she managed to behave with creditable evenness of manner after all, and the rest welcomed him warmly.

"I have been to Brabazon Lodge," he said at length to Aimée. "I spent Monday evening there, and was startled at the change I found in your sister. I did not know she was ill."

Aimée started herself, and looked up at him with a frightened face.

"Ill!" she said. "Did you say ill?"

It was his turn to be surprised then.

"I thought her looking ill," he answered. "She seemed to me to be both paler and thinner. But you must not let me alarm you,—I thought, of course, that you would know."

"She has never mentioned it in her letters," Aimée said. "And she has not been home for three months, so we have not seen her."

"Don't let me give you a false impression," returned Gowan, eagerly. "She seemed in excellent spirits, and was quite her old self; indeed, I scarcely should imagine that she herself placed sufficient stress upon the state of her health. She insisted that she was well when I spoke to her about it."

"I am very glad you told me," answered Aimée. "She is too indifferent sometimes. I am afraid she would not have let us know. I thank you, very much."

He had other thanks before he left the house. As he was going out, Mollie, in her character of porteress, opened the hall door for him, and, having opened it, stood there with Tod's new garment half concealed, a pair of timid eyes uplifted to his face, a small, trembling, feverish hand held out.

"Mr. Gowan," she said, in a low, fluttering voice. "Oh, if you please—"

He took the little hot hand, feeling some tender remorse for not having tried to draw her out more and help her out of her painful shyness and restraint.

"What is it, Mollie?" he asked.

"I want—I want," fluttering all over,—"I want to thank you better than I did that—that dreadful night. I was so frightened I could scarcely understand. I understand more—now—and I want to tell you how grateful I am—and how grateful I shall be until I die—and I want to ask you to try not to think I was very wicked. I did not mean to be wicked—I was only vain and silly, and I thought it would be such a grand thing to—to have plenty of new dresses," hanging her sweet, humble face, "and to wear diamonds, and be Lady Chandos, if—if Mr. Chandos came into the title. Of course that was wicked, but it was n't—I was n't as bad as I seemed. I was so vain that—that I was quite sure he loved me, and would be very glad if I married him. He always said he would." And the tears rolled fast down her cheeks.

"Poor Mollie!" said Gowan, patting the trembling hand as if it had been a baby's. "Poor child!"

"But," Mollie struggled on, penitently, "I shall never be so foolish again. And I am going to try to be good—like Aimée. I am learning to mend things; and I am beginning to make things for Tod. This," holding up her work as proof, "is a dress for him. It is n't very well done," with innocent dubiousness; "but Aimée says I am improving. And so, if you please, would you be so kind as not to think quite so badly of me?"

It was all so humble and pretty and remorseful that he was quite touched by it. That old temptation to kiss and console her made it quite dangerous for him to linger. She was such a lovable sight with her tear-wet cheeks, and that dubious but faithfully worked-at garment of Tod's in her hand.

"Mollie," he said, "will you believe what I say to you?"

"Oh, yes!" eagerly.

"Then I say to you that I never believed you wicked for an instant,—not for one instant; and now I believe it less than ever; on the contrary, I believe you are a good, honest little creature. Let us forget Gerald Chandos,—he is not worth remembering. And go on with Tod's pinafores and dresses, my dear, and don't be discouraged if they are a failure at first,—though to my eyes that dress is a most sumptuous affair. And as to being like Aimée, you cannot be like any one better and wiser and sweeter than that same little maiden. There! I mean every word I have said."

"Are you sure?" faltered Mollie.

"Yes," he replied, "quite sure."

He shook hands with her, and, bidding her goodnight, left her standing in the narrow hall all aglow with joy. And he, outside, was communing with himself as he walked away.

"She is as sweet in her way as—as the other," he was saying. "And as well worth loving. And what a face she has, if one only saw it with a lover's eyes! What a face she has, even seeing it with such impartial eyes as mine!"

"My dear Dolly!" said Aimée.

"My dear Aimée!" said Dolly.

These were the first words the two exchanged when, the evening after Ralph Gowan's visit, the anxious young oracle presented herself at Brabazon Lodge, and was handed into Dolly's bedroom.

Visitors were expected, and Dolly had been dressing, and was just putting the finishing touches to her toilet when Aimée came in, and, seeing her as she turned from the glass to greet her, the wise one could scarcely speak, and, even after she had been kissed most heartily, could only hold the girl's hand and stand looking up into her changed face, feeling almost shocked.

"Oh, dear me, Dolly!" she said again. "Oh, my dear, what have you been doing to yourself?"

"Doing!" echoed Dolly, just as she would have spoken three or four months ago. "I have been doing nothing, and rather enjoying it. What is the matter with me?" glancing into the mirror. "Pale? That is the result of Miss MacDowlas's beneficence, you see. She has presented me with this grand black silk gown, and it makes me look pale. Black always did, you know."

But notwithstanding her readiness of speech, it did not need another glance to understand what Ralph Gowan had meant when he said that she was altered. The lustreless heavy folds of her black silk might contrast sharply with her white skin, but they could not bring about that subtle, almost incomprehensible change in her whole appearance. It was such a subtle change that it was difficult to comprehend. The round, lissome figure she had always been so pardonably vain about, and Grif had so admired, had fallen a little, giving just a hint at a greater change which might show itself sooner or later; her face seemed a trifle more clearly cut than it ought to have been, and the slender throat, set in its surrounding Elizabethan frill of white, seemed more slender than it had used to be. Each change was slight enough in itself, but all together gave a shadowy suggestion of alteration to affectionately quick eyes.

"You are ill," said Aimée. "And you never told me. It was wrong of you. Don't tell me it is your black dress; your eyes are too big and bright for any one who is well, and your hand is thinner than it ever was before. Why, I can feel the difference as I hold it, and it is as feverish as it can be."

"You good, silly little thing!" said Dolly, laughing. "I am not ill at all. I have caught a cold, perhaps, but that is all."

"No you have not," contradicted Aimée, with pitiful sharpness. "You have not caught cold, and you must not tell me so. You are ill, and you have been ill for weeks. The worst of colds could never make you look like this. Mr. Gowan might well be startled and wonder—"

"Mr. Gowan!" Dolly interrupted her. "Did *he* say that he was startled?"

"Yes, he did," Aimée answered. "And that was what brought me here. He was at Bloomsbury Place last night and told me all about you, and I made up my mind that minute that I would come and judge for myself."

Then the girl gave in. She sat down on a chair by the dressing-table and rested her forehead on her hand, laughing faintly, as if in protest against her own subjugation.

"Then I shall have to submit," she said. "The fact is, I sometimes fancy I do feel weaker than I ought to. It is n't like me to be weak. I was always so strong, you know,—stronger than all the rest of you, I thought. Miss MacDowlas says I do not look well. I suppose," with a half-sigh, "that every one will see it soon. Aimée," hesitating, "don't tell them at home."

Aimée slipped an arm around her, and drew her head—dressed in all the old elaborateness of pretty coils and braids—upon her own shoulder.

"Darling," she whispered, trying to restrain her tears, "I must tell them at home, because I must take you home to be nursed."

"No, no!" said Dolly, starting, "that would never do. It would never do even to think of it. I am not so ill as that,—not ill enough to be nursed. Besides," her voice sinking all at once, "I could n't go home, Aimée,—I could not bear to go home now. That is why I have stayed away so long. I believe it would *kill* me!"

It was impossible for Aimée to hear this and be silent longer. She had, indeed, only been waiting for some reference to the past.

"I knew it was that," she cried. "I knew it the moment Mr. Gowan told me. And I have feared it from the first. Nothing but that could have broken you down like this. Dolly, if Grif could see you now, he would give his heart's blood to undo what he has done."

The pale little hands lying upon the black dress began to tremble in a strange, piteous weakness.

"One cannot forget so much in so short a time," Dolly pleaded. "And it is so much,—more than even you think. One cannot forget seven years in three months,—give me seven months, Aimée. I shall be better in time, when I have forgotten."

Forgotten! Even those far duller of perception than Aimée could have seen that she would not soon forget. She had not begun in the right way to forget. The pain which had made the pretty figure and the soft, round face look faintly worn, was sharper to-day than it had been even three months before, and it was gaining in sharpness every day, nay, every hour.

"The days are so long," she said, plaiting the silk of her dress on-the restless hands. "We are so quiet, except when we have visitors, and somehow visitors begin to tire me. I scarcely ever knew what it was to be tired before. I don't care even to scatter the Philistines now," trying to smile. "I am not even roused by the prospect of meeting Lady Augusta tonight. I forgot to tell you she was coming, did n't I? How she would triumph if she knew how I have fallen and—and how miserable I am! She used to say I had not a thought above the cut of my dresses. She never knew about—*him*, poor fellow!"

It was curious to see how she still clung to that tender old pitying way of speaking of Grif.

Aimee began to cry over her again.

"You must come home, Dolly," she said. "You must, indeed. You will get worse and worse if you stay here. I will speak to Miss MacDowlas myself. You say she is kind to you."

"Dear little woman," said Dolly, closing her eyes as she let her head rest upon the girl's shoulder. "Dear, kind little woman! indeed it will be best for me to stay here. It is as I said,—indeed it is. If I were to go home I should *die!* Oh, don't you *know* how cruel it would be! To sit there in my chair and see his old place empty,—to sit and hear the people passing in the street and know I should never hear his footstep again,—to see the door open again and again, and know he would never, never pass through. It would break my heart,—it would break my heart!"

"It is broken now!" cried Aimée, in a burst of grief, and she could protest no more.

But she remained as long as she well could, petting and talking to her. She knew better than to offer her threadbare commonplace comfort, so she took refuge in talking of life at Bloomsbury Place,—about Tod and Mollie and Toinette, and the new picture Phil was at work upon. But it was a hard matter for her to control herself sufficiently to conceal that she was almost in an agony of anxiousness and foreboding. What was she to do with this sadly altered Dolly, the mainspring of whose bright, spirited life was gone? How was she to help her if she could not restore Grif,—it was only Grif she wanted,—and where was he? It was just as she had always said it would be,— without Grif, Dolly was Dolly no longer,—for Grif's sake her faithful, passionate girl's heart was breaking slowly.

Lady Augusta, encountering her ex-governess in the drawing-room that evening, raised her eyeglass to that noble feature, her nose, and condescended a questioning inspection, full of disapproval of the heavy, well-falling black silk and the Elizabethan frill.

"You are looking shockingly pale and thin," she said.

Dolly glanced at her reflection in an adjacent mirror. She only smiled faintly, in silence.

"I was not aware that you were ill," proceeded her ladyship.

"I cannot say that I am ill," Dolly answered. "How is Phemie?"

"Euphemia," announced Lady Augusta, "is well, and I *trust*" as if she rather doubted her having so far overcome old influences of an evil nature,—"I *trust* improving, though I regret to hear from her preceptress that she is singularly deficient in application to her musical lessons."

Dolly thought of the professor with the lumpy face, and smiled again. Phemie's despairing letters to herself sufficiently explained why her progress was so slow.

"I hope," said her ladyship to Miss MacDowlas, afterward, "that you are satisfied with Dorothea's manner of filling her position in your household."

"I never was so thoroughly satisfied in my life," returned the old lady, stiffly. "She is a very quickwitted, pleasantly natured girl, and I am extremely fond of her."

"Ah," waving a majestic and unbending fan of carved ivory. "She has possibly improved then. I observe that she is going off very much,—in the matter of looks, I mean."

"I heard a gentleman remark, a few minutes ago," replied Miss MacDowlas, "that the girl looked like a white rose, and I quite agreed with him; but I am fond of her, as I said, and you are not."

Her ladyship shuddered faintly, but she did not make any further comment, perhaps feeling that her hostess was too powerful to encounter.

At midnight the visitors went their several ways, and after they had dispersed and the rooms were quiet once again, Miss MacDowlas sent her companion to bed, or, at least, bade her good-night.

"You had better go at once," she said. "I will remain to give orders to the servants. You look tired. The excitement has been too much for you."

So Dolly thanked her and left the room; but Miss MacDowlas did not hear her ascend the stairs, and accordingly, after listening a moment or so, went to the room door and looked out into the hall. And right at the foot of the staircase lay Dolly Crewe, the lustreless, trailing black dress making her skin seem white as marble, her pretty face turned half downward upon her arm.

Half an hour later the girl returned to consciousness to find herself lying comfortably in bed, the chamber empty save for herself and Miss MacDowlas, who was standing at her side watching her.

"Better?" she said. "That is right, my dear. The evening was too much for you, as I was afraid it would be. You are not as strong as you should be."

"No," Dolly answered, quietly.

There was a silence of a few minutes, during which she closed her eyes again; but she heard Miss MacDowlas fidgeting a little, and at last she heard her speak.

"My dear," she said, "I think I ought to tell you something. When you fell, I suppose you must somehow or other have pressed the spring of your locket, for it was open when I went to you, and—I saw the face inside it."

"Grif," said Dolly, in a tired voice, "Grif."

And then she remembered how she had written to him about what this very *dénouement* would be when it came. How strange, how wearily strange, it was to think that it should come about in such a way as this!

"My nephew," said Miss MacDowlas. "Griffith Donne."

"Yes," said Dolly, briefly. "I was engaged to him."

"Was!" echoed Miss MacDowlas. "Did he behave badly to you, my dear?"

"No, I behaved badly to him—and that is why I am ill."

Miss MacDowlas blew her nose.

"How long?" she asked, at length. "May I ask how long you were engaged to each other, my dear? Don't answer me if you do not wish."

"I was engaged to him," faltered the girlish voice,—"we were all the world to each other for seven years—for seven long years."

CHAPTER XV.
IN WHICH WE TRY SWITZERLAND.

IN the morning of one of the hot days in June, Mollie, standing at the window of Phil's studio, turned suddenly toward the inmates of the room with an exclamation.

"Phil!" she said, "Toinette! There is a carriage drawing up before the door."

"Lady Augusta?" said Toinette, making a dart at Tod.

"Confound Lady Augusta!" ejaculated Phil, devoutly. "That woman has a genius for presenting herself at inopportune times."

"But it is n't Lady Augusta," Mollie objected. "It is n't the Bilberry carriage at all. Do you think I don't know 'the ark'?"

"You ought to by this time," returned Phil. "I do, to my own deep grief."

"It is the Brabazon Lodge carriage!" cried Mollie, all at once. "Miss MacDowlas is getting out, and—yes, here is Dolly!"

"And Tod just washed and dressed!" said Mrs. Phil, picking up her offspring with an air of self-congratulation. "Miracle of miracles! The Fates begin to smile upon us. Phil, how is my back hair?"

"All right," returned Phil. "I suppose I shall have to present myself, too."

It was necessary that they should all present themselves, they found. Miss MacDowlas wished to form the acquaintance of the whole family, it appeared, and apart from this her visit had rather an important object.

"It is a sort of farewell visit," she explained, "though, of course, the farewell is only to be a temporary one. We find London too hot for us, and we are going to try Switzerland. The medical man thinks a change will be beneficial to your sister."

They all looked at Dolly then,—at Dolly in her delicate, crisp summer bravery and her pretty summer hat; but it was neither hat nor dress that drew their eyes upon her all at once in that new questioning way. But Dolly only laughed,—a soft, nervous laugh, however,—and played with her much-frilled parasol.

"Miss MacDowlas," she said, "is good enough to fancy I am not so well as I ought to be, Tod," bending her face low over the pretty little fellow, who had trotted to her knee. "What do you think of Aunt Dolly's appearing in the character of invalid? It sounds like the best of jokes, does n't it, Tod?"

They tried to smile responsively, all of them, but the effort was not a success. Despite all her pretence of brightness and coquettish attire, there was not one of them who had not been startled when their first greeting was over. Under the triumph of a hat, her face showed almost sharply cut, her skin far too transparently colorless, her eyes much too large and bright. The elaborately coiled braids of hair seemed almost too heavy for the slender throat to bear, and no profusion of trimming could hide that the little figure was worn. The flush and glow and spirit had died away from her. It was not the Dolly who had been wont to pride herself upon ruling supreme in Vagabondia, who sat there before them making them wonder; it was a new creature, who seemed quite a stranger to them.

They were glad to see how fond of her Miss MacDowlas appeared to be. They had naturally not had a very excellent opinion of Miss MacDowlas in the past days; but the fact that Dolly had managed to so win upon her as to bring out her best side, quite softened their hearts. She was not so grim, after all. Her antipathy to Grif had evidently been her most unpleasant peculiarity, and now, seeing her care for this new Dolly, who needed care so much, they were rather touched.

When the farewells had been said, the carriage had driven away, and they had returned to the studio, a silence seemed to fall upon them, one and all. 'Toinette sat in her chair, holding Tod, without speaking; Mollie stood near her with a wondering, downcast air; Phil went to the window, and, neglecting his picture wholly for the time being, looked out into the street, whistling softly.

At length he turned round to Aimée.

"Aimée," he said, abruptly, "how long has this been going on?"

"You mean this change?" said Aimée, in a low voice.

"Yes."

"For three months," she answered. "I did not like to tell you because I knew *she* would not like it; but it dates from the time Grif went away."

Mrs. Phil burst into an impetuous gush of tears, hiding her handsome, girlish face on Tod's neck.

"It is a shame!" she cried out. "It is a cruel, burning shame! Who would ever have thought of Grif's treating her like this?"

"Yes," said Phil; "and who would ever have thought that Dolly would have broken down? Dolly! By George! I can't believe it. If I am able to judge, it seems time that she should try Switzerland or somewhere else. Aimée, has she heard nothing of him?"

"Nothing."

The young man flushed hotly.

"Confound it!" he burst forth. "It looks as if the fellow was a dishonorable scamp. And yet he is the last man I should ever have fancied would prove a scamp."

"But he has not proved himself a scamp yet," said Aimée, in a troubled tone. "And Dolly would not like to hear you say so. And if you knew the whole truth you *wouldn't* say so. He has been tried too far, and he has been impetuous and rash, but it was his love for Dolly that made him so. And wherever he may be, Phil, I know he is as wretched and hopeless as Dolly herself could be at the worst. It has all been misunderstanding and mischance."

"He has broken Dolly's heart, nevertheless," cried Mrs. Phil. "And if she dies—"

"Dies!" cried out Mollie, opening her great eyes and turning pale all at once. "Dies! Dolly?"

"Hush!" said Aimée, trembling and losing color herself. "Oh, hush!—don't say such things. It sounds so dreadful,—it is too dreadful to think of!"

And so it came about that on another of these hot June days there appeared at the *table à hôte* of a certain well-conducted and already well-filled inn at Lake Geneva two new arrivals,—a tall, thin, elderly lady of excessively English exterior, and a young person who attracted some attention,—a girl who wore a long black dress, and had a picturesque Elizabethan frill about her too slender throat, and who, in spite of her manner and the clearness of her bright voice, was too whitely transparent of complexion and too finely cut of face to look as strong as a girl of one or two and twenty ought to be.

The people who took stock of them, after the manner of all unoccupied hotel sojourners on the lookout for sensations, noticed this. One or two of them even observed that, on entering the room after the slight exertion of descending the staircase, the girl was slightly out of breath and seemed glad to sit down, and that, her companion evidently making some remark upon the fact, she half laughed, as if wishing to make light of it; and they noticed, too, that her naturally small hands were so very slender that her one simple little ring of amethyst and pearls slipped loosely up and down her finger.

They were not ordinary tourists, these new arrivals, it was clear. Their attire told that at once. They had removed their travelling dresses, and looked as if they had quite made up their minds to enjoy their customary mode of life as if they had been at home. They had no courier, the wiseacres had ascertained, and they had brought a neat English serving-woman, who seemed to know her business marvellously well and be by no means unaccustomed to travelling.

"Aunt and niece!" commented one gentleman, surveying Dolly over his soup. "A nice little creature,—the niece." And he mentally resolved to cultivate her acquaintance. But it was not such an easy matter. The new arrivals were unlike ordinary tourists in other respects than in their settled mode of life. They did not seem to care to form chance acquaintance with their fellow guests. They lived quietly and, unless when driving out together or taking short, unfatiguing strolls, remained much in their own apartments. They appeared at the *table d'hôte* occasionally; but though they were pleasant in manner they were not communicative, and so, after a week or so, people tired of asking questions about them and lapsed into merely exchanging greetings, and looking on with some interest at any changes they observed in the pretty, transparent, though always bright face, and the pliant, soft young figure.

Thus Miss MacDowlas and her companion "tried Switzerland."

"It will do you good, my dear, and brace you up," the elder lady had said; and from the bottom of her heart she had hoped it would.

And did it?

Well, the last time Dolly had "tried Switzerland," she had tried it in the capacity of Lady Augusta's governess, and she had held in charge a host of rampant young Bilberrys, who secretly loathed their daily duties, and were not remarkable in the matter of filial piety, and were only reconciled to existence by the presence of their maternal parent's greatest trial, that highly objectionable Dorothea Crewe. So, taking Lady Augusta in conjunction with her young charges, the girl had often felt her lot by no means the easiest in the world; but youth and spirit, and those oft-arriving letters, had helped her to bear a great deal, and so there was still something sweet about the memory. Oh, those old letters—those foolish, passionate, tender letters—written in the dusty, hot London office, read with such happiness, and answered on such closely penned sheets of foreign paper! How she had used to watch for them, and carry them to her small bedroom and read them again and again, kneeling on the floor by the open window, the fresh, soft summer breezes from the blue lake far below stirring her hair and kissing her forehead! How doubly and trebly fair she had been wont to fancy everything looked on that "letter day" of hers,—that red-letter day,—that golden-letter day!

The very letters she had written then lay in her trunk now, tied together in a bundle, just as Grif had brought them and laid them down upon the table when he gave her up forever. Her "dead letter" lay with them,—that last, last appeal, which had never reached his heart, and never would. She had written her last letter to him, and he his last to her.

And now she had been brought to "try Switzerland" and Lake Geneva as a Lethe.

But she had determined to be practical and courageous, and bear it as best she might. It would not have been like her to give way at once without a struggle. She did not believe in lovelorn damsels, who pined away and died of broken hearts, and made all their friends uncomfortable by so doing. She made a struggle, and refused to give up. She grew shadowy and fair; but it was under protest, and she battled against the change she felt creeping upon her so slowly but so surely. She showed a brave face to people, and tried to be as bright and ready-witted as ever; and if she failed it was not her own fault. She fought hard against her sleepless nights and weary days; and when she lay awake hour after hour hearing the clock strike, it was not because she made no effort to compose herself, it was only because the delicate wheels of thought *would* work against her helpless will, and it was worse than useless to close her eyes when she could see so plainly her lost lover's desperate, anguished face, and hear so distinctly his strained, strangely altered voice: "No, it is too late for that now,—that is all over!" And he had once loved her better than his life!

So it was that, try as she might, she could not make Switzerland a success. When she went down to the table d'hôte, people saw that instead of growing stronger she was growing more frail, and the exertion of coming down the long flight of stairs tried her more than it had seemed to do that first day. Sometimes she had a soft, lovely, dangerous color on her cheeks, and her eyes looked almost translucent; and then again the color was gone, her skin was white and transparent, and her eyes were shadowy and languid. When the hot July days came in, the ring of pearls and amethyst would stay on the small worn hand no longer, and so was taken off and hung with the little bunch of coquettish "charms" upon her chain. But she was not conquered yet, and the guests and servants often heard her laughing, and making Miss MacDowlas laugh as they sat together in their private parlor.

The two were sitting thus together one Saturday early in July,—Dolly in a loose white wrapper, resting in a low basket chair by the open window, and fanning herself languidly,—when a visitor was announced, and the moment after the announcement a tall young lady rushed into the room and clasped Dolly unceremoniously in her arms, either not observing or totally ignoring Miss MacDowlas's presence.

"Dolly!" she cried, kneeling down by the basket chair and speaking so fast that her words tumbled over each other, and her sentences were curiously mingled. "Oh! if you please, dear, I know it was n't polite, and I never meant to do it in such an unexpected, awfully rude way; and what mamma would say, I am sure I cannot tell, unless go into dignified convulsions, and shudder herself stiff; but how could I help it, when I came expecting to see you as bright and lovely as ever, and caught a glimpse of you through the door, as the servant spoke, sitting here so white and thin and tired-looking! Oh, dear! oh, dear! how ever can it be!"

"My dear Phemie!" said Dolly, laughing and crying both at once, through weakness and sympathy,—for of course poor, easily moved Phemie had burst into a flood of affectionate tears. "My dear child, how excited you are, and how pleasant it is to see you! How did you manage to come?"

"The professor with the lumpy face—poor, pale darling—I mean you, not him," explained the eldest Miss Bilberry, clinging to her ex-governess as if she was afraid of seeing her float through the open window. "The professor with the lumpy face, Dolly; which shows he is not so horrid as I always thought him, and I am very sorry for being so inconsiderate, I am sure—you know he cannot help his lumps any more than I can help my dreadful red hands and my dresses not fitting."

Dolly stopped her here to introduce her to Miss MacDowlas; and that lady having welcomed her good-naturedly, and received her incoherent apologies for her impetuous lack of decorum, the explanation proceeded.

"How could the professor send you here?" asked Dolly.

"He did not exactly send me, but he helped me," replied the luckless Euphemia, becoming a trifle more coherent. "I saw you at the little church, though you did not see me, because, of course, we sit in the most disagreeable part, just where we can't see or be seen at all. And though I only saw you at a distance, and through your veil, and half behind a pillar, I knew you, and knew Miss MacDowlas. I think I knew Miss MacDowlas most because she *wasn't* behind the pillar. And it nearly drove me crazy to think you were so near, and I gave one of the servants some money to find out where you were staying, and she brought me word that you were staying here, and meant to stay. And then I asked the lady principal to let me come and see you, and of course she refused; and I never should have been able to come at all, only it chanced that was my music-lesson day, and I went in to the professor with red eyes,—I had cried so,—and when he asked me what I had been crying for, I remembered that he used to be fond of you, and I told him. And he was sorry for me, and promised to ask leave for me. He is a cousin of the lady principal, and a great favorite with her. And the end of it was that they let me come. And I have almost flown. I had to wait until to-day, you know, because it was Saturday."

It was quite touching to see how, when she stopped speaking, she clung to Dolly's hands, and looked at her with wonder and grief in her face.

"What is it that has changed you so?" she said. "You are not like yourself at all. Oh, my dear, how ill you are!"

A wistful shadow showed itself in the girl's eyes.

"*Am* I so much changed?" she asked.

"You do not look like our Dolly at all," protested Phemie. "You are thin,— oh, so thin! What *is* the matter?"

"Thin!" said Dolly. "Am I? Then I must be growing ugly enough. Perhaps it is to punish me for being so vain about my figure. Don't you remember what a dread I always had of growing thin? Just to think that *I* should grow thin, after all! Do my bones stick out like the Honorable Cecilia Howland's, Phemie?" And she ended with a little laugh.

Phemie kissed her, in affectionate protest against such an idea.

"Oh, dear, no!" she said. "They could n't, you know. They are not the kind of bones to do it. Just think of her dreadful elbows and her fearful shoulder-blades! You couldn't look like her. I don't mean that sort of thinness at all. But you seem so light and so little. And look here," and she held up the painfully small hand, the poor little hand without the ring. "There are no dimples here now, Dolly," she said, sorrowfully.

"No," answered Dolly, simply; and the next minute, as she drew her hand away, there fluttered from her lips a sigh.

She managed to change the turn of conversation after this. Miss MacDowlas had good-naturedly left them alone, and so she began to ask Phemie questions,—questions about school and lessons and companions, about the lady principal and the under-teachers and about the professor with the lumpy face; and, despite appearances being against her, there was still the old ring in her girl's jests.

"Has madame got a new bonnet yet," she asked, "or does she still wear the old one with those aggressive-looking spikes of wheat in it? The lean ears ought to have eaten up the fat ones by this time."

"But they have n't," returned Phemie. "They are there yet, Dolly. Just the same spikes in the same bonnet, only she has had new saffron-colored ribbon put on it, just the shade of her skin."

Dolly shuddered,—Lady Augusta's own semi-tragic shudder, if Phemie had only recognized it.

"Phemie," she said, with a touch of pardonable anxiety, "ill as I look, I am not that color, am I? To lose one's figure and grow thin is bad enough, but to become like Madame Pillet—dear me!" shaking her head. "I scarcely think I could reconcile myself to existence."

Phemie laughed. "You are not changed in one respect, Dolly," she said. "When I hear you talk it makes me feel quite—quite safe."

"Safe!" Dolly echoed. "You mean to say that so long as I preserve my constitutional vanity, your anxiety won't overpower you. But—but," looking at her curiously, "did you think at first that I was not safe, as you call it?"

"You looked so ill," faltered Phemie. "And—I was so startled."

"Were you?" asked Dolly. "Did I shock you?"

"A little—only just a little, dear," deprecatingly.

Then strangely enough fell upon them a silence. Dolly turned toward the window, and her eyes seemed to fix themselves upon some far-away point, as if she was pondering over a new train of thought. And when at last she spoke, her voice was touched with the tremulous unsteadiness of tears.

"Do you think," she said, slowly,—"do you think that *any one* who had loved me would be shocked to see me now? Am I so much altered as that? One scarcely sees these things one's self,—they come to pass so gradually."

All poor Phemie's smiles died away.

"Don't let us talk about it," she pleaded. "I cannot bear to hear you speak so. Don't, dear—if you please, don't!"

Her pain was so evident that it roused Dolly at once.

"I won't, if it troubles you," she said, almost in her natural manner. "It does not matter,—why should it? There is no one here to be shocked. I was only wondering."

But the shadow did not quite leave her face, and even when, an hour later, Euphemia bade her good-by and left her, promising to return again as soon as possible, it was there still.

She was very, very quiet for a few minutes after she found herself alone. She clasped her hands behind her head, and lay back in the light chair, looking out of the window. She was thinking so deeply that she did not even stir for a while; but in the end she got up, as though moved by some impulse, and crossed the room.

Against the wall hung a long, narrow mirror, and she went to this mirror and stood before it, looking at herself from head to foot,—at her piteously sharpened face, with its large, wondering eyes, eyes that wondered at themselves,—at the small, light figure so painfully etherealized, and about which the white wrapper hung so loosely. She even held up, at last, the slender hand and arm; but when she saw these uplifted, appealing, as it were, for this sad, new face which did not seem her own, she broke into a little cry of pain and grief.

"If you could see me now," she said, "if you should come here by chance and see me now, my dear, I think you would not wait to ask whether I had been true or false. I never laid this white cheek on your shoulder, did I? Oh, what a changed face it is! I know I was never very pretty, though you thought so and were proud of me in your tender way, but I was not like this in those dear old days. Grif, Grif, would you know me,—would you *know* me?" And, turning to her chair again, she dropped upon her knees before it, and knelt there sobbing.

CHAPTER XVI.
IF YOU SHOULD DIE.

THE postman paid frequent visits to Bloomsbury Place during these summer weeks. At first Dolly wrote often herself, but later it seemed to fall to Miss MacDowlas to answer Aimée's weekly letters and Mollie's fortnightly ones. And that lady was a faithful correspondent, and did her duty as readily as was possible, giving all the news, and recording all Dolly's messages, and issuing regular bulletins on the subject of her health. "Your sister," she sometimes wrote, "is not so well, and I have persuaded her to allow me to be her amanuensis." Or, "Your sister is tired after a rather long drive, and I have persuaded her to rest while I write at her dictation." Or sometimes, "Dolly is rather stronger, and is in excellent spirits, but I do not wish her to exert herself at present." But at length a new element crept into these letters. The cheerful tone gave way to a more dubious one; Dolly's whimsical messages were fewer and farther between, and sometimes Miss MacDowlas seemed to be on the verge of hinting that her condition was a weaker and more precarious one than even she herself had at first feared.

Ralph Gowan, on making his friendly calls, and hearing this, was both anxious and puzzled. In a very short time after his return he had awakened to a recognition of some mysterious shadow upon the household. Vagabondia had lost its spirits. Mrs. Phil and her husband were almost thoughtful; Tod disported himself unregarded and unadmired, comparatively speaking; Mollie seemed half frightened by the aspect affairs were wearing; and Aimee's wise, round face had an older look. And then these letters! Dolly "trying Switzerland" for her health, Dolly mysteriously ill and far away from home,—too weak sometimes to write. Dolly, who had never seemed to have a weakness; who had entered the lists against even Lady Augusta, and had come off victorious; who had been mock-worldly, and coquettish, and daring; who had made open onslaught upon eligible Philistines; who had angled prettily and with sinful success for ineligible Bohemians! What did it mean? And where was Donne? Certainly he was never to be seen at Bloomsbury Place or in its vicinity in these days.

But, deeply interested as he was, Gowan was not the man to ask questions; so he could only wait until chance brought the truth to light.

He came to the house upon one occasion and found Aimée crying quietly over one of Miss MacDowlas's letters in the parlor, and in his sympathy he felt compelled to speak openly to her.

Then Aimée, heavy of heart and full of despairing grief, handed him the letter to read.

"I have known it would be so—from the first," she sobbed. "We are going to lose her. Perhaps she will not live to come home again."

"You mean Dolly?" he said.

"Yes," hysterically. "Miss MacDowlas says—" But she could get no further.

This was what Miss MacDowlas said:—

"I cannot think it would be right to hide from you that your sister is very ill, though she does not complain, and persists in treating her increasing weakness lightly. Indeed, I am sure that she herself does not comprehend her danger. I am inclined to believe that it has not yet occurred to her that she is in danger at all. She protests that she cannot be ill so long as she does not suffer; but I, who have watched her day by day, can see only too plainly where the danger lies. And so I think it best to warn you to be prepared to come to us at once if at any time I should send for you hurriedly."

"Prepared to go to them!" commented Aimée. "What does that mean? What can it mean but that our own Dolly is dying, and may slip out of the world away from us at any moment? Oh, Grif! Grif! what have you done?"

Gowan closed the letter.

"Miss Aimée," he said, "where *is* Donne?"

Aimée fairly wrung her hands.

"I don't know," she quite wailed. "If I only did—if I only knew where I could find him!"

"You don't know!" exclaimed Gowan. "And Dolly dying in Switzerland!"

"That is it," she returned. "That is what it all means. If any of us knew—or if Dolly knew, she would not be dying in Switzerland. It is because she does not know, that she is dying. She has never seen him since the night you brought Mollie home. And—and she cannot live without him."

The whole story was told in very few words after this; and Gowan, listening, began to understand what the cloud upon the house had meant. He suffered some sharp enough pangs through the discovery, too. The last frail cords that had bound him to hope snapped as Aimée poured out her sorrows. He had never been very sanguine of success, but even after hoping against hope, his tender fancy for Dolly Crewe had died a very lingering death; indeed, it was not quite dead yet, but he was beginning to comprehend this old love story more fully, and he had found himself forced to do his rival greater justice. He could not see his virtues as the rest saw them, of course, but he was generous enough to pity him, and see that his lot had been a terribly hard one.

"There is only one thing to be done," he said, when Aimée had finished speaking. "We must find him."

"Find him! We cannot find him."

"That remains to be proved," he answered. "Have you been to his lodgings?"

"Yes," mournfully. "And even to the office! He left his lodgings that very night, paid his bills, and drove away in a cab with his trunk. Poor Grif! It was n't a very big trunk. He went to the office the next morning, and told Mr. Flynn he was going to leave London, and one of the clerks told Phil there was a 'row' between them. Mr. Flynn was angry because he had not given due notice of his intention. That is all we know."

"And you have not the slightest clew beyond this?"

"Not the slightest. He spent all his spare time with Dolly, you know; so there is not even any place of resort, or club, or anything, where we might go to make inquiries about him."

Gowan's countenance fell. He felt the girl's distress keenly, apart from his own pain.

"The whole affair seems very much against us," he said; "but he may—I say he *may* be in London still. I am inclined to believe he is myself. When the first passion of excitement was over, he would find himself weaker than he fancied he was. It would not be so easy to cut himself off from the old life altogether. He would long so inexpressibly to see Dolly again that he could not tear himself away. I think we may be assured that even if he is not in London, at least he has not left England."

"That was what I have been afraid of," said Aimée, "that he might have left England altogether."

"I cannot think he has," Gowan returned.

They were both silent for a moment. Aimée sat twisting Miss MacDowlas's letter in her fingers, fresh tears gathering in her eyes.

"It is all the harder to bear," she said next, "because Dolly has always seemed so much of a *reality* to us. If she had been a pale, ethereal sort of girl, it might not seem such a shock; but she never was. She even used to say she could not bear those frail, ethereal people in books, who were always dying and saying touching things just at the proper time, and who knew exactly when to call up their agonized friends to their bedside to see how pathetically and decorously they made their exit. Oh, my poor darling! To think that she should be fading away and dying just in the same way! I cannot make it seem real. I cannot think of her without her color, and her jokes, and her bits of acting, and her little vanities. She will not be our Dolly at all if they have left her. There is a dress of hers up-stairs now,—a dress she couldn't bear. And I remember so well how she lost her temper when she was making it, because it would n't fit. And when I went into the parlor she was crying over it, and Grif was trying so hard to console her that at last she laughed. I can see her now, with the tears in her eyes, looking half-vexed and half-comforted. And Tod, too,—how fond she was of Tod, and how proud of him! Ah, Tod," in a fresh burst, "when you grow up, the daisies may have been growing for many a year over poor little Aunt Dolly, and you will have forgotten her quite."

"You must not look at the matter in that desponding way," said Gowan, quite unsteadily. "We must hope for the best, and do what we can. You may rely upon me to exert myself to the utmost. If we succeed in finding Donne I am sure that he will do the rest. Perhaps, next summer Vagabondia will be as bright as ever,—nay, even brighter than it has been before."

All his sympathies were enlisted, and, hopeless as the task seemed, he had determined to make strenuous efforts to trace this lost lover. Men had concealed themselves from their friends, in the world of London, often before, and this, he felt sure, Griffith Donne was doing; and since this poor little impassioned, much-tried Dolly was dying in spite of herself for Griffith Donne's sake, and seemed only to be saved by his presence, he must even set himself the task of bringing him to light and clearing up this miserable misunderstanding. Having been Dolly Crewe's lover, he was still generous enough to wish to prove himself her friend; yes, and even her luckier lover's friend, though he winced a trifle at the thought. Accordingly, he left the house that night with his mind full of half-formed plans, both feasible and otherwise.

During the remainder of that week he did not call at Bloomsbury Place again, but at the beginning of the next he made his appearance, bringing with him a piece of news which excited Aimee terribly.

"I know I shall startle you," he said, the moment they were alone together, "but you can scarcely be more startled than I was myself. I have been on the lookout constantly, but I did not expect to be rewarded by success so soon. Indeed, as it is, it has been entirely a matter of chance. It is as I felt sure it would be. Donne is in London still. I know that much, though that is all I have learned as yet. Late last night I caught a glimpse—only a glimpse—of him hurrying through a by-street. I almost fancied he had seen me and was determined to get out of the way."

"The pretty English girl," said the guests at the inn, "comes down no longer to the *table d'hôte?*" "The pretty English girl," remarked the wiseacres, "does not even drive out on these days, and the doctor calls every morning to see her."

"And sometimes," added one of the wisest, "again in the evening."

"Consumption," observed another.

"Plainly consumption," nodding significantly. "These English frauleins are so often consumptive," commented a third. "It is astonishing to remark how many come to 'try Switzerland,' as they say."

"And die?"

"And die,—as this one will."

"Poor little thing!" with a sigh and a pitying shrug of the shoulders.

And in the meantime up-stairs the basket chair had been taken away from the window, and a large-cushioned, chintz-covered couch had been pushed into its place, and Dolly lay upon it. But luxurious as her couch was, and balmy as the air was, coming through the widely opened window, she did not find much rest. The fact was, she was past rest by this time, she was too weak to rest. The hot days tried her, and her sleepless nights undermined even her last feeble relic of strength. Sometimes during the day she felt that she could not lie propped up on the pillows a moment longer; but when she tried to stand or sit up she was glad to drop back again into the old place. She lost her breath fearfully soon,—the least exertion left her panting.

"If I had a cough," she said once to Miss MacDowlas, "I could understand that I was ill—or if I suffered any actual pain, but I don't, and even the doctor admits that my lungs are safe enough. What is it that he says about me? Let me see. Ah, this is it: that I am 'below par—fearfully below par,' as if I was gold, or notes, or bonds, or something. My ideas on the subject of the money market are indefinite, you see. Ah, well; I wonder when I shall be 'above par'!"

She never spoke of her ailments in any other strain. Even as she lay on her couch, too prostrate to either read or work, she made audacious satirical speeches, and told Miss MacDowlas stories of Vagabondia, just as she used to tell them to Grif himself, only that in these days she could not get up to flourish illustratively; and often after lying for an hour or so in a dead, heavy, exhausting day-sleep, she opened her eyes at last, to jest about her faithful discharge of her duties as companion. Only she herself knew of the fierce battles she so often fought in secret, when her sore, aching heart cried out so loud for Grif and would not—*would* not be comforted.

She saw Phemie frequently. The much-abused professor had proved himself a faithful friend to them. He had never been quite able to forget the little English governess, who had so won upon him in the past, even though this same young lady, in her anxiety to set Lady Augusta at defiance, had treated him somewhat cavalierly. Indeed, hearing that she was ill, he was so touched as to be quite overwhelmed with grief. He gained Euphemia frequent leaves of absence, and sent messages of condolence and bouquets,—huge bunches of flowers which made Dolly laugh even while they pleased her. There was always a bouquet, stiff in form and gigantic in proportions, when Phemie came.

At first Phemie caught the contagion of Dolly's own spirit and hopefulness, and was sustained by it in spite of appearances; but its influence died out at the end of a few weeks, and even she was not to be deceived. An awful fear began to force itself upon her,—a fear doubly awful to poor, susceptible Phemie. Dolly was getting no better; she was even getting worse every day; she could not sit up; she was thinner and larger-eyed than ever. Was something going to happen? And at the mere thought of that possible something she would lose her breath and sit looking at Dolly, silent, wondering, and awe-stricken. She began to ponder over this something, as she tried to learn her lessons; she thought of it as she went to bed and she dreamed of it in the night. Sometimes when she came in unexpectedly and found Dolly in one of those prostrate sleeps, she was so frightened that she could have cried out aloud.

She came in so one evening at twilight,—the professor had brought her himself and had promised to escort her home,—and she found Dolly in one of these sleeps. So, treading lightly, she put the bouquet in water, and then drew a low chair to the girl's side and sat down to watch and wait until she should awaken. Miss MacDowlas was in her own room writing to Aimée; so the place seemed very quiet, and it was its quietness, perhaps, which so stirred Phemie to sorrowful thoughts and fear.

Upon her brightly flowered chintz cushions Dolly lay like the shadow of her former self. The once soft, round outlines of her face had grown clear and sharp-cut, the delicate chin had lost its dimple, the transparent skin upon the temples showed a tracery of blue veins, the closed eyelids had a strange whiteness and lay upon her eyes heavily. She did not move,—she seemed scarcely to breathe. Phemie caught her own breath and held it, lest it should break from her in a sob of grief and terror.

This something awful *was* going to happen! She could not recover herself even when Dolly wakened and began to talk to her. She could not think of anything but her own anguish and pity for her friend. She could not talk and was so silent, indeed, that Dolly became silent too; and so, as the dusk fell upon them, they sat together in a novel quiet, listening to a band of strolling musicians, who were playing somewhere in the distance, and the sound of whose instruments floated to them, softened and made plaintive by the evening air.

At last Dolly broke the silence.

"You are very quiet, Phemie," she said. "Are you going to sleep?"

"No," faltered Phemie, drawing closer to her. "I am thinking."

"Thinking. What about?"

"About you. Dolly, do you—are you very ill—worse than you were?"

"Very ill!" repeated Dolly, slowly, as if in wonder. "Worse than I was! Why do you ask?"

Then Phemie lost self-control altogether. She left her seat and fell down by the couch, bursting into tears.

"You are so altered," she said; "and you alter so much every week. I cried over your poor, thin little hands when first I came to see you, but now your wrist looks as if it would snap in two. Oh, Dolly, darling, if—if you should die!"

Was it quite a new thought, or was it because it had never come home to her in such a form before, this thought of Death? She started as if she had been stung.

"If I should die!" she echoed. "*Die!*"

"Phemie, my dear," said Miss MacDowlas, opening the door, "the professor is waiting down-stairs."

And so, having let her sorrow get the better of her, Phemie had no time to stay to see if her indiscretion had done harm. If she did not go now, she might not be allowed fresh grace; and so she was fain to tear herself away.

"I ought n't to have said it!" she bewailed, as she kissed Dolly again and again. "Please forget it; oh, do, please, forget it! I did not mean it, indeed! And now I shall be so frightened and unhappy!"

"Phemie," said Dolly, quietly, "you have not frightened *me*; so you haven't the least need to trouble yourself, my dear."

But she was not exactly sorry to be left alone, and when she was alone her thoughts wandered back to that first evening Phemie had called,—the evening she had gone to the glass to look at her changed face. She had sat in the basket-chair then,—she lay back upon her cushions now, and a crowd of new thoughts came trooping through her mind. The soft air was scented and balmy; the twilight sky was a dome of purple, jewel-hung; people's voices came murmuring from the gardens below; the far-off music floated to her through the window.

"If I should *die!*" she said, in a wondering whisper,—"I, Dolly Crewe! How strange it sounds! Have I never thought that I could die before, or is it strange because now it is so real and near? When I used to talk about death to Grif, it always seemed so far away from both of us; it seemed to me as if I was not good enough or unreal enough to be near to Death,—great, solemn Death itself. Why, I could look at myself, and wonder at the thought of how much I shall see and know if I should die. Grif, how much I should have to tell you, dear,—only that people are always afraid of spirits, and perhaps you would be afraid, too,—even of me! What would they say at home? Dear, old, broken-hearted fellow, what would *you* say, if I should die?"

She could not help thinking about those at home; about Aimée and Mollie and Phil and Toinette, sitting together in the dear old littered room at Bloomsbury Place,—the dear old untidy room, where she had sat with Grif so often! How would they all bear it when the letter came to tell them she was gone, and would never be with them and share their pleasures and troubles again! And then, strangely enough, she began to picture herself as she would look; perhaps, laid out in this very room, a dimly outlined figure, under a white sheet,—not her old self, but a solemn, wondrous marble form, before whose motionless, mysterious presence they would feel awed.

"And they would turn down the white covering and look at me," she found herself saying. "And they would wonder at me, and feel that I was far away. Oh, how they would wonder at me! And, at the very last, before they hid my face forever under the coffin-lid, they would all kiss me in that tender, solemn way,—all but Grif, who loved me best; and Grif would not be there!"

And the piteous rain of heavy tears that rolled down her cheeks, and fell upon her pillow, was not for herself,—not for her own pain and weariness and anguish,—not' for the white, worn face, that would be shut beneath the coffin-lid, but for Grif,—for Grif,—for Grif, who, coming back some day to learn the truth, might hear that she had died!

CHAPTER XVII.
DO YOU KNOW THAT SHE IS DYING?

IT had come at last,—the letter from Geneva, for which they all had waited with such anxious hearts and so much of dread. The postman, bringing it by the morning's delivery, and handing it through the opened door to Aimée, had wondered a little at her excited manner,—she was always excited when these letters came; and the moment she had entered the parlor, holding the hurriedly read note,—it was scarcely more than a note,—there was not one of them who did not understand all before she spoke.

Mrs. Phil burst into tears; Phil himself laid down his brush and changed color; Mollie silently clung to Tod as a refuge, and looked up with trembling lips.

Mrs. Phil was the first to speak.

"You may as well tell us the worst," she said; "but it is easy enough to guess what it is, without being told."

"It is almost the *very* worst," answered Aimée.

"Miss MacDowlas wants me to go to them at once. *She* is so ill that if a change does not take place, she will not live many weeks, and she has asked for me."

They all knew only too well that "she" meant Dolly.

"Then," said Phil, "you must go at once."

"I can go to-day," she answered. "I knew it would come to this, and I am ready to leave London at any moment."

There was no delay. Her small box was even then ready packed and corded for the journey. She had taken Miss MacDowlas's warning in time. It would not have been like this heavy-hearted wise one to disregard it. She would have been ready to go to Dolly at ten minutes' notice, if she had been in India. She was not afraid, either, of making the journey alone. It was not a very terrible journey, she said. Secretly, she had a fancy that perhaps Dolly would like to see her by herself first, to have a few quiet days alone with her, in which she could become used to the idea of the farewell the rest would come to say. And in her mind the poor little oracle had another fancy, too, and this fancy she confided to Mollie before bidding her good-by.

"Mollie," she said, "I am going to leave a charge in your hands."

"Is it anything about Dolly?" asked Mollie, making fruitless efforts to check her affectionate tears.

"I wish you would leave me something to do for Dolly, Aimée."

"It is something connected with Dolly;" returned Aimée. "I want you to keep constantly on the watch for Griffith."

"For Griffith!" Mollie exclaimed. "How can I, when I don't know whether he is in England or not?"

"He is in England," Aimée replied. "He is in London, for Mr. Gowan has seen him."

"In London—and Dolly in Switzerland, perhaps dying!"

"He does not know that, or he would have been with her before now," said Aimée. "Once let him know that she is ill, and he will be with her. I know him well enough to be sure of that. And it is my impression that if he went to her at the eleventh hour, when she might seem to us to be at the very last, he would bring her back to life. It is Grif she is dying for, and only Grif can save her."

"And what do you want me to do?" anxiously.

"To watch for him constantly, as I said. Don't *you* think, Mollie, that he might come back, if it were only into the street to look at the house, in a restless sort of remembrance of the time when they used to be so happy?"

"It would not be unlike him," answered Mollie, slowly. "He was very fond of Dolly. Oh, he was very fond of her!"

"Fond of her! He loved her better than his life, and does still, wherever he may be. Something tells me he will come, and that is why I want you to watch. Watch at the window as constantly as you can, but more particularly at dusk; and if you should see him, Mollie, don't wait a second. Run out to him, and *make* him listen to you. Ah, poor fellow, he will listen eagerly and penitently enough, if you only say to him that Dolly is dying."

"Very well," said Mollie, "I will remember." And thus the wise one took her departure.

It was twilight in Bloomsbury Place, and Mollie crouched before the parlor window, resting her chin upon her hands, and looking out, pretty much as Aimée had looked out on that winter evening months ago, when Mr. Gerald Chandos had first presented himself to her mind as an individual to be dreaded.

Three days had passed since the wise one left London,—three miserable, dragging days they had seemed to Mollie, despite their summer warmth and sunshine. Real anxiety and sorrow were new experiences in Vagabondia; little trials they had felt, and often enough small unpleasantnesses, privations, and disappointments; but death and grief were new. And they were just beginning to realize broadly the blow which had fallen upon them; hard as it was to believe at first, they were beginning slowly to comprehend the sad meaning of the lesson they were learning now for the first time. What each had felt a fear of in secret was coming to pass at last, and there was no help against it.

Phil went about his work looking as none of them had ever seen him look before. Mrs. Phil's tears fell thick and fast. Not understanding the mystery, she could blame nobody but Grif, and Grif she could not forgive. To Mollie the house seemed like a grave. She could think of nothing but Dolly,—Dolly, white and worn and altered, lying upon her couch, her eyes closed, her breath fluttering faintly. She wondered if she was afraid to die. She herself had a secret girlish terror of death and its strange solemnness, and she so pitied Dolly that sometimes she could not contain her grief, and was obliged to hide herself until her tears spent themselves.

She had been crying during all this twilight hour she had knelt at the window. She was so lonely that it seemed impossible to do anything else. It would have been bad enough to bear the suspense even if Aimée had been with her, but without Aimée it was dreadful. The tears slipped down her cheeks and rolled away, and she did not even attempt to dry them, her affectionate grief had mastered her completely. But she was roused at length. Some one crossed the street from the pavement opposite the house; and when this some one entered the gate and ascended the steps, she rose slowly, half-reluctant, half-comforted, and with a faint thrill at her heart. It was Ralph Gowan, and she was not wise enough or self-controlled enough yet to see Ralph Gowan without feeling her pulses quicken.

When she opened the door he did not greet her as usual, but spoke to her at once in a low, hurried tone.

"Mollie, where is Aimée?" he asked.

Her tears began to flow again; she could not help giving way.

"You had better come in," she said, half turning away from him and speaking brokenly. "Aimée is not here. She left London three days ago. Dolly—"

"Dolly is worse!" he said, because she could not finish.

She nodded, with a heart too full for words.

He stepped inside, and, closing the door, laid his hand upon her shoulder.

"Then, Mollie," he said, "I must come to you."

He did not wait a moment, but led her gently enough into the parlor, and, blinded as she was by her tears, she saw that instant that he had not come without a reason.

"Don't cry," he said. "I want you to be brave and calm now,—for Dolly's sake. I want your help,—for Dolly's sake, remember."

She recollected Aimée's words—"Mr. Gowan has seen him"—and a sudden light flashed upon her. The tears seemed to dry of their own accord all at once, as she looked up.

"Yes," she answered.

He knew, without hearing another word, that he might trust her.

"Can you guess whom I have just this moment seen?" he said.

"Yes," sprang from her lips, without a second's hesitation. "You have seen Grif."

"I have seen Grif," he answered. "He is at the corner of the street now. If I had attempted to speak to him he would have managed to avoid me; and because I knew that, I came here, hoping to find Aimée; but since Aimée is not here—"

"I can go," she interrupted him, all a-tremble with eagerness. "He will listen to me; he was fond of me, too, and I was fond of him. Oh! let me go now!"

That bright little scarlet shawl of Dolly's lay upon the sofa, and she snatched it up with shaking hands and threw it over her head and shoulders.

"If I can speak to him once, he will listen," she said; "and if he listens, Dolly will be saved. She won't die if Grif comes back. She can't die if Grif comes back. Oh, Dolly, my darling, you saved me, and I am going to try to save you."

She was out in the street in two minutes, standing on the pavement, looking up and down, and then she ran across to the other side. She kept close to the houses, so that she might be in their shadow, and a little sob broke from her as she hurried along,—a sob of joy and fear and excitement. At the end of the row of houses somebody was standing under the street lamp,—a man. Was it Grif,—or could Grif have gone even in this short time? Fate could never have been so cruel to him, to her, to them all, as to let him come so near and then go away without hearing that Dolly was lying at death's portals, and no one could save her but himself and the tender power of the sweet, old, much-tried love. Oh, no, no! It was Grif indeed; for as she neared the place where he stood, she saw his face in the lamp-light,—a grief-worn, pallid face, changed and haggard and desperate,—a sight that made her cry out aloud.

He had not seen her or even heard her. He stood there looking toward the house she had left, and seeing, as it seemed, nothing else. Only the darkness had hidden her from him. His eyes were fixed upon the dim light that burned in Dolly's window. She had not meant to speak until she stood close to him; but when she was within a few paces of him her excitement mastered her.

"Grif," she cried out; "Grif, is it you?"

And when he turned, with a great start, to look at her, she was upon him,—her hands outstretched, the light upon her face, the tears streaming down her cheeks,—sobbing aloud.

"Mollie," he answered, "is it *you?*" And she saw that he almost staggered.

She could not speak at first. She clung to his arm so tightly that he could scarcely have broken away from her if he had tried. But he did not try; it seemed as though her touch made him weak,—weaker than he had ever been before in his life. Beauty as she was, they had always thought her in some way like Dolly, and, just now, with Dolly's gay little scarlet shawl slipping away from her face, with the great grief in her imploring eyes, with that innocent appealing trick of the clinging hands, she might almost have been Dolly's self.

Try as he might, he could not regain his self-control. He was sheerly powerless before her.

"Mollie," he said, "what has brought you here? Why have you come?"

"I have come," she answered, "for Dolly's sake!"

The vague fear he had felt at first caught hold upon him with all the fulness of its strength.

"For Dolly's sake!" he echoed. "Nay, Dolly has done with me, and I with her." And though he tried to speak bitterly, he failed.

She was too fond of Dolly, and too full of grief to spare him after that. Unstrung as she was, her reproach burst forth from her without a softened touch. "Dolly has done with earth. Dolly's life is over," she sobbed. "Do you know that she is dying? Yes, dying,—our own bright Dolly,—and you—*you* have killed her!"

She had not thought how cruel it would sound, and the next instant she was full of terror at the effect of her own words. He broke loose from her,—*fell* loose from her, one might better describe it, for it was his own weight rather than any effort which dragged him from her grasp. He staggered and caught hold of the iron railings to save himself, and there hung, staring at her with a face like a dead man.

"My God!" he said,—not another word.

"You must not give way like that," she cried out, in a new fright. "Oh, how could I speak so! Aimée would have told you better. I did not mean to be so hard. You can save her if you will. She will not die, Grif, if you go to her. She only wants *you*. Grif,—Grif,—you look as if you could not understand what I am saying." And she wrung her hands.

And, indeed, it scarcely seemed as if he did understand, though at last he spoke.

"Where is she?" he said. "Not here? You say I must 'go' to her."

"No, she is not here. She is at Lake Geneva. Miss MacDowlas took her there because she grew so weak, and she has grown weaker ever since, and three days ago they sent for Aimée to come to her, because—because they think she is going to die."

"And you say that *I* have done this?"

"I ought n't to have put it that way, it sounds so cruel, but—but she has never been like herself since the night you went away, and we have all known that it was her unhappiness that made her ill. She could not get over it, and though she tried to hide it, she was worn out. She loved you so."

He interrupted her.

"If she is dying for me," he said, hoarsely, "she must have loved me, and if she has loved me through all this,—God help us both!"

"How could you go away and leave her all alone after all those years?" demanded Mollie. "We cannot understand it. No one knows but Aimée, and Dolly has told her that you were not to blame. Why did you go?"

"*You* do not know?" he said. "You should know, Mollie, of all others. *You* were with her when she played that miserable coquette's trick,—that pitiful trick, so unlike herself,—you were with her that night when she let Gowan keep her away from me, when I waited for her coming hour after hour. I saw you with them when he was bidding her goodnight."

They had hidden their secret well all these months, but it was to be hidden no longer now. It flashed upon her like an electric shock. She remembered a hundred things,—a hundred little mysteries she had met and been puzzled by, in Aimee's manner; she remembered all she had heard, and all she had wondered at, and her heart seemed turned to stone. The flush of weeping died out of her face, her hands fell and hung down at her side, her tears were gone; nothing seemed left to her but blank horror.

"Was it because she did not come that night, that you left her to die?" she asked, in a labored voice. "Was it because you saw her with Ralph Gowan— was it because you found out that she had been with him, that you went away and let her break her heart? Tell me!"

He answered her, "Yes."

"Then," she said, turning to face him, still cold, and almost rigid, "it is *I* who have killed her, and not you."

"You!" he exclaimed.

She did not wait to choose her words, or try to soften the story of her own humiliation.

"If she dies," she said, "she has died for me."

And without further preface she told him all. How she had let Gerald Chandos flatter and gain power over her, until the climax of her folly had been the wild, wilful escapade of that miserable long-past day. How Ralph Gowan had discovered her romantic secret, and revealed it to Dolly. How they had followed and rescued her; even how Dolly had awakened her from her dangerous dream with that light touch, and had drawn her away from the brink of an abyss, with her loving, girlish hands; and she ended with an outburst of anguish.

"Why did n't she tell you?" she said. "For my sake she did not want the rest to know; but why did not she tell you? I cannot understand."

"She tried to tell me," he said, in an agony of self-reproach, as he began to see what he had done,—"she tried to tell me, and I would not hear her."

All his bygone sufferings—and, Heaven knows, he had suffered bitterly and heavily enough—sank into insignificance before the misery of this hour. To know how true and pure of heart she had been; to know how faithful, unselfish, sweet; to remember how she had met him with a tender little cry of joy, with outstretched, innocent hands, that he had thrust aside; to remember the old golden days in which she had so clung to him, and brightened his life; to think how he had left her lying upon the sofa that night, her white face drooping piteously against the cushions; to have all come back to him and know that he only was to blame; to know it all too late. Nay, a whole life of future bliss could never quite efface the memory of such a passion of remorse and pain.

"Oh, my God!" he prayed, "have mercy upon me!" And then he turned upon Mollie. "Tell me where to go to; tell me, and let me go. I must go to her now without a moment's waiting. My poor, faithful little girl,—my pretty Dolly! Dying,—dying! No, I don't believe it,—I won't. She cannot die yet. Fate has been cruel enough to us, but it cannot be so cruel as that. Love will *make* her live."

He dashed down Mollie's directions in desperate, feverish haste upon a leaf of his memorandum-book, and then he bade her good-by.

"God bless you, dear!" he said. "Perhaps you have saved us both. I am going to her now. Pray for me."

"I ought rather to pray for myself," she said; "but for me you would never have been separated. I have done it all."

And a few minutes after he had gone, Ralph Gowan, who had awaited her return before the window, turned to see her enter the room like a spirit and fling herself down before him, looking white and shaken and pale.

"I have found it all out now," she cried. "I have found it all out. I have done all this, Mr. Gowan; it is through me her heart is broken, and if she dies, I shall have caused her death, as surely as if I had killed her with my own hand. Oh, save me from thinking she will die,—help me to think she will live,— help me!"

There was no one else to help her, and the blind terror of the thought was so great that she must have help, or die. To have so injured Dolly, whom she so loved,—to have, by her own deed, brought that dread shadow of Death upon Dolly, who had saved her! Her heart seemed crushed. If Aimée had been there; but Aimée was not, so she stretched out her hands to the man she had so innocently loved. And as she so knelt before him,—so fair, in the childlike *abandon* of her grief, so guileless and trusting in her sudden, sweet appeal, so helpless against the world, even against herself,—his man's heart was touched and stirred as it had never been before,—as even Dolly herself had not stirred it.

"My poor child!" he said, taking her hands and drawing her nearer to himself. "My poor, pretty Mollie, come to me."

And why not, my reader? If one rose is not for us, the sun shines on many another as sweet and quite as fair; and what is more, it is more than probable that if we had seen the last rose first, we should have loved the first rose last. It is only when, like Dolly and Grif, we have watched our rose from its first peep of the leaf, and have grown with its growth, that there can be no other rose but one.

"*Le roi est mort—Vive le roi!*"

CHAPTER XVIII.
GRIF!

THERE was a hush upon the guests at the pretty little inn. Most of them were not sojourners of a day, who came and went, as they did at the larger and busier hotels,—they were comfortable people who enjoyed themselves in their own quiet way and so had settled down for the time being. Accordingly they had leisure to become interested in each other; and there were few of them who did not feel a friendly interest in the pretty, pale English girl, who, report said, was fading silently out of life in her bright room up-stairs. When Aimée arrived, the most sympathetic shook their heads dubiously.

"The sister is here," they said; "a thoughtful little English creature with a child's face and a woman's air. They sent for her. One can easily guess what that means."

Any one but Aimée would have been crushed at the outset by the shock of the change which was to be seen in the poor little worn figure, now rarely moved from its invalid's couch. But Aimée bore the blow with outward quiet at least. If she shed tears Dolly did not see them, and if she mourned Dolly was not disturbed by her sorrow.

"I have come to help Miss MacDowlas to take care of you, Dolly," she said, when she gave her her greeting kiss, and Dolly smiled and kissed her in return.

But it was a terribly hard matter to fight through at first. Of course, as the girl had become weaker she had lost power over herself. She was restless and listless by turns. Sometimes she started at every sound, and again she lay with closed eyes for hours, dozing the day away. The mere sight of her in this latter state threw poor Phemie into an agony of terror and distress.

"It is so like Death," she would say to Aimée. "It seems as if we could never rouse her again."

And then again she would rally a little, and at such times she would insist upon being propped up and allowed to talk, and her eyes would grow large and bright, and a spot of hectic color would burn on her cheeks. She did not even mention her trouble during the first two days of Aimée's visit, but on the third afternoon she surprised her by broaching the subject suddenly. She had been dozing, and on awakening she began to talk.

"Aimée," she said, "where is Miss MacDowlas?"

"In her room. I persuaded her to go and lie down."

"I am very glad," quietly. "I want to do something particular. I want Grif's letters, Aimée."

"Where are they?" Aimée asked.

"In a box in my trunk. I should like to have them now."

Aimée brought them to her without comment. The box had not been large enough to hold them all, and there was an extra packet tied with that dear old stereotyped blue ribbon.

"What a many there are!" said Dolly, when she came to the couch with them. "You will have to sit down by me and hold some of them. One can write a great many letters in seven years."

The wise one sat down, obediently holding the box upon her knee. There were so many letters in it that it was quite heavy.

"I am going to look them over and tie them in packages, according to their dates," said Dolly. "He will like to have them when he comes back."

It would not have been natural for her to preserve her calmness all through the performance of her task. Her first glance at the first letter brought the tears, and she cried quietly as she passed from one to the other. They were such tender, impetuous letters. The very headings—"My Darling," "My pretty Darling," "My own sweetest Life"—impassioned, youthful-sounding, and Grif-like, cut her to the heart. Ah! how terrible it would be for him to see them again, as he would see them! She was pitying him far more than she was pitying herself.

It was a work not soon over, but she finished it at length. The packets were assorted and tied with new ribbon, and she lay down for a few minutes to rest.

"You will give them to him, Aimée?" she said. "I think he will come some day; but if he does not, you must keep them yourself. I should not like people to read them—afterwards. Love-letters won't stand being read by strangers. I have often laughed and told him ours would n't. I am going to write a last one, however, this afternoon. You are to give it him, with the 'dead' letter—but they are all dead letters, are they not?"

"Dolly," said Aimée, with a desperate effort, "you speak as if you were sure you were—going."

There was a silence, and then a soft, low, tremulous laugh,—the merest echo of a laugh. Despite her long suffering Dolly was Dolly yet. She would not let them mourn over her.

"Going," she said, "well—I think I am. Yes," half reflectively, "I think I must be. It cannot mean anything else,—this feeling, can it? It was a long time before I quite believed it myself, Aimée, but now I should be obliged to believe it if I did not wish to."

"And do you wish to, now?"

That little silence again, and then—

"I should like to see Grif,—I want Grif,—that is all."

She managed to write her last love-letter after this, and to direct it and tie it with the letter which had returned to her,—the "dead" letter. But the effort seemed to tire her very much, and when all was done and her restless excitement had died out, she looked less like herself than ever. She could talk no more, and was so weak and prostrate that Aimée was alarmed into summoning Miss MacDowlas.

But Miss MacDowlas could only shake her head. "We cannot do anything to rouse her," she said. "It is often so. If the end comes, it will come in this way. She feels no pain."

That night Aimée wrote to those at home. They must come at once if they wanted to see Dolly. She watched all night by the bedside herself; she could not have slept if she had gone to her own room, and so she remained with Dolly, watching her doze and waken, starting from nervous sleeps and sinking into them again.

"There will not be many nights through which I can watch," she said to herself. "Even this might be the last." And then she turned to the window, and cried silently, thinking of Grif, and wondering what she should say to him, if they ever met again.

How could she say to him, "Dolly is dead! Dolly died because you left her!"

Another weary day and night, and then the old change came again. The feverish strength seemed to come once more. Dolly would be propped up, and talk. Before very long Aimée began to fancy that she had something she wished to say to Miss Mac-Dowlas. She followed her movements with eager, unsatisfied eyes, and did not seem at ease until she sat down near her. Then when she had secured her attention the secret revealed itself. She had something to say about Grif.

Gradually, during the long weary weeks of her illness she had learned to place much confidence in Miss MacDowlas. Her affectionate nature had clung to her. In telling anecdotes of life in Vagabondia, she had talked of Grif,— Vagabondia would not have been Vagabondia without Grif,—and there was always a thrill of faithful love in her simplest mention of him. Truly, Miss

MacDowlas beheld her reprobate nephew in a new light, surrounded by a halo of innocent romance and unselfish tenderness. This poor little soul, who was breaking her heart for his sake, showed him sinned against but never sinning, unfortunate but never to blame, showed him honest, sweet of nature, true, and faultless. Where were his faults in the eyes of his first and last love? The simple, whimsical stories of their loves and lovers' quarrels, of their small economies and perfect faith in the future,—a faith so sadly wrecked, as it seemed, by cruel Fate,—brought tears into Miss MacDowlas's eyes. Eloquent, affectionate Dolly won her over before she knew what she was thinking about. He could not have been such a reprobate, after all,—this Griffith Donne, who had so often roused her indignation. Perhaps he could not help being literary and wearing a shabby coat and a questionable hat. And Dolly had in the end begun to see how her long-fixed opinion had softened and changed. So she had courage to plead for Grif this afternoon. She wanted to be sure that if he should ever come back, there would be a hand outstretched to help him.

"He only wanted help," she said; "and no one has ever helped him, though he tried so hard and worked so. Aimée knows how hard he worked, don't you, Aimée?"

"Yes," answered Aimée, turning her working face away.

"I should like you to promise," said Dolly, wistfully, to Miss MacDowlas. "It would make me so much happier. You have been so kind to me,—I am sure you will be kind to him,—poor Grif,—poor fellow!"

Miss MacDowlas bent over her, touched to the heart.

"My dear," she said, "he shall never want help again. He must have been worthy of so much love, or he would never have won it. I owe him some recompense, too. If I had not been so stupidly blind I might have saved you both all this pain. I have grown very fond of you, Dolly," she ended; and then, being quite overcome, she kissed the pretty hair suddenly, gave the thin hand an almost motherly squeeze, and made the best of her way out of the room.

"Aimée," said Dolly, "do you remember how often I have made fun of her, when we were all so happy together? We made a good many mistakes, even in Vagabondia, did n't we?" And then she closed her eyes and lay silent, with wet lashes resting on her cheek.

In speaking of this afternoon, long afterwards, Aimée said it seemed the longest and weariest she had ever known. It was extremely hot, and the very air seemed laden with heavy languor. The sun beat down upon the outer world whitely, and scarcely a leaf stirred. Miss MacDowlas did not return, and Dolly, though she was not asleep, lay quite still and did not open her eyes again. So Aimée sat and watched at her side, wondering how the day would end,—wondering if Phil and 'Toinette and Mollie would arrive before it was too late,—wondering what that strange last hour would be like, and how Dolly would bear it when it came, and how they themselves would bear to think of it when it was over.

She was not quite sure how long she sat watching so, but she fancied that it must have been two or three hours, or even more. She got up at last and drew down the green blinds as noiselessly as possible, and then went back to her place and rested her head upon the pillow near Dolly's, feeling drowsy and tired,—she had slept so little during the past few nights.

Dolly moved restlessly, stretching out her hand to Aimée's and opening her eyes all at once—ah! what large, hollow, shadowy eyes they were!

"I am very tired," she murmured, "so tired and so weak, Aimée," dreamily. "I suppose this is what you would call dying of a broken heart. It seems so queer that I should die of a broken heart." "Oh, Dolly—Dolly!" Aimée whispered, "our own dearest dear, we never thought such pain could come to you."

But even the next moment Dolly seemed to have lost herself, her eyes closed again and she did not speak. So Aimée lay holding her hand, until the indoor silence, the shadow of the room, and the sound of the droning bees outside lulled her into a sort of doze, and her own eyelids fell wearily.

A minute, was it, five or ten, or more than that?

She could not say. She only remembered her own last words, the warmth, the shadow, the droning of the bees, and the gradual losing consciousness, and then she was wide awake again,—awakened by a strange, wild cry, which, thrilling and echoing through the room, made her start up with a beating heart and look towards the door.

"Grif!"

That was all,—only this single rapturous cry, and Dolly, who had before seemed not to have the strength of a child, was sitting up, a white, tremulous figure, with outstretched arms and fluttering breath, and Grif was standing upon the threshold.

Even when she had blamed him most, Aimée had pitied him also; but she had never pitied him as she did when he strode to the couch and took the weak, worn, tremulous little figure in his arms. He could not speak,—neither spoke. Dolly lay upon his breast crying like a little child. But for him—his grief was terrible; and when the loving hand was laid upon his cheek and Dolly found her first words, they only seemed to make it worse.

"Don't cry," she said. "Don't cry, dear. Kiss me!" He kissed her lips, her hands, her hair. He could not bear it. She was so like, yet so fearfully unlike, the winsome, tender creature he had loved so long.

"Oh, my God!" he cried, in his old mad way, "you are dying, and if you die it will be I who have murdered you!"

She moved a little nearer, so that her pretty face rested against his shoulder and she could lift her streaming eyes to his, her old smile shining through her tears.

"Dear old fellow," she said, "darling old fellow, whom I love with all my soul! I shall live just to prove that you have done nothing of the kind!"

It was only Grif she wanted,—only Grif, and Grif had come.

CHAPTER XIX.
ROSE COLOR.

OF course she recovered. What else could she do? If a man is dying for want of bread and you give him bread enough and to spare, he will regain strength and life, will he not? And so with Dolly. Having found Grif, she had nothing to die for and so much to live for, that she lived. It seemed, too, that even if she had been inclined to die, Grif would have held her fast to earth. It was worse than useless to attempt to delude him into leaving her side, even for an hour; he hung over the invalid's couch, in such an anguish of half-despairing anxiety that the hearts of the unceremoniously deposed nurses were quite touched. He watched every change in Dolly's face, every brightening or fading tint in her cheek, every glance of her eyes; he followed her every movement. If she was tired of her posture, he could raise her or lay her down and settle her cushions as no one else could; if she was strong enough to listen, he could talk to her; if she was too weak, he could be silent.

But naturally there was much to talk about. Not that the period of his absence had been a very eventful one. It was as Ralph Gowan had fancied,—he had been living quietly enough in a secluded London street during the whole of the time; but Dolly found the history of his self-banishment both interesting and soul-moving. The story of his miseries brought the tears into her eyes, and his picture of what he had suffered on that unhappy night, when he had rushed out of the house and left her insensible upon the sofa, made her cling to his hand convulsively and sob outright.

"I can scarcely believe you are here,—quite safe," she would say; "you might have killed yourself."

And indeed he had been in no small danger of so doing.

Among all this, however, there was one bit of brightness,—a wonderful piece of news he told her that very day after his return. Fortune had, with her usual caprice, condescended to smile upon him at last. Incredible as it appeared, he had "got into something," and this "something" was actually remunerative,—reasonably remunerative, if not extravagantly so. Four hundred a year would pay the rent of the figurative house in Putney or elsewhere, and buy the green sofa and appurtenances, at least. Dolly could scarcely believe it, and, indeed, he scarcely believed it himself.

"It seemed as if, when I had lost all else, this came to add to the bitterness of the loss," he said. "I am afraid I was far from being as grateful, at first, as I ought to have been. I could only remember how happy such luck would have made us both if it had only come a year or so earlier. And the very day I got the place I passed the upholsterer's where the parlor furniture was,—

green sofa and all. And I went home with the firm intention of blowing my brains out. The only thing that saved me that day was the fact that my landlady met me at the door with a miserable story about her troubles and her taxes, and by the time I had listened for half an hour, and done something she wanted done, I had cooled down a little, though I was wretched enough."

"The 'something' was paying the taxes, was n't it?" questioned Dolly.

"Something of that kind," admitted Griffith.

"Ah," said Dolly, "I thought so."

Very naturally Griffith felt some slight embarrassment on encountering Miss MacDowlas, having a rather unpleasant recollection of various incidents of the past. But Miss Berenice faced the matter in a different manner and with her usual decision of character. She had made up her mind to receive Griffith Donne as a respectable fact, and then, through Dolly's eloquence, she had learned to regard him with even a sort of affection,—a vague affection, of course, at the outset, but one which would ripen with time. Thus she rather surprised him by confronting him upon an entirely new ground. She was cordial and amiable, and on the first opportunity she explained her change of feeling with great openness.

"I have heard so much of you from Dolly," she said, "that I am convinced I have known nothing of you before. I hope we shall be better friends. I am very fond of Dolly. I wish I had known her three or four years ago."

And there was such a softened tenderness in her thin, unpromising face, that from thenceforward Griffith's doubts were removed and his opinion altered, as hers had done. The woman who had loved and pitied Dolly when she so sorely needed pity and love, must be worthy of gratitude and affection.

Phil and 'Toinette and Mollie arriving, in the deepest affliction, to receive Dolly's last farewell, were rather startled by the turn affairs had taken. Changed as she was, the face she turned to greet them was not the face of a dying girl. She was deplorably pale and shrunken and thin, but the light of life was in her eyes and a new ring was in her voice. She had vitality enough to recognize fresh charms in Tod, and spirit enough to make a few jokes.

"She won't die," commented Phil to his wife when they retired to their room.

"No," said Mrs. Phil, discreetly, "it is not likely, now Grif has come back. But it won't do to waste the journey, Phil, so we may as well stay awhile. We have not been anywhere out of London this summer."

Accordingly, with their usual genius for utilizing all things, they prolonged their visit and made it into a kind of family festival; and since their anxiety on Dolly's behalf was at an end, they managed to enjoy it heartily. They walked here, and rode there, and explored unheard-of points and places; they kept the quiet people in the quiet hotel in a constant state of pleasant ferment with their good spirits and unceremonious friendliness. Mollie and Aimée and Mrs. Phil excited such general admiration that when they made their appearance at the *table d'hôte* there was a visible stir and brightening, and Dolly was so constantly inquired after, that there were serious thoughts entertained of issuing hourly bulletins. The reaction of high spirits after their fears was something exhilarating even to beholders.

And while they enjoyed themselves, and explored, and instituted a high carnival of innocent rejoicing, Dolly directed all her energies to the task of getting well and filling Grif's soul with hope and bliss. As soon as she had fully recovered they were to be married,—not a day, not an hour, longer would Grif consent to wait. His only trouble was that she would not be strong enough to superintend the purchase of the green sofa and appurtenances. Aimée had, however, proved his rock of refuge as usual They were to return to London together and make the necessary preparations, and then the wedding was to take place in Geneva, and the bride would be carried home in triumph.

"We have been so long in travelling toward the little house at Putney that it will be the nicest bridal tour we could have," said Dolly.

Then, of course, came some pleasant excitement in connection with the trousseau, in which everybody was involved. The modest hotel had never before been in such a state of mind through secret preparations, as it was when Dolly was well enough to sit up and walk about and choose patterns. Her instinct of interest in worldly vanities sustained that young person marvellously. When Grif and Aimée had returned to London she found herself well enough to give lengthy audiences to Mrs. Phil, who, with Miss MacDowlas, had taken the business of purchasing in hand, and to discuss fabrics and fashions by the hour. She remembered Grifs enthusiasm on the subject of her toilets, and she was wholly ruled by a secret and laudable ambition to render herself as irresistible as possible. She exercised to its utmost her inventive genius, and lay awake at night to devise simple but coquettish feminine snares of attire to delight and bewilder him in the future.

She might well progress rapidly toward health and strength. By the time the house was ready for her reception she was well enough to drive out and explore with the rest, though she looked frail and unsubstantial by contrast with Mollie's bloom and handsome Mrs. Phil's grand curves. She was gaining flesh and color every day, but the slender throat and wrists and transparent hands were a bitter reproach to Grif even then, and it would be many weeks before she could again indulge in that old harmless vanity in her dimples and smooth roundness of form.

Mollie mourned over her long, in secret, and, indeed, was so heart-wrung by the sight of the change she found in her, that the very day of her arrival had not drawn to its close before she burst upon her with a remorseful appeal for forgiveness.

"But even if you forgive me I shall not forgive myself," she said. "I shall never forget that dreadful night when I found out that it was all my fault, and that you had borne everything without telling me. If—if it had not been for—for Mr. Gowan, Dolly, I think I should have died."

"If it had not been for whom?" asked Dolly.

"Mr. Gowan," answered Miss Mollie, dropping her eyes, her very throat dyed with guilty blushes.

"Ah!" said Dolly. "And what did Mr. Gowan do, Mollie?"

"He was very kind—and sympathizing," replied Mollie.

"He always is sympathizing," looking at her with affectionate shrewdness. "He is very nice, is n't he, Mollie?"

"Yes," said Mollie. "Very nice, indeed."

"And I dare say you were so frightened and wretched that you cried?"

"Yes," confessed the abashed catechised.

"I thought so." And then, conjuring up in her mind's eye a picture of Mollie, heart-broken, appealing and in tears, beauteous, piteous, and grief-abandoned, she added, with tender impulsiveness, "I don't wonder that he sympathized with you, Mollie."

It revealed itself shortly afterward that his sympathy had not confined itself to the night Mollie called "dreadful." Since that night he had been a frequent visitor at Bloomsbury Place,—as frequent a visitor as he had been in the days when Dolly had been wont so to entertain him.

A week after the return of Aimée and Grif from London, there fell again upon the modest hotel a hush; but it was not the hush of sympathetic silence which had fallen upon it before,—it was merely a sort of reaction after a slight excitement. The pretty English girl had, to every one's wonder, suddenly returned to earth and had been married! The wisest were bewildered, but such was the fact, nevertheless; nobody could exactly comprehend, but who could deny it? It was a mystery, indeed, until one day, some time after, a usually phlegmatic matron was struck with an idea, and accordingly propounded to her friends a somewhat vaguely expressed problem.

"After the appearance of the lover one heard no more that she was dying?"

"Just so."

"Perhaps the lover had something to do with the matter?", "Ah!"

"Perhaps she was dying for him, and his coming cured her?"

"Exactly. That must have been the case."

And thenceforth the matter was deemed settled. However, the gay, light-hearted party of English had taken their departure,—the friendly young artist who sketched and smoked and enjoyed himself; his handsome young wife, who sketched and played with her handsome child, and enjoyed *herself*; the beautiful younger sister, who blushed and was charmingly bashful, but enjoyed herself; the fair little saint with the grave youthful face, who took care of them all, and yet enjoyed *herself*,—the lover, the elder lady, the guest who came to be groomsman, the bride,—they were all gone at last, and their absence was the cause of the hush of which I speak.

There had been a wedding,—a joyous, light-hearted wedding, in which the bride had looked pretty and flower-like and ethereal,—a fragile creature enough in her white dress and under her white veil, but a delightfully happy creature, notwithstanding,—in which the bridegroom had been plainly filled with chivalric tenderness and bliss,—in which the two sisters had been charming beyond measure, and the awkward, affectionate girl friend from the seminary had blushed herself into a high fever. There could not have been a more prettily orthodox wedding, said the beholders. Somehow its glow of young romance touched people, it was so evident that the young couple were fond of each other, and happy and hopeful. There were those who, seeing it solemnized in the small church, shed a few tears, they knew not why, when Grif lifted Dolly's veil and kissed her without a word.

"It is all rose color to them," said one of these soft-hearted ones, apologetically, to her neighbor.

Rose color! I should think it was.

But if it was all rose color then, what was it that first evening they spent at home,—in their own home, in the little house which was so bright and pretty that it seemed more like a dream than a reality? What color did life look when Grif led Dolly across the threshold, half trembling himself for very joy? What color did it look when he shut the door of the little parlor, and, turning round, went to her and folded her in his arms close to his beating heart?

Rose color! It was golden and more than golden! And yet, for the first minute, Dolly could not speak, and the next she laid her cheek in her favorite place, on the lapel of Grif's coat, and burst into a great gush of soft, warm tears,—tears without a touch of any other element, however, than love and happiness.

"*Home*, Grif!" she said.

He was quite pale and he had almost lost his voice, too, but he managed to answer her, unsteadily.

"Yes, Dolly," he said; "home!" And he stroked the bright hair upon his breast, with a world of meaning in his touch.

"Do you think," she said next, "that I am good enough and wise enough to take care of it, and to take care of *you*, Grif?"

"Do you think," he said, "that I am good enough and wise enough to take care of *you*?"

She lifted up her face and kissed him.

"We love each other," she whispered, "we trust each other, and so we can help each other, and God will help us both. Ah, Grif, how bright and sweet life is!"

And she scarcely knew, tender little soul, that instead of "life" she should have said "love."

There we will leave them both, merely hinting at the festivities that followed,—merely hinting at the rejoicings at Bloomsbury Place, the gatherings at Brabazon Lodge, and the grand family reception at the house of the bride,—a reception at which Dolly shone forth with renewed splendor, presiding over a gorgeous silver tea-service, which was one of Miss MacDowlas's many gifts, dispensing tea and coffee with the deportment of a housekeeper of many years' standing, and utterly distracting Grif with her matronly airs and graces.

Vagabondia was itself again in these days, but it was turning its brighter side outward. Phil was winning success, too, his position in the world of art was becoming secured, and Bloomsbury Place was to be touched up and refurnished gradually. Aimée had promised to make her home with Dolly until such time as her sweet little saint's face won her a home of her own. Miss MacDowlas had been adopted into the family circle, and was conscious of being happier than she had ever felt since her long-past youth slipped from her grasp. Tod's teeth were "through," as Mrs. Phil phrased it, and convulsions had not supervened, to the ecstasy of his anxious admirers. And Mollie,—well, Mollie waltzed with Ralph Gowan again on the night of Dolly's reception, and when the dance was at an end, she went and seated herself near her hostess upon the green sofa—it was a green sofa, though a far more luxurious one than Dolly and Grif had ever dared to set their hearts upon in the olden days.

"Dolly," she said, blushing for the last time in this history of mine, and looking down at her bouquet of waxen-white camellias and green leaves,— "Dolly, I suppose Aimée has told you that I am engaged to—to—"

"To Mr. Gowan," suggested Dolly.

"Yes," answered Mollie, "to Mr. Gowan."

9 789362 091642